THE PO
OF
MIND

THE POWER
OF
MIND

Muriel Nayes Gillchrest

Crest Publishing House

(A JAICO ENTERPRISE)
G-2, 16 Ansari Road, Darya Ganj
New Delhi-110 002

THE POWER OF MIND
ISBN 81-242-0077-7

First Edition: 1998
Reprinted: 1999

Published by:
CREST PUBLISHING HOUSE
(A Jaico Enterprise)
G-2,16 Ansari Road, Darya Ganj,
New Delhi-110002

Printed by:
Efficient Offset Printers
215, Shahzada Bagh Industrial Complex,
Phase II, Delhi-110035

What This Book Will Do For You

This Book will lift you out of the doldrums of ordinary existence—the boredom of the sameness of continuously repeating past experiences. It will open up new activities that are of interest to you and extend your information into knowledge and better experiences. It will awaken you to what will appear to you as a larger, more comfortable world. In this world you will be appreciated, rather than maligned—helped, rather than hindered.

You will begin at once, regardless of circumstances and present surroundings, to let go of tensions and anxieties and establish the feeling of calm, serene peace. From this will come wise decisions upon which you will act insuring better and happier experiences, less limitation and more real joy.

You will discover your own unique gift—that one expression of your best self which not only gives you more joy as you develop skill in expressing it, but for which you can be handsomely rewarded.

Your motivations—your reasons for doing—will become correctly based, and you'll no longer reap dissatisfactions and disappointments.

As you learn to cast away morbid opinions and poor policies that bring wrong results, you become aware that what follows in these pages is not merely theory, but some-thing which has been practised by the wise of all time.

When something within me prompted me to write this book, I did so because I had met so many who, in reading other books along the same line, had so many misconceptions.

Listening to their interpretations, I knew the language used was either too mystical or too ponderous and scientific. Enlightening as I know these books are, if they were being misinterpreted by many readers, a way must be made to make clear what is stumbled over and becomes a further obstacle.

In working with persons whose knotty problems required nothing less than a miracle, I have learned that it is often the result of these misinterpretations. I have also discovered what questions come up the most. This book will enlighten you on both, as well as showing you how to find the answers you seek for yourself, by yourself.

By showing you how the creative power reveals itself to others, you are able to follow the example and let it be revealed to you; so that you, too, may utilize your energy, originality, and innate charm.

You can become a magnet, attracting nothing but good to you; for as you perceive that this creativeness is limitless, you quickly comprehend how to remove from you all that is undesirable.

The many individuals who have sincerely followed the basics as given herein, now have an enjoyable, satisfying life. While the cases cited carry fictitious names, they are all real and true—actual happenings.

Whether you are one who is just beginning to be interested in how you can help yourself to better living or one who has studied long and hard with no appreciable results, this book will point out exactly where the trouble lies *Trouble* is always a *lie* about the Truth.

PROLOGUE

Your *mind* tells you that the Universe is a masterpiece of perfection. Everything needed for its perfect running is already here—every element, every law. If you do not discern this, it is due to your viewpoint; for, in viewing the Universe with your sensory equipment, much may seem to be missing. Just as your vision is limited when you stand in a valley, and much more can be seen by your eyes when you stand upon a hilltop or mountain-top, so do things known by the mind change when attention is moved from the valley of the senses to the higher place of mind.

The Law of Mind, like the multiplication table, is exact and mathematical. It is not a theory, or something Mankind invented; Man *discovered* it and the rules pertaining to it. Until we know those rules, we are like a ship sailing in fog, with no radar. The rocks and hazards are no less real because undiscernable.

As a child, you knew nothing of the laws of science or nature, but you were taught to be cautious of fire, electricity, and other things which might be dangerous to your well-being. Such warnings produced a curiosity and a desire to learn how to safely handle such things so that they might benefit rather than harm.

Watching how individuals think and seeing the effect of their thoughts led to the discovery of the rules which, if Man followed, his life would be peaceful and joyous.

CONTENTS

Clairaudience. Spiritism. Apparitions and Poltergeists. Communication With Those Not in the Flesh. Trance-Mediumstup. Your Guardian Angel. Telekinesis and Psychometry. All Unusual Effects Must Have a Cause Hitting the Control Center. From the Sense Standpoint. The Progress of Spirit.

Believe. Refuse to Respond Emotionally. All Are Here by the Power of God. The God Concept of the Senses. Your Changed Viewpoint Affects Others for Good. You know What Conscience Is. What Have You Been Telling Yourself? The Greatest Glory. What Would It Be Worth to You?

CHAPTER 1

The Heart of Humanity: The Invisible Master

You own a fabulous treasure that nestles within you, hidden in the heart of you, awaiting your discovery.

How would you like knowing that whatever you needed would be present, when and as you needed it? How would you like being free from mental and emotional turmoil?

Why is it folks blindly make error after error, suffering anguish, loss, even pain—letting problems harass them because the solutions are not known?

Why, when the treasures of wisdom and energy are already within you, do you not tap this source? Do you remember, as a child, how you loved fairy tales, ideas about magic, Santa Claus, and play-acting? The joys of a small child fade all too quickly from memory. Can you remember, when as a child, you were loved and cared for? You can have that same faith and trust again, if you are willing to follow instructions.

To find the way, you need a map; this book is that map. A map is not the transportation; you will have to do the travelling.

The heart of you is like a cave filled with gold and jewels, against which boulders of false beliefs have been piled along with the jagged rocks of misunderstanding and long-entertained hurts of past injustices. Then, there's the debris of doubt, despair, disgust and disappointment, piled high against the gold of integrity, the pearls of wisdom, the diamonds of intelligence. Also, there is your own heart are the rubies of true love and the wealth of emeralds, waiting for you to find them.

Is it possible to remove this debris, the rocks and boulders which are now showing forth as your problems? Yes, it is.

Perhaps, in some categories of your experience you have, at times, been aware of drawing upon this inner wisdom, or you may have had flashes of intuition. You may have attributed it all to "luck", not knowing that beneficial circumstances are within your own jurisdiction or that you had a "built-in" guidance system to which you might turn.

Have you been taught that you are a sinner? Do you understand that a sinner is one who makes a mistake? Do you know that there are certain kinds of thinking habits which are *mistakes*? Such mistakes are what bring about the effect called a *problem*. Small problems when not corrected make larger ones.

Let us glance at some common problems; that is, results produced by certain kinds of thinking habits. Then, we can see why beliefs of a specific nature create actions which result in further problems.

Acquaintances of Katherine T. say she is a lonely woman because she is a great fault-finder and speaks unkindly of others behind their backs. What causes her to deride and ridicule others?

She acts in this manner because she does not have a good opinion of herself. Belittling others will not give her a better regard for herself or give her any real self-esteem, for she has made herself a cause of unpleasantness to others. If she knew about her treasures within, she would build herself into the sort of person she would like to know.

Here is another sort of problem. Carl W. took his 19-year-old son Willard to Las Vegas. He bought him drinks and introduced him to the gambling tables. Four months later, Willard was still drinking steadily and making every effort to get something for nothing. Can a parent lead his child in the right direction if he isn't headed that way himself?

Then there is Kenny D., a teenager in trouble with the school authorities.

Kenny observes that, "The people who make the rules, break them themselves. Mom and Dad fight all the time; they argue and yell at each other, but if my kid brother and I fight, we get licked by my Dad. Same way with lies. We get punished, but my Mom lies to her friends all the time. If what they tell us is the right way, then why don't they do it that way?"

What Kenny wants is an ideal, something to pattern his own behavior after. He isn't rejecting values, he's trying them out.

Young Josie C. is making a mistake in another direction. Loving her little four-year-old Suzie well but not wisely, she now has a small tyrant on her hands. Suzie's Mom and Dad have quarreled to the point of breaking up their home because Josie exercises love without wisdom. These common problems of lack of wisdom are forerunners of greater ones.

None of these individuals knew of the treasures within, nor how to reach and express them.

Correct Instruction Essential

Teeming millions go uninstructed as to a better way of life simply because they have a misconception of the Bible and an incorrect idea of what prayer is. To many, the word *prayer* is thought to be merely religious terminology, just as church attendance is believed to be religion.

This Book Is About You

This book is not about a new religion; it is about you and for you. It is not a religious book if what is meant by "religious book" is that it follows beliefs taught by any denomination. It is a book of instruction for you, the reader, to help you cease suffering, find your treasures, and experience a wealth of good. It is a book of instruction for you. It Must, of necessity, include your beginning. Therefore, the use of the word *God* must be employed, just as it is necessary for you to comprehend what "heaven" is. Mainly, this book is a vocational guide that will help you discover what gives you a happy, successful, and worthwhile life.

The Way to Wisdom

Prayer is the method; it is the actual way to the discovery of these treasures within you, for it opens the door to Wisdom. Wisdom is not looking at past errors with regret, but discovering the Perfect Intelligence within yourself which is always ready to apprise you of a better way. Prayer is not asking for something you believe you do not have but is recognition of the treasure already present and waiting to be expressed.

The real heart of humanity is God, and the life and perfection of God, which is God, are in your heart at your beginning.

God Is Not Three-Dimensional

How could you ever understand this if you have been taught to believe that God is a somebody apart from you, up in the sky, or a being you might meet only after your demise? Is it any wonder that so many have a "tongue-in-cheek" attitude about God and prayer, when they have been given a faulty interpretation of what God is, where heaven is, and have been told Bible stories built strictly upon sense concepts at the three-dimensional level?

Foes and Enemies Are Erroneous Beliefs

A MAN'S FOES SHALL BE THEY OF HIS OWN HOUSEHOLD.   (Matt. 10: 36)

Your *household,* then, is not where your family is gathered but your own mental realm. Your foes are your incorrect beliefs. A belief is said to be incorrect when it deals solely with sense perceptions. Why? Because sense perception is limited to time and space. The forms your eyes see have not always been there, nor will they always remain. What you hear may be factual only of that moment, and you quite possibly do not know the whole story. Therefore, appearances have furnished your mental realm with many false beliefs.

Likewise, what you have no perception of does not seem to exist for you. Yet, every now and then someone breaks through this wall of carnal thought and finds a new viewpoint. He is truly a "new creature," living a life free of the tyranny of what others believe. His code of conduct is improved; the government of his life runs smoothly. He has stopped judging by what has appeared to his senses, and gradually, as his new viewpoint becomes stronger, what appears to his senses is all good.

Becoming Aware of Your Wisdom

You, too, can live in this charmed safety without seat-belts, for you will find God is more powerful than a strip of fabric, no matter how well-anchored. It has become clear to you that a safety-belt is not a substitute for sane driving. You understand the difference between a lock which any accomplished burglar can pick and having faith in a power which keeps thoughts of burglary out of your mental realm.

You can rid yourself of other "foes" of your "household," such as the malfunctioning of some organ or disease-causing germs, once you understand that the Great Healer is in your heart. No medicine or surgery will bring you closer to God, and death does not open up the gates to heaven.

"I am come that ye might have life, and have it more abundantly," will come to mean something more to you than waiting for a vision of a man to appear in the sky.

You want to know the "How?" Close your eyes and relax for a moment. Take a deep breath. Think: *"My life is God. God's life is my life."*

Do this frequently; it will occur to you that God is the All-Good, that you can breath deeply as often as you like, and that your breathing is a function you seldom give much attention to. Many other ideas will come to you which will expand your ideas of what God is to you.

Professed Religious Beliefs Worthy, But Unpracticed

Many modern religious teachings may have given you the idea that you are to be far more noble than is practicable. Perhaps you have sincerely tried to be high minded, honest, loyal, sincere, and chaste and have found it to be quite an ordeal. Possibly your associates seemed to have made your good resolves a bit hard to stick to. Many have found that the good deeds they've done have put them on the short end, and no one really appreciated their efforts.

Human goodness is a fine thing, but it often builds up the intolerance of those who fall short of its standards. Know this: You are not disliked for your goodness, but for your lack of tolerance.

A good many persons turn away from the study of religion because it has come to mean to many the giving up of certain activities and pleasures in which they believe they find enjoyment. Such dogmas are man-made and have nothing to do with the doctrine. Teachings which dictate that you shall not wear certain colors, eat certain foods, or engage in some activities because of a day of the week are pure ignorance of the gospel. They have kept more individuals from studying the Bible and really learning its laws than anything else. You need give up nothing which really gives you joy; what you give up are those things that cause you trouble, grief, despair and despondency.

Giving Up Wrong Beliefs

I once said to a man who came to me for lessons. "I know you are willing to relinquish this ailment which is giving you so much pain, but are you equally willing to give up the kind of thinking which is causing it?"

"It isn't caused by thought," he objected, "it is an organ which isn't functioning properly."

"But that is a belief, and a belief is a thought, isn't it?" I pursued.

"Well, yes, I've tried to believe that I'm all right, but nothing changes."

"No," I agreed, "because you haven't changed the belief which arrested the right activity of this organ. Let us see if we can find what most irritates you, for that will be the thought, or conviction, which has brought about this tension. It is this tension which is preventing the right action of the organ."

After a moment of thought, he said, "Oh, I see what you mean! It is the way I think about something else, unrelated to my health!"

Emotions Affect Thoughts

Those who are ignorant of the law of mind and how it works, often remark, "I wasn't thinking of becoming sick, or having an automobile accident, or losing my job." They believe that by tossing the whole subject off in this way, they have made their point.

We never say to another, "Oh, you just think you're sick," nor, "Think you are well, and you will be." If illness and pain are pictured as experiences, they are seen to be due to beliefs which are heavily laden with the wrong kind of emotions. Fault-finding, nagging, and bickering are ways of thinking due to emotions which produce all the ills Man is prone to get. If such attitudes coming from others set your teeth on edge, how much greater is the effect upon those who thusly engage themselves? It makes them headachey, nervous, and sickly.

Those who tell themselves that they are justified in hating someone who has been cruel, unfair, or despicable have yet to learn that hating harms only the hater. Thus, "Love your enemies." How?

1. By forgiving. First of all, you must know how to forgive. Second, you must want to, for your own sake.

2. Change one dominant idea about yourself. You have believed that you are one individual among many. Change that to: "I (the thinker), and *the Father* (who created me as a thinker) are' ONE."

3. Now see that the reason you have witnessed this unpleasant appearance, is that it is coming from one of your own beliefs, taken into your mental realm by means of sense perception. (You have seen persons like this before, read about them, heard about them.)

4. Are you ready to take a good look at your own behavior pattern and see if in some other area you have been cruel, unfair, or whatever the disliked state was? Can you spot the point where your own thoughts caused you to act in some similar manner? It may have been ridicule; it might have been vindictiveness.

The person you are hating is yourself. Can you forgive *yourself?* Yes, you can. You can stop making the mistake.

How is this going to help you forgive the other person? Try it, and then you'll know.

A Waste of Time

In some circles it is considered quite smart to sit and talk over what is "wrong" with nearly everything and everybody. Hours are wasted in such petty, small-minded, and futile pastimes. To attempt to justify this is called "being realistic," but it in no way minimizes the damage done.

Before long, these persons are caught in the web of their own thought forms, and the magnitude of their own problems increases. They are erecting a pile of boulders of discontent, which make even more difficult the finding of their own inner treasures.

Eventually, though, they can come upon the question, "What can I do to remedy this situation?"

By using the method cited above, they can alter their manner of thought and find their own inner treasures, thus restoring their mental and physical health.

Your Beginning

Once you begin to ponder this idea that God is "closer than breathing, nearer than hands and feet," something wonderful, as well as extremely practical, begins to take place. You ask yourself, "How could God know everything I do, unless He is within me?"

Early teachers of the Bible, as well as some present ones, looked at the verse in Genesis 1;27, "God created man in his own image and likeness," and too quickly reached a conclusion that God had the same form as Man or the form of a man. Starting from a faulty premise, many have believed that God was a "somebody else," an invisible but three-dimensional being. Yet, if invisible to mortal sight, certainly we are out of the realm of dimensions!

Heaven then had to be set up as an after-death habitation. Such a "heaven" is as mythical as all the rest of the three-dimensional concepts of the Bible. Are you, who profess to believe in the divinity of Jesus ignoring that Jesus said, "The Kingdom of God is within you?" How would you follow Jesus' instruction to "Seek ye first the Kingdom of Heaven," if heaven were a location to which you would go after you gave up life in the body? It is almost the same as saying that you should commit suicide, isn't it?

You are praying when you begin to ponder how it is that God and His Kingdom are within you. You are praying when you have stopped asking for things and begin to seek this source of your life, intelligence, love, joy, and substance. When you find this source, ask for Wisdom, for that is where you'll find it. With Wisdom, you can discern that the things God has in His Kingdom are not things of form, but qualities, like strength, harmony, peace.

AND WHEN HE WAS DEMANDED OF THE PHARISEES, WHEN THE KINGDOM OF GOD SHOULD COME, HE

ANSWERED THEM AND SAID, THE KINGDOM OF GOD COMETH NOT WITH OBSERVATION.

NEITHER SHALL THEY SAY, LO HERE! OR, LO THERE! FOR, BEHOLD, THE KINGDOM OF GOD IS WITHIN YOU.

(Luke 17:20, 21)

This is the treasure which is within you, and you perceive that true wisdom could never cause an act which would later bring regret.

What is Unwise?

To some, being "wise" means to be quick enough to "outsmart" someone else or to reveal another's weakness by voicing unkind and cutting remarks. Such persons learn, in time, that sowing seeds of discontent reaps nothing of value. Retaliation, "getting even," is as ridiculous as it is damaging, and it builds even greater problems.

To think and act in such a way as to give you an unfavorable picture of yourself is unwise. Much incorrect thinking and many unpleasant emotional attitudes are due to a false idea of what prayer really is. This has come about because of a three-dimensional sense-concept of the Bible and religion. The world, as it appears to your sences, looks to be anything but the perfection God is aid to have created. Theology preaches the reality of evil as something in contrast to what God is, yet adds that God is "All." You must have a correct premise upon which to start.

In the examples of Carl and his son Willard and Josie and her baby Susie you are well aware that love was administered without intelligence. Had these parents known what true prayer is, and utilized it, an equal amount of intelligence would have balanced their affection. In the example of Katherine T. there was no love evinced. It was within her, unexpressed and, therefore, unexperienced.

Human misfortunes like blighted affections are common emotional problems which stem from false beliefs long indulged, from no real knowledge of God and prayer. Prayer doesn't change God's nature; it changes yours. Actually, it changes your beliefs, for your true nature is a permanent identity of which you may not be aware. All things that you experience or see reflected are the results of your own beliefs; so, it is desirable for you to change those beliefs which are damaging to your peace of mind.

If You are around those who think they smell "danger" in anything new to them and who declare that to study anything bearing any religious terminology in it will cause "madness," you have probably absorbed a belief you'd do well to change right away. There is nothing more sane than what I have to present to you, for self-improvement is the best thing you can do for yourself as well as others. Those who lose mental stability aren't reflecting God; they are reflecting their own faulty concepts.

Get the Correct Idea

Come away from the three-dimensional belief of God, His Son, His Kingdom of Heaven, and become aware the God that is real, unlimited, and omnipresent. Come away from the belief that heaven is a location to which you enter upon leaving this life or that it is a place in the sky. It is not a place fenced off with entrance gates, studded with the pearls which come from oysters. Jesus never posed for the pictures or statues you have seen of him.

Thinking of God, Jesus Christ and Heaven from the standpoint of your senses has made the whole idea vague, foggy, and greyed. Your physical senses apprise you of what is going on outside of you, so how would you find God when He is within?

What good thoughts do you have? Think about these. No, not the thoughts about personalities and things you enjoy, nor where you'd like to go on your vacation, although this would be an improvement over thinking only about what you deplore. As a suggestion, you might consider what "loyalty" means, how much of it you express, or why "honesty is the best policy." You might take stock of your own good qualities, the ones you do express, such as your efficiency, your kindness, or generosity.

Sense Consciousness

If entertainment is all you desire and attending church bores you, studying out anything tires you, and if reading the Bible only confuses you, you are steeped in *sense consciousness*. You are too concerned with conditions, objects, personalities, and status symbols. This state of mental attention is called in the Bible the "carnal mind," or "mortal mind," and is said to be "enmity to God." *Enmity* means displeasing hostility.

This "carnal mind" usually thinks it is praying. when it is asking the Supreme Being to relieve it of the effect, or result, of some mistake it knows it has made. Unless you are willing to take your attention off the world of the senses—that is, what you see, hear, taste, smell and touch—and find the way to do so, you haven't "prayed" in a real sense.

You Have a Choice

God is your ability to think. What you think about is your choice. Now do you see how it is that God is in the "midst" of you? If you so choose, you are free to think about the world of the senses, the effects that you see, touch, smell, taste, and hear.

A Real Thrill in Store for You

What is discovery to find the meaning of your own life! You have the ability to discover an unlimited intelligence within yourself when you choose to ponder what God's nature is, rather than always thinking of what comes to you by means of your senses. If you are always thinking of objects and forms, you have left no time to tap the source of inspiration.

Suppose you ponder the word *strength*. You think of its meaning, don't you? Can you express it? Of course you can, in some degree. The more you express it, the more you have. Try the word *peace*. Consider its meaning. Are you expressing it to those around you? The more you express it, the more of it you'll feel.

This is what we mean by "good thoughts." Do you love harmonious conditions? Think of what they are. What can you do to produce them? It is very simple, for in the same manner as *you* express them, they will grow. Ponder the word *harmony*. Are you always expressing it, or are there times when you express the opposite, such as temper or quarrelsomeness?

These "good" thoughts are the treasures within you, which, when expressed consistently by you, bring in their wake similar good back to you. If you deny the existence of them in others, it is because you are not fully expressing them yourself.

The peace of mind which has been so often disturbed by thoughts about the effects perceived by the senses; the love you would like to share; the wealth you long for; and the life of health, optimism, and serenity; are already within you. All perfect ideas are established, built-in, as it were, requiring only that you learn what they are and express them yourself. What has kept you from realizing this? Nothing but your continued and seldom-interrupted use of the sense-mind.

Barriers dissolve when you realize that prayer is union with your treasures. The rocks and boulders of misconceptions and hurts crumble away. Doubt and superstition are known to be nothing but a sticky nothingness which holds hard thoughts and wrong feelings in place.

Every Problem an Opportunity

Incorrect judgments, wrong companionships, and disharmonies of all sorts harass humanity until the treasure within is found and expressed. Since wrong ideas tend to produce wrong actions, so will correct thoughts produce beneficial results in action. Adversities and obstacles merely show you what particular character-trait needs reform or reinforcement.

We all know those to whom the practise of the presence of God is something ridiculous and the subject for scorn. They may gaze at your present effects and ask, "What good has it done you?" Be careful that you do not condemn that person, or persons, still thinking in terms of sense consciousness. They only represent an area in your own thought realm where you are asking yourself that question.

No need to feel hurt; just ask yourself, "Which belief is it?"

The Difference Between Beliefs and Ideas

In Jesus' teachings, it is said, "It is done upto you according to your belief."

What are these wrong ideas which produce unwanted results? They aren't "ideas" at all; they are beliefs. An "idea" is a pattern, a standard or ideal, an abstract principle. The word *idea* has been used interchangeably to mean also a mental image or belief. However, for the sake of clarity, let us use the word *belief* to mean "mental image of something known by means of sense perception."

A belief then, would pertain to that which has to do with time, space and form. In other words, a belief is something over which you do have control. You can refuse to accept as true and lasting anything adverse or negative. When you realize that what your senses perceive is always of the present moment, you can understand that no condition of the moment is final. It is always subject to change.

You need not panic when your senses inform you of a specific condition or situation. Just remember that all of the senses "see only in part, through a glass, darkly." What your eyes see does not remain that way forever. Neither do they see all sides of everything at once. Your ears can be fooled. Consider the sound effects in radio or the movies—you may think you actually hear a storm or an explosion. All the senses can be fooled to some extent; so if you are going to rely solely upon them for what you know, your knowledge might be extremely faulty.

Superstitions

Sense beliefs build superstitions, and a superstition is a fear of the unknown. Have you tried to justify your fears by claiming that everyone has them? Don't confuse fear with caution. What we are dealing with here is the irrational, injurious, false approach to life.

Some folks declare they are not superstitious because they don't cringe and expect the worst when a black kitty crosses their path, especially if it's Friday the thirteenth.

But they are scared out of their wits when told about an afterlife of burning in hell-fire. We can't help asking, "What kind of a God, do you believe in?"

Believing what has come to you through any of your senses, from anyone, can build a superstition. Can you, and will you, think? God is the Power to Think.

Here are some of the categories into which sense beliefs and superstitions fall:

1. That Time has something to do with success or failure. This is expressed by such thoughts as:
    "I'm too old to start now."
    "It's too late for me to bother with it."
    "World conditions are not timely."

2. That other people are somehow responsible. This belief is voiced in this manner:
    "The bank refused to make the loan."
    "My wife (or husband) doesn't approve."
    "The doctor said this condition is incurable."

3. That outer conditions are unsuitable. This belief is expressed thusly:
    "Business everywhere is too slow."
    "There might be a war around the corner."
    "Election year is a bad time to begin."

Time Is of the Senses

Believing that you are too old to begin something new is a most ridiculous mental attitude. If you have been counting the chronological years from the date of your birth to the present calendar date, stop it right now. The only reason the mirror gives you the evidence of the passing of time is because you have been holding before you the belief of Age. Your senses behold the *belief*.

Interest enthusiasm, and joy come from starting new protects. Why cheat yourself when you are actually ageless?

To say, "I am too young," is equally silly if there were something beneficial for you to do. There is always something to be done now-even if it is only making up your mind what it is and deciding what your first step will be.

What Is the First Step?

Wouldn't the first step have to be the discovery that what you have been calling "death" is not the end? How have you accounted for the "born genius"? Or can you? There are no tricks of fate in life; everything moves forward with mathematical precision. The great composer Mozart could produce melodies on the violin at the age of five. Nicola Tesla's inventive mind displayed its workings at the same age, and his original experiment in power production was made at the age of nine. You must understand that nothing you learn is ever lost, for going on in another vehicle is the plan of life. There is no such thing as not having a chance to finish whatever you begin.

If you want to learn music and have no instrument, try studying the sheet music. "God sends the thread for the web begun." No matter what it is which interests you, the time to begin is now, and the place to start is right where you are.

No One Hinders You

If you have been thinking someone is hindering you, recognize that you have a belief here which you can change. While it may appear to you that one individual blocks your progress in some specific direction, just remember there are many others, some of whom who would be only too glad to help you. Move your attention always from the limited to the unlimited. This is the "how" of discovering your own authority. As long as it seems to you that authority is outside of you rather than in your own mind, you will continue to be weak in your convictions.

Unless you find this place of authority within you, you are like an amnesia victim with no home or identity.

On the other hand, we are not talking about your being stubborn in getting your way with others. This is not the meaning here at all. All You change is your own belief.

The Right Idea of Strength

Some individuals have interpreted strength to mean becoming a tyrant, a dictator, having others carry out their will or cater to their whims. Such persons always meet up with those who will not do as they demand or an obstacle they cannot remove.

Pushing others about is not strength, for strength is in knowing how to gain co-operation. You have tapped the source, of right ideas when you have learned how to gain constructive co-operation. When all the parts work together for the good of the whole idea, the overall design will give forth its perfect picture. Success, then, is a *must*.

Strength has so long been thought of as physical prowess or armament and financial wealth that when someone speaks of God as strength, those who know not God cannot even imagine such a thing as an unlimited power which knows no opposition! A strong man can always meet up with one who is stronger; armed forces might be misplaced or out-numbered; financial wealth may not buy what you want or need at a specific moment, such as shelter from a storm or water on a desert.

You cannot be held back by other conditions when you know your strength comes from an unlimited source.

Every Moment Is the Right Time

There is always someone making a huge success of something when someone else is saying, "Times aren't right." At fifty, it isn't the wintry blast or the sight of his receding hairline that makes a man shiver; it is realizing how many opportunities to grow into a better person he has passed up. A woman of the same age, never stretching anything but her girdle and interested only in her bridge game and a new recipe, feels life has passed her by. What joys they might have known!

Yet, all can begin NOW. The discovery that you have merely been making excuses for your lack of joy, or health, or whatever appears to you to be missing from your experience, is only a beginning. The interesting part lies ahead, continually infolding your treasures and the ways in which they may be expressed.

Revamping your beliefs in order to attain better conditions requires determined effort, and it is upon this that you use your will-power. It may not seem easy at first to give up your self-pity, resentments, and blaming of others, but you will find it a simple thing to do if you just put prayer in place of such emotional thoughts.

Love Is Not Possessiveness

The feeling that you have called "love" for some member of the human race should be studied carefully to make sure that it isn't a rather unpleasant attachment which spells bondage to either of you.

Holding another subservient to you, or being under the spell of another's will-power is not love, for love is a great freeing agent. It is a great power, a healing force that may be used to eliminate every wrong condition which harasses humanity. The right interpretation of this word love will gradually come to you as you read further and put into practise what is presented, if you do not already know.

Lifting the Veil

The startling facts about this design of life have been discovered by an amazingly small minority, yet when any individual makes this discovery, he immediately becomes joyful. No matter what his present circumstances may be, nor how distressing, a ray of light and a new trust enters into him. He has no outer evidence to go on, but it is as though a veil had been lifted. He observes that he has been concerned with the body of things, not the spirit; and that only the manifestation, the tangible things, have seemed to be important. He sees the advantage of knowing what is true and believing it, rather than the ever-shifting scenery known to the senses.

Those who have steadfastly refused to give allegiance

to any power but God have a magical "something" in their make-up which draws them forward, always safely. Others feel their beneficent influence. (We refer to those who really know God; not just those who talk *about* God, yet condemn their neighbors and constantly "see wrongs" which they think they are qualified to attempt to correct.)

Everything that the senses recognize as power, such as the tremendous force of a high waterfall, the mighty action of a huge steam engine, jet and rocket power, are all simply shadows of the intelligence coming from Divine Power. Not one of them represents the All.

Teamwork

There must be teamwork among your thoughts and beliefs.

Mean and ugly thoughts have no real power other than to stand in the way of the correct ones. Displays of temper, anger, and self-pity are thought habits which must be overcome. Before you find yourself in a painful illness, an economic crisis, or the loss of something or someone you love, you'd better make the effort to change the kind of thinking and acting which is the cause of them.

Men and women wept for joy when our astronauts successfully orbited the earth. Few realized they were saluting something called "teamwork." Much discipline, cooperation, skill, labor, and the dedication of many persons went into this project.

You are called upon to employ these qualities also if you desire success. Your thoughts must keep you in control of your emotions.

How to Achieve Teamwork Among Your Beliefs

1. Let no thought anchor itself which troubles. The instant you have a negative emotional response, such as anger, take your attention away from that which appeared to bring it about:

      a. Place your attention upon an inanimate object.

      b. Think of what composes this object (wood, metal, glass, paper).

      c. Then, consider that whatever shape this object has is an *idea*.

2. Now, think of God as the acme of Pure Intelligence, Perfect Love.

If you will use this little exercise consistently, you'll discover that it is quite as sensible as disconnecting an electrical appliance before you go to work to take it apart.

It is most interesting that the answer to any problem is called a "solution." As you know, the word *solution* can also mean "a liquid." What you are doing with the above exercise is making the problem into a liquid, and re-forming it into an effect to your liking. Both the problem and the solution are ideas, or thoughts. The problem, however, is only half of the idea, the *question half*; whereas, the solution is the complete idea.

Others Have Found the Way

Some persons apply these ideas the moment they are presented; others waste time trying to get their families and friends to apply them. You will advance most rapidly if you disregard anyone's needs, including your own, centering your attention upon what is already within you and expressing it to the best of your abilities.

After only a short period of study, one middle-aged. unmarried woman got the whole idea rather swiftly.

"It was better than finding a goldmine," she told us joyfully, "for I'd been one who was always scraping the bottom of the barrel. No matter how much effort I made, someone else always got there first. I couldn't even find anyone to marry me, so I just let myself get fat."

Sitting in her beautifully appointed home across from the pleasant, white-haired man who was now her husband, we enjoyed hearing her tell her story.

"I lived in a dreary little two-room apartment in a rundown neighborhood when the revelation came," she went on, her dark eyes sparkling. "That didn't matter, those sordid surroundings, for I suddenly knew 'here it is, all within me.' And I knew it with every fiber of my being. I had but little cash and no employment at the moment, but I'd found the Pearl of Great Price!"

Her husband smiled and put in, "Oh, she had, all right! When I first saw her. I was sure she must be someone of real importance. I used to watch her pass my place of business, and I *had* to find a way to know her."

She laughed gaily, "It never occurred to me that he might be flirting! Oh, I'd longed for male companionship and love, but it had seemed hopeless. But, you know, from the first day after I had this revelation, nice things began happening to me.

"For instance, I had played the piano for years, even memorized some of the classics; but right then, I didn't even have a piano. Anyway, for years I had longed to learn to play an electric organ. I ran into a man on the street who had heard me play a friend's piano. Out of the clear blue sky as we say, he offered me a job in a music store with lessons on the organ thrown in!"

My eyes took in the Steinway Grand, and I asked, "This was some time ago?"

"A year and a half," her husband answered. "It was when she was on her way to this job that I kept seeing her with that radiant look of happiness. I want to say too, that she didn't look fat to me. She says she has lost some pounds, but that wouldn't have made any difference."

"You see," she added, "when I changed my viewpoint, or base of consciousness, everything that was right came about. I played the sheet music on the piano at the store and soon got onto the organ and would play inbetween customers and selling things."

"A crowd would gather, when she did," he put in, so it didn't take me long to make her acquaintance."

"You see," she explained, "I played the way I felt, and I felt real good! I believe that sound carries the vibrations of one's thought, and I believed that those listeners were stimulated into happier thinking." Then she rose and glided gracefully across the room to the piano and played for us.

CHAPTER 2

The Key to the Riddle of Life

Whether or not you are aware of the contents of the Christian Bible, you have at least heard that it contains the key to the riddle of life. Do you know that it also carries the correct solution to every problem which could confront mankind?

If you are a moderately educated person, you do understand the use of simile, metaphor, and allegory. Every word is the symbol of some idea, and groups of words take care of the more complex thoughts and ideas. The Bible is filled with this figurative manner of treating a subject by the use of terminology which is linked by resemblance.

Your physical senses deal entirely with the world of form, of three-dimensional objects that take up space or are measured by time. All that you know by means of your senses only has a measurement of durability. Neither God nor His Son is perceived or cognized by means of these physical senses. Therefore, the Bible does not give up its secrets by the mere reading of the words.

The Law Which Produces Miracles

If what you want will take a miracle, isn't it about time that you discovered what produces miracles? If you practise the exercises in this lesson every day, you shall open the doors to a wonderful discovery—the Law which produces miracles.

Your First Exercise

Let this thought become so familiar to you that you cannot forget it: "*God is my spirit, my mind, my life itself.*"

24

BE STILL, AND KNOW THAT I AM GOD. I AM THE HOLY ONE IN THE MIDST OF THEE.

You have discovered God to be Spirit. Now, you are discovering that God (Spirit) made you in His image and, likeness; therefore, you are spirit. For so long, you have thought of yourself as a body of flesh, blood, and bones and of a certain race or color. Unless you are extremely careful, you will forget that you are spirit, for the senses have convinced you that you are the physical form you behold when you look into a mirror.

God created the idea of you, and that idea is still perfect. *Your* belief about your body is far different, is it not? When your thought has encased the Unlimited within a body or a form, you have *curtailed*, as far as you are concerned, its unlimited perfection and power.

Think about that for a while. See if you can find that feeling of being spirit. When I mention God the Father, I capitalize the word *Spirit* to designate that I mean all Life, all Mind. When I speak of your spirit or mine, I use the small letter "s"; but I want you to comprehend that it is the same Spirit.

Remember, "The Father and I are one, but the Father is greater than I . . . the Father death the work."

Your Concept of Self

You must also know that your sense concept of yourself is important, so that you don't slip into behavior patterns which make problems for you.

Are you deceitful? Do you play both ends to the middle? Do you ever scheme to get your own way? Are you careless, slovenly, inconsiderate of others?

A good way to find out what you really think about yourself is to ask yourself frequently, "If someone I admire and whose opinion of me I feel I'd want to be good should walk in right now, how would I look?" Carry it further and ask, "What if that person could see into my mind and heart? Would I feel ashamed of what I know myself to be?" (This may be news to you, but there are those who can do exactly that.)

Once it is clear to you that your human concept of yourself is also important, you won't slip into carelessness about personal neatness which engenders criticism from others. You should have such a high opinion of your-self that you want to look and be your best at all times.

Think of yourself as neat, clean, sincere, tactful, considerate, and gracious; then suit the action to the thought.

Think of yourself as trustworthy, dependable, and efficient, then do as much as you can to prove that you are. Suppose that you see yourself as a timid person, afraid of new situations, strangers, or being alone. Do you shy off from going to gatherings where you'll meet new people who, so far, are strangers to you? Do you put the chain on the door when you are alone?

This lesson is to make you take a look at the person you think you are and see that you could not be that person. These fears for your comfort or safety prove that you have not fully discovered your spiritual being. If you are leaning upon any physical being for anything at all—help, companionship, or material aid—you still have a false belief about what God is and where He is located. As these false beliefs are replaced by your new awareness, all the help, companionship, and aid will be present for you at all times wherever you may be, with no long, embarrassing gaps.

How to Have the Benefits

A good beginning is always orderliness. It begins in the mind. When your mental realm is disordered and you feel "all mixed up" inside, you can begin by taking an outer action of cleaning things up.

A bath, a shampoo, and clean fingernails have been known to cause sickly persons to suddenly take a turn for the better.

Go into action; get rid of unnecessary mental and material "junk." Many who have found themselves to be in financial need have discovered some item which could be sold and thus relieved the pressure of the moment.

Orderliness is a worthwhile jewel. When you express it, it has a way of leading you to more pricelesss possessions. It keeps you on time for important meetings and helps you to be ready when opportunities are presented.

Think of Yourself as Being Capable

How often do you drop into the gloom of self—pity? Do you feel ignored, pushed around by a cruel fate? Do you think others don't like you? Have you ever asked yourself why? And what is your answer?

If it is a fact that you are not well-liked by others, they must have a reason. Could it be that there is something *you do* which causes this? Are you willing to remedy *it*?

What is the mistake you habitually make which you dislike so much you don't even want to admit it to yourself?

Begin to think of yourself as being capable of discovering it and correcting it, as well. You can if you want to.

Realizing that there is within you an unlimited Divine Intelligence, ask of it what it is you do or don't do. Ask it to show you how you can change. It will be shown so clearly you can't miss it. Now, know that you are capable of this change. Whether it is easy or hard, it will be worth the effort you make.

Your Self-Opinion Shows Through

Are you as courteous and congenial with your family and employees, if you have any, as you are in a social gathering? It won't matter how nicely you are able to behave at an important social function if you are sharp-tongued and gruff with your daily associates. Your honest opinion of yourself will show through, like a toothing shirt which reveals more than it hides.

Everything you give mental attention to you'll some day act upon, so woe to you if your thoughts are of an unsavory nature.

Do Only What You Approve Of

If you like to be ridiculed, criticized, yelled and screamed at, by all means do the same to others. If you enjoy being teased and argued with, you'll find the companions who will give you the same treatment. You are dealing with a law of mind which gives back to you exactly, measure for measure, what you give out.

Perhaps you have noticed that you have a tendency to perpetuate any condition that you feel deeply about—the more it bothers you, the more it holds your attention and the longer it takes to get rid of it. Let us say that you have someone around you who enjoys belittling you and who looks down on you with a smug smirk that not only irritates but angers you. You think of this often and perhaps even discuss it with others. As you nurse your grievance, the bigger it grows. *What should you think and do*?

Recognize immediately that it is a belief you are holding about yourself. Want to argue the point? You can jettison this belief with this thought:

> *God is present with me at all times. I do nothing of which I do not approve. God's power, intelligence, and love now move this false belief out.*

You may have to do this more than one time; you will have to do it until the belief is changed. You will also change whatever it is that you are doing of which you do not approve.

What Is Self-Approval?

Is self-approval just confidence in yourself which comes from an assurance that you have integrity? As an example, would you say that a married man who indulges himself with a romance which he hides from his wife is expressing the quality of loyalty? He may say that he approves of his actions and that he "sees nothing wrong in it," since he takes care that his wife doesn't learn of his escapades and, therefore, isn't hurt by them. He knows that he isn't expressing loyalty, and he has to live with that knowledge.

Whenever there is any doubt in your mind about your integrity, your confidence in yourself is weakened.

Sincerity is another quality which, when unexpressed, shows up as lack of self-approval. Anxiety, negligence, oversight, and impatience show up when sincerity is lacking, and discontent and pessimism soon follow.

Comprehension of the Law of Mind is an inner feeling which is the result of having *lived* the qualities. Living These qualities develops your faith and eliminates irritability, intolerance, and indiscretions which lead to future problems.

No matter what you have done in the past, today is a new day. Determine that henceforth you shall express sincerity and loyalty. In the long run, it is yourself who is hurt the most when good qualities are unexpressed.

One Day at a Time

Constructive thinking is learned by degrees. For now, don't try to make long-range plans; take one hour at a time, one day at a time. You can think correctly for the next hour, can you not? And the one after that? You can be happy, smiling, and sincere, speaking gently and kindly. You can be at your best and look your best for one day. Give full attention to whatever you are doing at the moment and do it well.

Which Self Is Perfect?

The question is often asked, "Won't I become conceited if I begin to think of myself as perfect?"

The self you now believe you are is far from perfect, just as the friends and acquaintances you have are a far cry from your idea of perfection. These beliefs you have been entertaining about the self you think you are all deal with the limited, mortal side of you.

The self you really are, is the God Life. Perhaps you are not too well acquainted with it. What good experiences you do enjoy are but faint glimpses of your God Self. Whatever degree of intelligence you show is inside of you and being expressed by you; it is unlimited and perfect and becomes apparent as used.

As you change these false beliefs about the self you think you are, as you would change errors in arithmetic, you allow more of this perfect. Self to be reflected, expressed, and experienced by you. No, you will not become conceited.

Admit Your Mistakes

Should there be times when you feel tempted to re-hash events that led up to some quarrel or otherwise miserable experience, have the strength of character to recognize your own part in the fiasco. You indulged thoughts and emotions which produced the happening.

Have any of your apparently "unselfish actions" been an attempt to curry favor, show off, or gain something still more favorable in return?

Gifts or services given with the hope to put another in your debt so that he must respond in kind, are a sure way to disappointment. Even though he may respond as you planned, this in no way insures the success of your project. Almost everyone has tried this at some time and wound up questioning the advisability of generosity. It isn't generosity; it is bargaining.

Steadfastness Gets Results

Make your first thought each morning: "The Father and I are one." Consider that God the Father is the Spirit which is your own Life—not the effects you see with your physical senses, but the *life force* flowing through you.

Do this whenever you are tempted to self-pity, wanting sympathy, or inclined to dramatize your "hard luck."

Do this when you feel momentarily irritated, angered, or uncomfortable in any way.

Do it instead of making the sharp, caustic remark.

Do it when you are nervous or greatly frightened.

Do it when your body hurts somewhere.

Do it when you see or hear about illness.

Do it when everything seems to be going wrong.

Do it when others complain.

Do it when trouble seems to be brewing, or when you feel the pain of anxiety.

Remind Yourself What the Life Force Is

Its basic nature is Peace. It is Love, for it gives of itself whenever it is recognized. It is Unlimited Intelligence and Power. Not only is it in yourself, but everywhere.

Your perseverance will be rewarded, for this quick turning away from what the senses inform you about, which is only a belief, is what changes the faulty belief.

Discipline your thinking as you would train yourself to any skill, remembering that all which comes to you via your senses reports only a *temporary* condition.

At least once every day, remind yourself that:

1. I am not thinking thoughts about anything I do not want to happen.
2. I am not blaming anyone else for anything.
3. I am careful about choosing what thoughts I harbor.

4. I am making an effort to praise sincerely when praise
    is due.
5. I am learning how to distinguish a sense belief from
    a truth, and know the difference between a truth and
    a present fact.
6. I am now aware that every unwanted, distasteful, or
    troublesome condition is temporary.

Every now and then, someone protests, "Well, here is
a condition you could hardly call temporary; it has been this
way for years!"

Nevertheless, it was not always thus, was it? You'll have
to admit that it is changing, even though it may appear to
be changing for the worse. You are able to comprehend
that, since it is changing, it might change for the better.
Often there are other equally faulty beliefs supporting the
major one. You feed these beliefs with the only sustaining
substance they have—your own life force.

God did not create the unpleasant condition; God
created the Perfect Pattern. You will know your real self
within by widening the aperture for its expression.

Now that you understand that God is the essence of your
life, you have glimpsed the "Pearl of Great Price".

BE STILL, AND KNOW THAT I AM GOD; I WILL BE
EXALTED AMONG THE HEATHEN, I WILL BE EXALTED IN
THE EARTH.

(Psalms 46:10)

Let this be your last thought as you go to sleep every
night.

CHAPTER 3

The Divinity Within You

Divinity is that state of equality which comes from God. The Lord God is One, a primal truth with no opposite whatsoever. Clearly stated in the opening verses of the book of Genesis in the Bible is this Great Principle. This is often repeated in what appears to be historic narrative, as well as in allegory in the teachings of Jesus.

There Is One Truth

Earnest and sincere persons will not fail to discover this single truth. Your understanding of just what Divinity is will come about when you want to *know God more* than you want a holing in your body, a new car, success in business, or a satisfying romance. Your sincerity will do the job.

Often, a correct concept is reached more easily by looking at the things we know it is *not*. Maybe it has never occurred to you that shifting sense impressions around in your mental realm is not real thinking. The organ you call your brain is similar to the tape on an adding machine, simply recording what has been visually observed, heard, smelled, tasted and touched. The life force enables you to do this. This life is the unseen Intelligence, which is the Real Thinker.

A simple way of comprehending this is to consider the last meal you consumed. Consciously, you have no idea of what activity is required, nor what digestive juices may be needed to convert this food into energy, new cells, tissues, or whatever is needed. Your stomach is one place where

33

you know this Intelligence is active. It also causes your heart to beat and causes you to inhale and exhale. It is the divinity within you. It is the Real Thinker.

Let me tell you the story of Janet, for this incident may be the answer to one of your own questions at this point.

Janet was not a student of mine, but we had attended many of the same classes in terms past and occasionally visited each other when time and location permitted. From these visits and our infrequent correspondence, I learned that she was constantly embroiled in one thing or another. After 15 years of study and application, it seemed to me that she should have developed more serenity.

She dropped in to see me at my office one day while I was finishing a telephone conversation. Since she had come a distance of some 50 miles, I waved a welcome and indicated that I would soon be finished. I watched her flop into a chair and reach for a book nearby. She read passages, shaking her head, making little grimaces and thrusting out her lower lip in disapproval.

I knew it was an enlightening book, written by a highly regarded man who had helped many to understand.

When I put down the receiver and greeted her, she said, "I thought he was fine. until I met him." Then, she tossed the book on my desk with a petulant air. "He doesn't look anything like the kind of man you'd expect!"

"I don't need to remind you that we don't judge by appearances," I chided.

For the next several minutes Janet produced stories of the faults she had found in several of the teachers she'd known, with items about their personal lives.

"You didn't come all this distance just to tell me that," I stopped her.

"Not exactly, but it's a good beginning," she sighed. "I don't experience all this good they're all so glib about-saying it is right here, and so on."

As she spoke, I realized this was a thought which I'd had to deal with frequently. I had often been asked why, if what I believed was true, I did not have a house with a swimming pool, servants, and a chauffeur and a limousine. The fact that I was in excellent health, did not have to wear glasses, and was sufficiently supplied passed by these questioners unnoticed.

Janet was voicing my own belief that there were persons who could not believe unless they could see the outer evidence, in a way they thought it should be.

She added, "Mr. Blank recently was divorced. Does that look as though he believes what he is teaching?"

I surprised her when I replied, "Yes, it does. If harmony is lacking in any union, then, of course, it is not a 'union,' is it? When harmony is an established idea in consciousness, all that disturbs is eliminated."

"But don't you see? I want a teacher who is practising perfection, that is, giving me a correct example to follow."

"Janet, I know you do know that the real teacher is within *you.* It is you who are to become the good example. Surely, the Intelligence within you tells you that to deny God's goodness at several points, and then attempt to affirm it *only* for oneself is a 'house divided against itself.'"

"I have to see evil and recognize it as such so that I can avoid making the same errors, don't I?" she objected.

"Then, you *deny* God's Allness?" I pursued.

"Not at all, but out here on the relative plane, there is evil. We see it and hear about it all the time. Aren't people telling you, all the time, their troubles and problems?"

When Janet said this, I had to smile. She had supplied her own answer. "Out *here*?" I grinned.

"Do you recognize that these come from their own beliefs, Janet? As long as you, or they have a belief in evil, it will be there to observe. Will it not? Isn't it practical to postulate a perfect life?"

Her mouth dropped open in amazement, "I've been confused, but I see it all now! Why, I've been double minded all this time—not single—eyed to the Truth at all."

I added, "I believe this thought will help you to hang on to directing your attention properly; while there is only one Mind which we all use, it is helpful to consider that we get impressions from two sources when we first begin to grasp this idea."

"How do you mean that?"

"The senses give us most of our impressions; but now and then, something from within impresses itself upon our awareness."

"Intuition?"

"Yes, the instinctive knowledge or perception. You just experienced it," I laughed.

"That's right, I did!" Her eyes were sparkling. "It's a feeling, a wonderful feeling."

"Sure it is, because that's the Divinity within you. When all the impressions are coming only from the outside, that feeling is submerged. But It is always there."

She left me, bubbling over with joy.

Your Divinity Does Not Come and Go

While this wonderful feeling of peace and joy is forever present, it can be so clouded over with other impressions that it seems to be missing. It is somewhat like trying to see a city through the mist of fog. Even though you know all the buildings are still there, you cannot discern them.

A childlike trust, coupled with sincerity and a willingness to be patient will yourself as you persevere, will help you to understand how to go about constructing right beliefs.

If you are one who has regarded the Bible as a number of books telling of historical events which happened to peoples hundreds of years ago, it has had scant meaning for you. Perhaps you have sometimes had a glimmer of light from the Psalms, the Proverbs, or the Gospels, but wouldn't you like to be able to read it from the standpoint of understanding its universal laws? Wouldn't you like to live in such a way that joy was always yours? Isn't it thrilling to contemplate the possibility of being able to solve every kind of problem which you might encounter?

Some folks dabble lightly at this subject, nibbling around the edges, and delay the good they might experience now. They wind up disgruntled because they think they have been misinformed.

Has anyone been saved from making more mistakes simply by saying, "I believe in Jesus Christ"? Or by believing that He died so that they might go right on sinning, making the same errors over and over, yet "be saved" just the same? He, whose teaching is "Go, and sin no more," meant exactly that.

It is necessary to know whether your mistake is one of omission or commission. You must understand the Law of Mind.

Your Personal Will Must Be Used Correctly

A man whom I shall call Mr. Allen was in excellent health, had a fine, successful business, and a lovely family. Having bought several books on the subject, he was teaching himself; but he called me and asked for an appointment.

After the introduction and his explanation of all this, he bristled as he told me, "If there is anything to this, this stuff ought to work for me."

I could hardly contain my amusement, for I remember that one of my own teachers had once said that beginners usually thought this was a method of acquiring anything one wanted, at anyone's expense. Fortunately for us all, it doesn't "work" that way.

Mr. Allen continued, "The idea I have is a good, sound one. I'm not trying to cheat anyone. I see no reason why it doesn't work."

"Then, it is working", I told him.

"No, it's not!" he said gruffly. I need some help. I don't believe in practitioners, so I wanted to do this myself; but apparently I'm not doing it right."

He didn't believe in practitioners? But here he was! I didn't try to suppress my grin. "Surely, Mr. Allen, you aren't believing that you are the one individual for whom the laws of life don't work?"

"Of course not, but I must be doing something wrong, or all of this is just a lot of malarkey!"

A man who had found Divinity wouldn't think of making such a remark. He was full of inner disharmony because he was striving to "get the best of" some situation by exerting his personal will over it. Full of self-concern and self-importance, he was causing himself to experience all sorts of unpleasant emotions.

Experience had taught me that persons who believed this study to be the exertion of their personal will over external events could not bear being told that they were wrong about anything. Even their faults have become virtues to them, so that any kind of recrimination sets up resistance. Such people as these build up tensions fast.

"Well," I said lightly, "suppose you tell me what it is that you strive to accomplish, and we can then see what needs to be added to what you have done so far."

He leaned back in his chair, saying, "I have seen a way to expand my business by taking in another one. I have worked out all the details. They are sound and fair, but this chap I want to buy out keeps refusing. I've talked my head off, but he still refuses."

Only at the sense level had his intellect grasped the idea of what could be done with the Law of Mind. There was something he wanted to get, and that was his only interest. The fact that some character trait might be improved or reinforced had not occurred to him.

"You assumed that he would see your sound reasoning in this proposition?" I asked.

"I offered him enough money. He admitted it was a good idea but said he didn't want to do it." Mr. Allen slammed his right fist into his left palm, a gesture which effectively indicated his desire to use his personal will to make another man do his bidding.

"Are you aware, Mr. Allen, that this forcing, or persuading, another person to follow your personal will is called 'mortal thinking? That this isn't the way to use the Law of Mind?"

He blustered, "I'm not trying to cheat him, he will benefit."

"He lives according to his own state of consciousness; he apparently doesn't see it that way," I said gently. "Suppose you did succeed in convincing him that he should do what you want done? Do you realize that this action on your part, opens a door, so to speak, for the same thing to happen to you? Surely, you'd like to retain your own authority?"

A frown puckered his brow. "What do you mean?"

"Hasn't it occurred to you that there are things not known by *your* conscious mind, that are known *in and by* Divine Mind?" I watched him stroke his chin thoughtfully and waited until he nodded, then I went on, "You see, we don't tell God how; He tells us. He gave you the idea for expansion, then you jumped to a conclusion, reaching it by means of what your senses knew about."

He looked for all the world like a little lad who has just discovered that two times two does not equal five.

"But I thought we were supposed to use our intelligence," he exclaimed. "I knew about this place, and it seemed to me just right."

"You knew of this place by means of your *senses,* didn't you? The senses are the carnal mind. And, what does the Bible have to say about the carnal mind?"

"It says it is *enmity* to God. Oh, I see! Then, this means God has a better plan."

"Exactly! Now you can say, 'Not my will, but thine be done."

"If I do that now, will this chap change his mind?"

"Not necessarily. You could be entertaining some belief which blocks the passage of divine thoughts. Discords and conflicts do occur among your thoughts; the Bible calls them 'storms.' The Savior knows how to quiet these storms. Your job at such times is to find the Divinity within you . . . to have the '*same* Mind that was in Christ, Jesus."

"Then, just tinkering with the thought, 'Not my will but thine' doesn't *do* anything?"

"It is *recognition* that God's laws are always operating. Suffering of any kind is caused by not obeying them."

He looked puzzled, "How can you obey them if you don't know all of them?"

"What you need to know the most and first is how to find Divinity within you." His expression made me add with a smile, "Oh, everyone knows it's there, but conscious knowledge is necessary. Yes, even though some deny they have any belief in God, they really *do* believe in God."

"Oh, I don't think they do. I've heard lots of arguments, and those folks have really convinced themselves."

"Mr. Allen, aren't they really saying that they don't believe God is something you can see, hear, or touch? And isn't what you hear them say a sense impression, as far as you are concerned?"

He was relaxed and grinning. "You have a way of making me perceive how often I slip back into sense consciousness. How do I find the Divinity within me?"

"Why not try thinking of Judas? I take it that you had read your Bible and know who he is, what he represents."

"Judas? Why Judas? He was a betrayer."

"A 'betrayer' because he revealed the whereabouts of the Christ, that's right. Judas has been hated and despised by those who interpret the Bible on the level of sense consciousness; but, Mr. Allen, if you have a thought which reveals to you where your Divinity is, the Christ Mind, you wouldn't dislike *that* thought."

"No, but I keep thinking of Judas as being the cause of the crucifixion."

"That's because you have accepted the Bible stories as being about personalities, rather than symbology which depicts the universal laws."

"What did Judas represent?"

"Judas is symbolic of your desire, the unfulfilled one. Because you have such a desire, you seek the Kingdom of Heaven, or place in mind where you recognize that everything is first a word. A 'word' is an idea."

"Then I say, 'I have the idea!'"

"Correct!"

"How are you going to explain away the crucifixion of Jesus?" he asked.

"I don't 'explain it away,' but you have gone back to dealing with the pictures you've formed in the sense mind. See how quickly your sense mind can move your attention from Divinity? Suppose you had been told since childhood to revere Oliver Twist? Would your reverence make you into a better person?"

"Not unless I followed in his footsteps and became like him; I get your point." He shook his head, "It isn't as easy as I thought. I was brought up to be honest, to do my work well ar.d to exercise a reasonable amount of good judgment, but I was also brought up to believe that Jesus was a man."

"There's no quarrel there; your father was a man; you are a man. The world, as it appears to the senses is full of men and women, as well as children, each of which has a mind of his own. One thing they all have in common, is that thing called life. Some love and protect their life, make the most of it; others farther down the scale do not understand what it is which sent them into expression and misuse it for a while.

"All have one Father, one Source, and that Father had only one Son, or idea of 'man in His image.' Jesus represents your own awareness of life, and he became the Christ, or Savior, when he discovered his own Divinity, your Divinity. The Son is the Divine Pattern and is within every man, though it may take him eons to become consciously aware of it."

Mr. Allen shifted his position and studied me. "You have proved this to your satisfaction, haven't you?"

"Yes. Judas is this sense of needing something, that sends you to look for the Christ Mind. It is there that your desire is fulfilled. Then, Judas 'dies!' That is, you no longer have that desire."

"Is the crucifixion the crossing out of the sense awareness?" He scowled, "No senses any more?"

"Oh dear no!" I said quickly. "you need to have them to know how you *are* believing. The crucifixion actually represents the discovery that you are not this mortal, physical thing you have so long believed you were."

"You know," he said thoughtfully, "*that* is a much more palatable idea, than the one about a good man who was so misunderstood and mistreated. As a kid, I used to wonder how anyone thought *that* encouraged anyone to be good. It always seemed to me that an ignominious ending in front of all one's family and friends would be about the worst possible thing that could happen."

"Yes, and I believe because it is palatable, as you say, you can digest its meaning. God's offspring, or Son, is the idea of mankind. It is a Perfect Idea. As you contemplate the natural of this Divinity within you, you'll be less and less troubled by 'things to get rid of.'

"A month later, this man came back to tell me how he had found a much better business for his expansion program. He told me, "Learning to keep my attention on Divinity is the most worthwhile, most rewarding, and most practical exercise I have ever learned!"

It Takes Care of Every Need

Whether your need is the alertness to jump out of the way of a skidding automobile or the consumption of right food for your own body needs, this Divine Intelligence within is ready to supply it. Things you need to know will be brought to your attention. This powerful Intelligence is always ready. It asks of you just one thing, that you take time to become aware of Its Presence *by thinking of Its nature.*

CHAPTER 4

How to Tap the Universal Energies

You have begun to understand why you have held the opinion of yourself that you have, and how it has come into existence due to your own actions. You know that those actions all stemmed from the way you think about everything, including yourself.

You began to want to be truthful, sincere, and trustworthy, rather than scheming, sly or covetous. You value your self-opinion and realize how important your own concept of yourself must be. That others do not know of something you do or think that is "not too nice," does not matter half so much as that you know it. You are important to you, and you must feel satisfied with yourself.

You have grasped the idea that God is not a "Something or Someone" far off, but is a Divine Spark within you. You understand that the senses are finite, therefore limited, and that God is Infinite and Unlimited.

If you now see the difference between what the senses report to you and God's ideas, you are aware of the "first day," which is a period of enlightenment.

The Second Day

This "day," or next period of enlightenment, you become aware that you are the life that lives the experiences you have. You are not the body of form, or even the personality, but you are the spirit of life.

You are aware that the senses always show you a dual state, both good and bad, with their numerous variations. This is why all sense testimony must be set aside during your prayer period. In order to turn your attention toward your Divinity, you do not deal in thought with any sense beliefs such as persons, places, or events.

Reach for the Right Feeling

Decide that you do not feel weak or inadequate. Push out the feelings of irritation, jealousy, and dislike. Let go of your disappointments. Stop all the cringing timidness, the suspicious imaginings. These feelings do you no good whatsoever. Make up your mind that you do not have to feel anxious or uneasy.

Now, with all the boldness you can summon, think that God has just taken over all of your affairs. You are intimately connected with this omnipresent Good. Would God the all-powerful tremble with fear? God is Peace, so how could He be troubled?

See if you can feel this Loving Presence taking charge of all your affairs as though they were His. God would be strong, intelligent, and thoroughly competent. Nothing is arduous or distasteful to God. Right at the point where you are, God is. God is the very substance of what you are.

God is waiting to think through you, to act by means of you. Are you beginning to experience, in some measure, an entirely different feeling?

Feel Grateful

Gratitude is a quality of God. Allow yourself to feel appreciative that now you know how to find your own Divinity. By recognizing that God is your own life and mind you have taken the limitations off yourself.

Say: *"Let this God Mind show forth in me as Peace and Love."*

Then add: *"And this God Mind does show forth in me as Peace and Love."*

Be very still until the spirit of this feeling uplifts your mood.

Old Grievances Slip Away

The kind of thoughts which caused anxiety slip out of your attention. Keep them out. If you rake the leaves your lawn on Tuesday, you wouldn't think of going out Wednesday and scattering them about again. You know more will be falling from time to time. Each day more other beliefs of your senses will accost you, so don't make your load heavier than it need be while you are learning. Don't hesitate to remind yourself that God is where you are, and that His Love and help and ways of showing it are more numerous than the leaves on your lawn.

Your Life Is Energy

When outer events become so interesting or engrossing, you may become forgetful of all this Divinity within. Then, the body begins to feel tired, achy, or painful. Headaches, colds, cramps, and all manner of pain-producing disturbances may ensue.

All that is really happening is that you are being called back to the Source of Energy and Life. Refill yourself with the awareness of your own Divinity. Get back to the feeling of inward confidence of an unlimited supply of energy. Remember once again that the Great Healer is within you, has never left you; but you, with your attention back in sense consciousness for so long, left It.

Tell yourself: "*I am energy, which is Perfect Life. I am energetic. I am that very Intelligence and Love which God is.*" Feel it; know it. Know it with all your heart. Forgive yourself for having moved away for so long into sense consciousness, where you forgot who, where, and what God is.

You are connected to the great ocean of life. Only the way you think needs to be changed when something seems to be amiss. You don't have to be changed; nothing is wrong with you. Discovery of the Real You is the greatest adventure you will ever know.

How to Make This Discovery

Think of the word *breathe*; this is something you are doing all of the time. Now, take a deep breath. Inhale deeply and exhale. What caused you to take that action? It was a thought. As your eyes read the words on the page, suggesting this action to your mind, you had a choice; you could accept that suggestion, or refuse to. Quite possibly, you automatically accepted it and took a deep breath. You could do so because you know there is nothing harmful in breathing deeply.

How many other suggestions do you accept as readily with no regard as to whether they are helpful?

I am showing you a point of control. At the point where you know your life is God's Livingness, you are one with the Father. Identical.

Think! What does that say to you?

By means of the power which God is, you walk talk, think, see, hear, digest, breathe. Name what you think God is not capable of doing.

If there is anything, then that is the place where you are denying God's Presence.

That's not what you want to do, is it?

Your body is an avenue for God's activity; your mental realm is also an avenue for this same activity, so how will you permit this activity to take place?

Relax. Gently, still all your thoughts. See how long you can keep from thinking about anything.

When it seems to you that you just must think something, this is: *"I AM ALL THERE IS."*

ONENESS

The wholeness of the Divine Presence is right here.
The Life Principle is everywhere in all its fullness.
Therefore It is where I am. It is what I am.

Hold it until your joy and peace increase. Hold it until the limited, tight feelings leave. The Spirit ALWAYS RESPONDS.

What understanding you feel after each time of this kind of exercise! Fascinating new ideas will occupy your attention; the feeling of love increases; the life in the body takes on a new exhilaration. Many areas of consciousness must be reached, so take this exercise often.

Bring Your Attention to Wholeness

Unhappiness of any kind shows you where your incorrect beliefs are hiding. Unpleasantness of any kind whatsoever is showing you where, as well as what, your belief in evil is.

Whenever you are believing in evil, the devil, or trouble, you are not believing in God, are you? I caution that this must become more than merely an intellectual-level thought; it must become a feeling.

Like plus and minus, the spiritual truth and the material fact I are opposites. While one is on the throne of attention, the other is absent. It takes training to keep your attention upon the Divine, for human thought tends to wander back to its dual activities; you must adopt single-mindedness.

God needs you for His expression, so He is going to take care of you. So, whatever appears to be wrong to you is a lie.

Why would you want to believe a lie?

Then only possible reason would be that you wanted to be punished and thought you deserved it. No one can possibly believe that God is within him when he continues to behave "like the devil." If you are sharp-tongued, moody, and grouchy and given to displays of temper, you will find it most difficult to make the discovery of your real self. Nevertheless, it can be done; it has been done. Consistently use these exercises, and the time will come when you will have no desire to return to your former behavior.

That sort of negative behavior only proves the adage. "Evil destroys itself." It is a feeling of being limited, of lacking good. The only cure for it is the discovery of the true nature, the unlimited Self.

Arrogance Brings Regret

High-handed, aggressive individuals, "swinging their weight around" as they say, are covering up (they think) some lack in themselves. What they lack is real love. Hostile to the world, as well as themselves, they gain attention by being disagreeable.

Arrogant persons do climb by the sheer strength of taking every advantage of those weaker than themselves, but these martinets who discipline others with such a heavy hand go only so far and then stop.

If you see yourself as one who has gone just so far and then been stopped, it could be that arrogance is your problem. Gentle kindness, tenderness, consideration for the rights of others, expressions of sincere praise will help you.

Aggressive, arrogant persons are seldom aware that they are rank materialists and see nothing wrong with themselves until they come to the end of their rope. History shows us how many have hung on the end of that rope. In the words of Jeremiah, they "have forsaken God, the fountain of living waters," and they are "broken cisterns that can hold no water."

If you have gone just so far and then stopped—the mill burned down, someone did some double-dealing, there was no demand for your product—what you need is not to get something, but to give more love.

What Motivates You?

Why do you wish to pamper yourself with luxuries? Do you feel greedy? What do you strive to prove? Are you a show-off? Whom do you wish to impress?

Isn't what you think of yourself more important than what others think of you? If not, why not?

Don't you have to live with yourself all the time?

Can you stand knowing about some of the things you've done?

The Remedy is to Understand

Finding the meaning of Divine Love gives you understanding. Every time any antagonism you feel causes you to act in such a way that you bring about an unpleasant feeling in another, whether it be envy, jealousy, worry, fear, or hate, you too will suffer. If you have become so hard of heart that you feel no remorse, Nature will find a way to give your body a pain.

Perhaps you have beard it said that you can't help it if another is envious; that is right, but you can help it if he is envious of *you*. Your own right thought will handle this.

Love is a giving of yourself. How could you "give of yourself" if there is nothing in you worth accepting? But there is, of course. You have but to find it and express it.

To the strictly material-minded person, love is only romance and physical pleasure, mostly expressed as "what I want" and not "how may I help you?"

Search deeply within yourself for the meaning of love. Ponder it often, remembering that it is one of your most precious jewels.

Sometimes the awareness of the real meaning of love comes like a flash of light, causing one to see the self-righteousness he has harbored, and to observe that all the time he was enumerating the faults of others, he was actually counting his own.

More often, it comes slowly. Only now and then does a person see that his so-called generosity was only a form of bargaining, and that he really expected back twice what he gave. The average individual dislikes admitting that he has tried to buy business or friendship, or that he has been generous only because such action promised some form of reward. If he will refuse to take refuge behind intellectual arguments, his true Self will reveal Itself as Love.

Clear Away the Rubble

If this lesson has brought you to the place where you will no longer look with disapproval at others whose errors you no longer make, you have cleared away some of the rubble. You won't be so quick to criticize and condemn now that you know that what you put your attention upon with any degree of feeling is apt to manifest itself as your own experience.

All that is suggested to you is that once you perceive that a certain way of thinking is wrong, you will stop thinking that way.

We have used the pronoun "you" interchangeably to mean the self you *think* you are and the Self you really *are*. One is real, the other fictitious.

There is nothing wrong with the Real You, and there never has been. Only the finite you, the limited, mortal being you have so long thought you were, has "wrought and suffered." The infinite you lies in smiling repose. Awake, Angel!

CHAPTER 5

Moving Toward Joy

That which is imperfect does not emerge from that which is Perfect. So many have taught and sincerely believed that God created sinners. *Failure to comprehend the meaning of what God has created, and of Man's relationship to that Deity, has brought about many ridiculous beliefs.*

Conflicting Beliefs

Attempting to accept an all-good God and a Kingdom of Heaven by contrasting them with the devil and hell has produced confusion in the reasoning of many. Apparently it has not occurred to these people that when they say, "God is All-Powerful" and then add that the devil has much power, that they are contradicting themselves.

Why does the Bible mention the devil? This is symbology to indicate Man's misuse of the intelligence and freedom of choice that God gave him. Ignorance of the Law of Mind causes Man to believe in much that is not true. Thus, as every belief is manifested in some way, it is most unfortunate that many of his beliefs are untrue.

Blaming another is a way in which you bring about conflict among your beliefs. Refusing to lay the blame for some unfortunate circumstance on another's doorstep is one of the quickest ways to real joy. It is a waste of time and energy to deal with the argument as to whether or not you should blame another. When it appears to you that another has acted either foolishly or maliciously, such appearance comes from your own beliefs.

Dislodge your own judgment and keep your eye focused on a universe of wisdom, harmony, and joy, and not only will the false belief be removed, but the outer result will benefit you and not be harmful.

Joy Is Your Goal

Since your objective is to find joy, you can see that discontent, allowing your attention to dwell upon past unpleasantness, condemning others, and finding fault are all joy robbers.

No one is beating you over the head to make you think such thoughts; they are your choice. Since you are always free to choose what you think about, why not learn to be happy each moment? In each moment there is something nice, pleasant, and good that you can think about. As you make the effort to do this it becomes easier to lift your attention to the Perfect Truth. You can reach the state of consciousness where you are no longer aware of any discord or inharmony, for you have observed that dissatisfaction and discontent are actually your way of denying the Presence of God.

Forgiving Brings Joy

It is not so much what others do to you that harms, hurts, and harasses, but the way in which you allow your-self to harbor and hug to yourself the feelings of anger and self-pity. Indulgence of such feelings acts just like poison in your system, and you are doing this to yourself! You must forgive the other person not for his sake, but for your own.

A woman student was telling me about a conversation she'd had with a neighbor who had been greatly upset because of some action of her daughter-in-law. The neighbor made the remark that she could never forgive this.

"Oh, but you must!" this lady exclaimed. "She is younger than you, and there is much she doesn't know. You are the one who must show understanding."

"How?" asked the neighbor.

There I stood, fumbling with words. All I could think of was that she should *try* to understand her better. I remembered later that there was a person I had never forgiven. Just *how* do you really forgive?" she asked me.

What Forgiveness Really Is

It is exchanging a wrong belief for a right one.

It is transferring your thought from the event to the goodness of God.

It is moving your attention to your own divine nature, and looking from there to the Perfection all around you.

It is the comprehension of why you were hurt by the person. Quite often the reason it hurts you so much is because you are continuing to make the *same* error. Lack of forgiveness is a sense of guilt coming from an inner knowledge that *you* still act upon some false belief.

Be courageous enough to take a good look at whatever you can't forgive, or haven't forgiven.

We often forget when we look at the acts of others how we ourselves have accepted beliefs, nourished and sustained them, until finally they appeared as a condition or situation. Unaware that we have passed up opportunities for our own growth and development, we are saddled with a guilty feeling. Into this area we must introduce a conscious awareness of the Presence of All Good.

It is always yourself that you have to forgive, never another person. Once this is clear to you, you are well on the way to Joy. See yourself in the center of the Kingdom of God. Acquaint yourself with it. Unforgiveness has deep roots.

You need all your power and all your love to get to these roots. Not by mental means alone will you change anything, but by "My Spirit."

Should You Blame Yourself?

No, you don't blame yourself. You discover which belief is false. Take Bonnie and Phil's case, for example. Bonnie was divorcing Phillip on the grounds of his excessive drinking. He was a successful salesman and claimed that his business demanded that he buy his clients drinks and drink along with them.

"I don't want our children to grow up as I had to," Bonnie told me, "for my dad was always drinking. I lost respect for him. Why, I was even ashamed of him! I think it had a lot to do with my feelings of inferiority in school and ever since. Phil knows this, and loves our little boy and girl. I just can't understand why he thinks he must continue to drink in order to sell, when he knows how I feel."

"Does he want the divorce, too?" I asked.

"He says not. In fact, he has become so disturbed about it now that he isn't selling anything, and so, no money! What shall I do?" she wailed.

At Bonnie's request, Phil came willingly to see me. "It's true," he said forlornly. "Without Bonnie and the kids, I've lost all incentive. I haven't made a sale since we parted, and I'm so bothered that I couldn't sell a sack of peanuts to a hungry man." Since their separation, Phil hadn't touched a drop of liquor.

When I talked with Bonnie again. I pointed out to her the basic pattern of her own childhood, and showed her how it had never been cleared out of her consciousness. She had met and married a man who out-pictured it. I explained how this belief had been resting there unforgiven.

"Then, I'm to blame," she said.

"No, but I'm going to show you how to rid yourself of that belief."

"It is really my dad who is to blame, isn't it?" she asked quickly.

"It is ignorance that is the cause, Bonnie; not yours, not his, but everyone's. Persons take on these beliefs about drinking to excess from seeing it, hearing about it, and having it continually held up before their mind's eye, we might say. They can accept these beliefs just by listening to others talk, just as some people take on unpleasant illnesses by thinking about them all of the time, fearing them, and looking for signs of them."

"Golly," she said, "that's hard to understand. I thought diseases were caused by germs."

"They are, but the germ has to be believed in."

"How about someone very ignorant of germs? They get sick, don't they? Also small children do."

"That's right, Bonnie, and these beliefs are all floating through race consciousness; anyone can accept them, until he learns how to think correctly. Individuals take on beliefs in hard times, poverty, disasters of all kinds. Some folks never talk about anything else; they are adding to the great swarm of negative thoughts."

"Good heavens! And drinking too much is just another one of those kinds of beliefs?" Bonnie gasped.

"Yes. Now, Bonnie, you and Phil have been married about eight years. Has he told you much about his work of selling and advertising?" I asked.

When she nodded, I continued, "Then, you know that good advertising makes you want to try the product, don't you? You know that selling is simply an art of convincing the buyer still further. Both the advertiser and the seller are dealing with beliefs, aren't they? I want to help you see how it is that we are all in the process of accepting or rejecting beliefs all the time.

"Most of our lives we accept what we see without a question. No one tells us that what we see isn't true. Until we see a theater magician do his act, we have become quite accustomed to thinking that everything we see is the way it looks."

Her brown eyes gazed at me thoughtfully. "I saw a bird once that looked like it was singing, but I couldn't hear a sound. I know that the sound it was making was just out of my range of hearing. I don't understand about sight, though.

"What I am getting at is that all of the senses can be fooled. Even when they are very sharp and accurate, it is the mind back of them which understands and comprehends. Skills are taught in every kind of school, manual arts, fine arts, chemistry, and so on, but who is teaching how to reject an unwanted belief, or an untrue one?"

"Like Dad's drinking problem?"

"Yes. Today there are such places, but when you were a little girl these ideas weren't common knowledge. Your mother believed a certain way, and that belief soon became your own. Do you want to change it?"

Bonnie's chin went up, "Oh yes! How do I do it?"

"Forgiveness, Bonnie." I saw the look on her face cloud. "It doesn't mean what you've been thinking it means. It doesn't mean to mouth the words, 'I forgive you' and act hypocritically, pretending something you still don't feel."

"Oh?" Her eyes widened. "If I change the belief about Dad, will it also be changed about Phil?"

"When you change the belief, it will not be manifesting anywhere, as far as you are concerned."

"Oh goody!" she clapped her hands. "Tell me, how."

"First, you must know that you are only going to change your own mind. You aren't to try to change your husband or your dad. Concern yourself not the slightest with what someone else is believing. Tell no one what you are trying to do."

"Why not? You mean not even my mother or my best friend?"

"Well-intentioned though they may be, it is better for you to wait until later to say anything about this. Since you are only going to deal with your own thought, you will find that you are hard put to explain it until you have done it."

"All right," Bonnie said excitedly, I won't say a word to anyone. I feel right now that I'm going to clear up a whole lot of things."

"First of all, every time you think of either one of these men, remember that what beats your heart also beats theirs. Then think that this is Life, and it is a perfect intelligence and love. This Life is God.

"Second, when you think about drinking, see if you can realize that the liquor, as such has no real power. Nobody craves it, nobody needs it. Joy comes from a belief. Persons who believe that the drinking of liquor makes them more relaxed and happier, only *think* they feel that way. They could be just as relaxed and happy without the expense." I smiled. "Or use it to try to stop thinking!"

"Oh, I understand," Bonnie said quickly, "and they could have all the money they spent that way for other things."

"You see, as long as you believe it is a bad thing, and harmful, you only *add to* a belief in it. By your belief that it is something with any kind of power, you make *it seem more real*."

"Then it isn't only those addicted to it that give it power?"

"That's right, Bonnie, and both those who fight against it with hate and those who use it are making the *belief* in it more *firmly entrenched*."

I know what you are saying to me—that *nothing* has more power than God."

"Nothing has any power but God," I corrected.

It took Bonnie four months to rid herself of this belief completely. Tangled up with it were other beliefs which supported it, and one by one they had to be weeded out. Even so, long before the four months had passed, she come in to tell me some good news.

"Daddy has quit drinking," she grinned at me. "I had avoided going over there when I knew he'd be at home, but one day I wanted to see Mom about something, and I just forgot he'd be at home at that hour. We chatted just as if I'd never been mad at him. In fact, I never even looked to see if there was his usual bottle around. He was painting the kitchen."

"That's the way it works," I said.

'A couple of days later, Mom told me that he had been tapering off for some time and she was now convinced that he really meant to give it up."

Necessity to make a living had put Phil into a different line of work temporarily. He felt he couldn't sell and keep his promise to Bonnie not to drink, or buy drinks, and since that was what he had promised, to be allowed back, he kept his word.

About the beginning of the fourth month of her determined effort to change these faulty beliefs, Bonnie came in to tell me this story:

"When I first came to you, we were broke," she broke off, laughing. "I mean, temporarily out of funds." She brushed her hair back, as though she had pushed the belief out too with the gesture.' "Mom gave me $200. She told me the other day that Daddy gave it to her and said to tell me it was her own private savings. Wasn't that sweet of him? I suppose he thought I wouldn't accept it from him; our relationship had been none too congenial. He understood . . . then . . . how I'd felt about him." Tears filled her eyes. "I'm so glad I changed my thought about him. He's really a darling."

"It *is* clear to you now that knowledge coming only through your senses is the *cause* of these kinds of beliefs, isn't it?"

"You mean judging by appearances instead of righteous judgment? Oh yes, and I see that the right thought brings about the right emotion and does change the appearance. The change appears to be a miracle, but it is only using a higher law. And Phil is so happy now. At first, I would only let him come and eat his dinner with us because I didn't want the children to have a wrong impression," she laughed.

"Now, Bonnie, you can explain this to someone else, for you really know how, having done it yourself."

"I know, I know! I have been explaining it all to Phil, and he was able to understand me. He's been busy changing some of his own false beliefs. Does it work this way always, for everyone? That all improve, I mean?"

"Yes. They always improve some, or they go out of your life. I have reason to believe that all do improve even if you cannot see them do so."

Harmony and Order Already Exist

That which is real and lasting is present even though the senses may not be currently perceiving it. Through placing the attention correctly, obstacles float away. Harmonious adjustments take place because harmony is a law of life.

As I took my place at the lecture one night for a regular class, I was startled at the appearance of the guest of one of my regular students. She was a young woman whose face was pulled awry by facial paralysis, one eyelid drooping and a sagging cheek with the lower side of her mouth hanging as though unsupported. I looked away from her quickly, and began my talk:

"Our purpose here in the study of this subject is to learn how to bring our thoughts into alignment with a harmony and order which already exists."

I didn't want to stare at my student's guest and increase her awareness of her malady. It was clear enough why she had been invited. At the time of this experience, I had been in the work only a few years, but had learned that if I kept looking at any unwanted condition, it was harder for me to reach a feeling that it wasn't real, or that it didn't have to be lasting. While it was easy for me to comprehend that any such condition was only temporary, it would have an appalling reality for me if I allowed my senses to even dwell upon it for a short time.

Not many months before this night, I had been treating a woman with a manifestation of skin cancer on her mouth. One morning I awoke to discover a horrible looking sore inside my own mouth. Knowing instantly what I had done, becoming too concerned with the physical aspect, I became busy with knowing the Truth. Consequently, we were both healed simultaneously. Alerted by this experience, I was, thereafter, careful to remember that God's life was in every muscle and tissue, beating every heart.

Continuing with the lesson, I said, "Before we knew about this orderly, harmonious, and perfect Life, we made no effort to be careful of what we thought, and judged everything by its present appearance. Quite unintentionally, because we were ignorant of what the outcome might be, we dropped a good many thought patterns to a level where they later became manifested as distressing conditions or events.

"Only what God *is* has real existence. Therefore, anything which can be classified as temporary, or unlike God, contrary to God the all-good, has to be unreal. It is like witnessing a mirage . . . while it seems to be there, all that supports it is *our belief.* We let go of the belief by taking our attention away from what appears to the senses and placing our thought upon the Presence of God as our perfect life. By pondering the aspects of this Truth, we have replaced the wrong belief with a correct idea."

As I said this, I must have forgotten all about our guest, for I didn't think about her again until she was brought to me after the class to be introduced. My subject became the only thing which was important.

"One must engage in a process of reasoning," I went on, "until a deep inner conviction moves the untrue belief out of the way. Then you cannot escape having a healing, a better condition, or a solved problem." I quoted Scriptural passages from which these ideas come until the students sitting before me were lifted out of their undivine states of consciousness. When a teacher's attention is fixed upon the Light that is Truth, it automatically charges others with that dynamic Spirit. There is a point in everyone's consciousness where he meets Divinity.

"When you can understand," I added, "that the Divine qualities in you exit in all others as well, then you will begin to observe them. If you deny these are present because you have not seen them expressed, you have allowed no passageway through which they might come. This is why we tell you to look to God for all the good you desire, such as love, appreciation, gratitude, sincerity, pleasantness, and peace.

"Perhaps you have noticed a certain person who is never grateful? Try thinking of God's Life in that person as being the quality of gratitude, and you will see changes that will amaze you.

"Take someone who is cross and grumpy. Turn your attention to the Life there as being serenity and peace. Remember then that God is also love and joy, and carry it further to think of harmony and order."

There were smiles on all their faces as I closed. As I stepped down from the platform several of the students rushed up to me, speaking excitedly, so that what they said was a bit incomprehensible. I was introduced to the guest, a charming, pretty young woman.

She said, "I knew something had happened to me by the feeling I had; it was so wonderful. I just had to take out my compact and look at my face."

Until that moment I had not given another thought to what I had seen earlier. Putting the appearance completely from my attention, I had apparently not looked her way again.

The disturbance in her consciousness gone, she resumed a normal state.

"When we saw what had happened," the student who brought this young lady said, "we got so excited and tickled I was afraid we were disturbing you. We both felt like shouting for joy."

I had to smile, for I was daily becoming more aware of how many there were who found the *manifestation* of some good far more interesting than what they were learning! How could I show them the naturalness of all good? How could I make them see that it was the Father's goodwill to give them the Kingdom?

"My doctor said it might take about six months," the young lady informed me. "He said it would leave gradually." Astonishment was still on her face.

"You experienced a perfectly natural thing, once you understood, and the belief you held gave way," I said. "Now forget the whole thing by remembering that you are divinely blessed."

When Your Feelings Are Hurt

Everyone else is running this race for greater understanding, just as you are. The runner in a foot race must be active, alert, and sure of his footing. So must you be. If you are a sensitive person, easily offended, it is not only difficult for you to find joy, but at times it is seemingly impossible. You are not sure that anything you do is the right thing, and because you have such a fear of being hurt, a good many of the acts you perform actually are mistakes.

Your whole problem is that you really don't know that you have a right to the good you want. Getting only a small glimmer of light on the subject, you interpret such a statement as meaning that all you have to do is take something which belongs to someone else. You mentally deal with the material things known to the senses. You find that your rights stop exactly where the other fellow's rights begin, even when it comes to robbing him of his peace of mind. Speak critically and caustically, and he goes you one better. Your feelings are hurt.

You have started out on the "wrong foot." In order to have "good footing" in this race, you will have to understand that taking vengeance, getting even, and kicking back cannot be classified as "good footing."

Stop scolding and giving vent to your temper and others will cease hurting your feelings. It is as simple as that.

Expedite your own development by ridding yourself of fuzzy thinking. Arouse yourself out of the habit of letting others do your thinking for you by realizing their prejudices.

Be Alert

How much of this unfavorable bias have you yourself assumed? How many opinions do you claim as your own without really knowing anything about the subject?

The next time you think of something you don't like, ask yourself why you don't like it. Do you have a good reason? Do you know all about the subject, or are you one-sided, knowing only one viewpoint?

Become aware that you are a thinker, too.

You don't have to be like a blotter, sopping up the venom of what others believe. The way you permit yourself to feel is up to you. It may be that you associate with those just as recalcitrant as yourself. The next time your feelings are hurt, look to see whose feelings *you* have injured.

Be Active

If you know stubbornness is one of your characteristics, why not be stubborn about improving *yourself*, instead of attempting to put others straight? Save your vocal cords and work on your beliefs about yourself. Suit action to the thought.

See how you can benefit by what now stings when said to you. If someone calls you "sloppy," try being neat. Often things hurt because they are facts. When they are not true, forget them.

Slights, real or imagined, often cause some folks to ingratiate themselves by an exceptional display of generosity; but a display of munificence does not indicate magnanimity. We do not buy favor; we earn it.

To be above pettiness and forgive personal injuries is to look at the faults and weaknesses of others with understanding compassion. If you have a propensity for self-pity, remind yourself of some of the hardships endured bravely and surmounted by others. Then, see how big *you* can be.

Everything is under your control, if you will take that control. Forgiveness is a major step toward joy. If you can reach the feeling that God is Love, the hurt feeling will dissolve. Not only that, but you will know there had been a place inside of you where love was unknown, and you hurt so that you could fill that vacant place.

You Are Always in the Right Place

Every soul is born into just the right family and conditions, taking up precisely where he left off in his last embodiment. All the accrued earnings are present, as well as all the unpaid debts (those things as yet unlearned), for Life does not balance Her books at the close of an earthly span of living. You are free to go forward or lag behind.

What is a Soul? It is the realm of your beliefs, true and false, and it belongs exclusively to you. You are making your soul. You "save" it by giving it right beliefs and correct ideas. No matter how small your idea of heaven may be right now, it is from here that the eternal Substance upon which it feeds will come. Your concept of the Kingdom of Heaven will continually unfold, and the reward for "seeking it" is always, immediate.

Great joy always follows the union of the soul with its Source. It is a state of awareness that the enlightened of all ages have discovered. You can have a complete emancipation from discord of any kind if you will be diligent about never hurting others, not even with a wrong thought about them.

CHAPTER 6

Words Which Heal

You are now ready to change your mind about believing in "sinners." This will require much time and effort on your part, for the senses have you well indoctrinated into believing that there is much "wrong." You must make yourself understand that such beliefs in "evil" deny the existence of God.

Have you been believing that the "serpent" in the Garden of Eden allegory was a snake? Was this snake one who talked, and probably spoke whatever language you do? Of course now you realize that these feelers you call the senses, which apprise you of what goes on around and about you, wind through your body as a serpent winds, and permit you to know both good and evil.

You believe the Bible means what it says. Read in Genesis:

BUT THE TREE OF THE KNOWLEDGE OF GOOD AND EVIL, THOU SHALT NOT EAT OF IT; FOR IN THE DAY THAT THOU EATEST THEREOF THOU SHALT SURELY DIE.

(Genesis 2:17)

To "eat" of anything is to accept it as true. It has often been supposed that if you believe in only the good everything is then all right; it is just the evil you are not to accept. What this verse is saying to you, is that the *senses* never impart to you the primal Truth.

A "tree" in Bible language, means a source of thought, so you are being told that if you acknowledge the senses as a source, and judge by appearances, you have "eaten" (accepted) the fruit of this forbidden tree. A sin is a

67

transgression of God's Law; it is estrangement from one's True Self; it is turning from God.

THE WAGES OF SIN IS DEATH; BUT THE GIFT OF GOD IS ETERNAL LIFE THROUGH JESUS CHRIST OUR LORD.

(Romans 6:23)

1. Realize what Life is.
    One and the same Spirit shows forth in different degrees.
    Spirit is vital essence, or energy.

2. This Perfect Life is yours.
    It belongs to you now.
    It expresses Itself.

3. You are an avenue for God's expression.
    By means of the Power which God is, you walk, talk, think, breathe, etc.
    Everything is possible to this Power, God.

The Third Day

During this period of your enlightenment, you perceive the difference between the expression of God's life, love, and intelligence, and the materialistic thoughts which were patterns for your actions and which caused you to be more inclined to care what others thought of you than what you knew you were.

You have become fully aware that you have to be the sort of person you want to know. You understand that you have to "be fit for yourself to know."

You have continued to seek the meaning of Divine Love by pondering It, and you have grasped the fact that God always loved *you*, your Real Self.

You cease to look upon other persons with disapproval, for you now comprehend that God's Spirit is the Life within all.

The Tree of Life

You are told quite simply that the tree of life is in the midst of the "Garden." Your senses would have you believe this allegory refers to a lovely landscape, replete with beautiful shrubbery and wooded hills. The "Garden" is you— body, soul, and spirit.

Your senses would also have you believe that God created the first Adam, much as a sculptor would make a statue out of clay. Now, you can see that such an idea is just as much a fallacy as the idea that the stork brings babies.

Spirit is the Tree of Life, the source of pure intelligence, completeness, and pure and perfect ideas.

How Do You Move From Sense to Spirit?

This question is asked so often, and the answer is rephrased in so many ways, that it may be said to you over and over before you "hear.

Let's try a few ways. We'll start with the senses. The sky is cloudy and grey, and no sun is visible, but you *know* the sun hasn't gone anywhere. It is still there, and still shining, even though not discernable. If the sun were not there you wouldn't have daylight. Suppose it is night. You know where the sun is, don't you? You *know* it is shining on another part of the earth.

God is still present, even though the senses are telling you the opposite.

Now, try thinking "love." At first your thought slips over into human love, affection, and sentiment. Your thought probably rests upon someone or some thing. Whether what you love is a plant, a pet, or a person, that *feeling*, not the outer object, is God. The object is of the senses. Suppose it is an activity which gives you joy. You love this activity for the joy you derive from it. That feeling is God. It is always present, but you are not aware of it because you confuse it with the forms and objects of the senses.

When you have this feeling and are interpreting it as being for or about some person, your senses are still strong. The serpent strives to keep you under its control. You find that you move back and forth between good, and bad.

The reason for this is that you have put yourself in the way again. (The self you have been thinking you are, personal, physical, and mortal.) Go back to No. 3, recalling to mind that this personal self is the avenue through which God is expressing himself. Now let this feeling expand to joy, to intelligence, to peace and serenity. Know that it will expand into correct thoughts and actions.

God Is What You Think He Is

In the first chapter of the Gospel of John, it says: "IN THE BEGINNING WAS THE WORD, AND THE WORD WAS WITH GOD, AND THE WORD WAS GOD."

A "word" is an idea. Your concept of God is an idea. When you have incorrect beliefs about what God is, where He is, or what He does, you do not *know* God.

Not only do some folks believe that God is the cause of all the trouble they have known, but they lay at God's doorstep every evil happening. "God willed it this way", they say. They accuse God of having created "us sinners," a ridiculous contradiction which only proves they do not *know* God. When something happens which pleases them, they say, "God is so good to me," with the implication that God is not good to others.

The words "good" and "evil" describe outer conditions which have resulted from their own concepts of God. The true God in the Bible is called Elohim, while the one believed in by the senses is called Jehovah—a human, or carnal-mind concept. If you doubt this, you might ask yourself why you find in Exodus this passage:

AND I APPEARED UNTO ABRAHAM, UNTO ISSAC, AND UNTO JACOB, BY THE NAME OF GOD ALMIGHTY, BUT BY MY NAME JEHOVAH WAS I NOT KNOWN TO THEM.

(Exodus 6:3)

Truth Comes From Only One Source

When you fall short of knowing the complete concept, it is because you have concluded that all thoughts come from the same place. In Jas. 3:11 we have, "Doth a fountain send forth at the same place both sweet water and bitter?"

If God created the idea of Man in the "image and likeness" of Himself, He did not "create" at the same time the opposite idea of "sinners." If this is what you believe you are dealing with an IMPOSSIBILITY!

Are you able to comprehend now that the idea of "sinners" comes from your senses, and that you have implanted that belief? Will you carry this further and see that such thinking is not "thinking" at all, but merely the acceptance of impressions coming to you via your senses?

Information is not Knowledge

Your senses inform you. True knowledge comes from God. God's *ideas* are always all good, always complete.

What About Human Love?

Can you have human love and pleasant companionship. Is it possible to have the right mate and children who are a credit to you? Is it feasible to expect to have right relationships with all persons? Is not loyal friendship something to be desired? These are normal questions and you have a right to ask them. The answer is yes, you are to have all this, and without the chaotic conditions and events which accompany the carnal mind's conception of love and companionship.

The correct *idea* of God brings all this.

The Bible's advice about this is found in Romans:

BE NOT CONFORMED TO THIS WORLD, BUT BE YE TRANSFORMED BY THE RENEWING OF YOUR MIND, THAT YE MAY PROVE WHAT IS THAT GOOD, AND ACCEPTABLE, AND PERFECT, WILL OF GOD.

(Romans 12:2)

You hadn't realized that you were "conformed to this world" while you credited God with the lack of good your senses told you of, had you? Once you *know* Divine Love is present all the time, just as the sun is present even though not always visible, what you call human love and friendship will all be present in your own experience.

How to Work With Your Beliefs

Since a changed belief means that you will never again have that particular problem, it is surely worth whatever effort you make.

For instance, suppose there is some act you are called upon to execute which you find distasteful. Remembering that God is the Power to Act, and that God is Joy and Love, you begin to do this job whatever it may be. How would God do it? Thoroughly and enjoyably. God works through you, by means of you.

Suppose you have a belief that someone is mean and nasty. Let us say that you see in this person all the un-lovely traits. Compared to this individual you think of yourself as a saint. You recognize that this person depicts for you some place in your own thought realm where you do not believe in God. Tell yourself that the Life there is God. Drop the physical appearance of that person from your attention as well his personality as you see it. What does God's life consist of? God is not unfair, nor inconsiderate; God is Love.

Continue to go right down the line, seeing what is true of God that is the opposite of what you have been thinking. Ask yourself, "Would God think of anyone in the same way I have been thinking?" God is too pure to behold evil. If you are going to align yourself with the correct ideas, you will transfer your attention to those same correct ideas.

Adjustments Made Only at Sense Level Return

How often have you quit a job because you didn't like someone, only to find the same kind of personality at the next place? Or seen someone get a divorce, only to remarry someone with the same faults?

How often have you been "cured" of an ailment, only to have another crop out in some other area of your body?

How often have you moved from one dwelling because of some unwanted condition, only to find the same condition developed at the new abode?

You know why, now, don't you?

Improving material conditions, seeking material gain or even a healthy body, cannot be done entirely from the outside. There are theories promoted by human education which are incorrect, and which have brought about a barrier of ignorance and superstition.

Instead of believing that outer things are your salvation, you are now understanding that only by reliance on the Law of Life—knowing that you are to use the all-intelligent Mind—will you rid yourself permanently of unfavorable results.

Discernment

A sense belief makes pictures. Can you learn to think such ideas as made *no* pictures; such ideas as: stability, strength, compassion, alertness, or judgment?

Ponder words which express qualities, such as: harmony, wisdom, righteousness, or peace.

Try to see yourself as a mind rather than a body, and then you will have the same viewpoint of yourself that God has. You are the thinker, the solver of problems.

You also, want to have the same viewpoint of others that God has. It won't seem hard if you remember that the Life Force in them is the same as the Life Force in yourself.

Words Which Heal

A word is, of course, an *idea*. The word "Peace," when considered as to its meaning, has often been known to stop pain. When it is followed by "Thank you, Father," spoken with conviction that the Father is present, it is all-powerful. Whatever was the reason for the pain is wiped out of consciousness, as well as all the effects coming from that belief.

It must be known and clearly understood that the Perfect Life is all that is expressing Itself.

"Love" is another word which, when knowledge of its full meaning is comprehended, will do away with temper, anger, and hurt feelings.

Again it must not be confused with personal, human love, as known by means of the senses. It is the comprehension of the Perfect Life that is *all* that is expressing.

When you feel that you aren't learning fast enough, use the word "Truth." Allow your mind to dwell upon what it must mean. Claim that you *now* know the Truth. To keep thinking, "I don't know it, yet," is to keep moving it away from you.

Declare that you are no longer double-minded, and mean it, for this is the Truth about you, the real YOU. Double-mindedness is believing that one person is well and another is sick, one poor and another wealthy, or one good and another evil. YOU don't believe that. The senses believe that.

When the meaning of the IDEA of the word "Truth" is clear, no one can deceive you, cheat you, or make you believe any falsehood. Nothing can obstruct your ongoing.

Your Prayer Period

You can pray anywhere. Your mind is your own private property and you can turn your thought to what God is at any time. It only takes an instant to remind yourself that Perfect Life is all that is expressing in all places. The time should come, and does come, when you do not have to set aside all other activities to pray. Until you reach this state of awareness, it is good that you arrange a time to be alone with these ideas. Make it a regular time, preferably a daily affair.

During this period do not ask God to give you one single thing of the sense world—not more money, a better job, good health, nor some person.

Seek only the Kingdom of Heaven, which is the right concept of God. You have already been told that if and when you do this, "all these things will be added."

WHEREFORE HENCEFORTH KNOW WE NO MAN AFTER THE FLESH; YEA, THOUGH WE HAVE KNOWN CHRIST AFTER THE FLESH, YET NOW HENCEFORTH KNOW WE HIM NO MORE.

(II Cor. 5: 16)

Your "good" must come from God. If you look for it to come from a person, an organization, or your own personality, you "pray amiss." Your Heavenly Father already knows what you want and how to get it to you.

Your entire task during your prayer is to become more aware of God's nature. Is there any other way except through your mind? Go over in your mind the meanings of *words which heal*, and the other words which make no pictures. Try for the feeling of what they all mean, and you are praying.

CHAPTER 7

For That Sense of Need

The serpent doesn't want you to set him down from his throne. The brain will come in, with its reasoning and planning, bringing pictures of past happenings. Recognize instantly that this is the brain, with all the sense impressions which are registered there.

Many persons not addicted to the use of dope or alcohol, or tobacco, coffee, sweets, and other physical indulgences, are addicted to something far more damaging to themselves—the habit of rehearsing troubles and wrongs they believe have been done to them. They heed not this passage:

THEREFORE THOU ART INEXCUSABLE, O MAN, WHOSOEVER THOU ART THAT JUDGEST; FOR WHEREIN THOU JUDGEST ANOTHER, THOU CONDEMNEST THYSELF; FOR THOU THAT JUDGEST DOEST THE SAME THINGS.

(Romans 2: 1)

When not doing this, they are seeing wrongs done to others, and fearing for the safety and security of someone else. Such a one's sense of need is great. It may or may not be a material need; it may be a need for love and kindness, or a need for respect.

If you find that this description in some way fits what you think of yourself, or the way in which you have been thinking, you only need to go over this lesson material carefully.

Much negative thinking often causes the body to lose some of its abilities; but anyone can, by fastening his attention upon the Healing Presence within, change these habits.

Union Is Established

Man, God's idea, or thought, is already unified with his Divinity. A human person is cognized by the senses, and so cannot be the Son of God. Since God is Spirit, the Son, *His* Son, is spirit also. This makes clear what the Bible says, "No man sees God and lives." Only the Son "sees" God. Only as you know yourself to be Spirit are you able to perceive God, to know what God is.

The human senses have been educated to believe that the Son of God is another man, named Jesus. The carnal mind, enmity to God, mind you, would have you believe that you must worship a man you never met. Remembering that "man" is an idea, let us re-phrase that last sentence to say, "You must worship a thought you never saw." Your senses have never seen this concept.

Only your Mind can entertain this concept of God's perfect idea. In many places the Bible says that if you affirm that you are a human person, you are a sinner. Since a sin is a mistake, it is telling you that you are mistaken. Who then, are you?

Why, this spark of Divinity in you is the Son, the spirit of God. And all the while many sincere persons have been teaching that the Son was Jesus. Well, he is! But he is not *someone else.* That belief is purely of the senses and comes from having read the Bible with only the senses. We have already observed that the senses are the serpent, the devil, and Satan, the Great Red Dragon that would rule the world!

Do you want to go on believing that way? For so long you have stumbled along being fooled by the senses, fighting evil, hating evil, recognizing evil. Now and then you had a little something good for a while, but it didn't last long. Something always happened to it.

How could you ever hope to find the Savior while teachings coming solely from the senses kept you going astray? You went to church or temple, *smelled* the flowers or the incense, *heard* the music, the priest, preacher, or rabbi, and *saw* all the people. Did you keep hearing that you were a sinner?

Perhaps you were one who wondered what good it did you. Possibly you attended church services only for appearance! The safety of your soul being beyond your comprehension, you clung to a vague hope that there was a "something" which wouldn't allow you to suffer beyond your endurance.

Now and then you might have felt peaceful enough to allow God to become known to you, and maybe you thought, as many have, that this feeling came from the services instead of from within you.

Churchgoers Do Find God Within

Every religious faith has its thread of Truth. What is said from the pulpit may be exceedingly real as a message, but the senses can garble it. Likewise the message might be purely of the senses, and yet God is still present.

Watch that you do not condemn those who have not grasped beyond the sense level, for to do so is to cloud your own perspective.

Getting Past the Intellect

Your control can become great enough to keep you from fastening your attention upon errors, if you will decide to dramatize the good for a change. You already are well acquainted with dramatizing the bad.

The next time you feel moody and despondent, wipe that look off your face with a smile. If you feel weak and weary, pull your shoulders back and put a spring into your step, no matter how much effort it takes. If you have just heard some unpleasant news, remind yourself that only good can come from it.

The owner of a thriving business who netted more than a million dollars a year, came in to see me one afternoon.

"I have always liked being a winner," he began. "I have believed in giving good service and a good product. When I first began to be a financial success, I was a happy man. I liked what I was doing."

I nodded, watching his mirthless smile. An interest in what is before one to do, coupled with a joyful attitude, is, of course, a requisite for getting the feeling of wealth. Individuals who dislike what they do seldom make much money. The emotional attitude toward the work one does has a great deal to do with the efficiency with which it is executed.

"I learned many years ago that God was my own intelligence," he went on. "Consequently, I gave much attention to feeling out for this intelligence, and knowing that God, present as my intelligence, kept me doing the wise things. It was great fun for a long time, but now the interest is gone. I have no love for my work. I just can't seem to get back that feeling. What shall I do?"

"Do you not also know that with that same intelligence, you can know God as Love and Joy?" I asked, studying his expression.

"With my intellect, yes, but I have somehow blocked it off. I just don't feel it. I think, perhaps, that I, not God, have become the center of my thought, but try as I do, I am not reaching the feeling."

I pursued my lips. He had just denied, vocally, his chances of reaching it. He had said, "I am not."

"When you were teaching yourself to feel wealthy and successful," I said slowly, "you disciplined your thought processes, didn't you? That is, you never for a moment allowed yourself to think what a failure you were. You never told yourself that you didn't have this intelligence, did you?"

"No, I didn't. But I have become impatient with those who don't use their intelligence, or who don't want to work. I see it all around me. It depresses me."

There it was. The reason. He had failed to discipline his thought about others.

So I said, "Since it is only your own thought which you can do anything about, why not forget what the senses are telling you regarding these others? You know that you influence the thoughts others have only by the example you set for them."

"I would like to express love for them, but all I feel is disgust. I don't know when or how it began; seems it just crept up slowly."

"How do you feel about those closest to you: your family, for instance?"

"Oh, so-so. They're okay, I guess," he shrugged.

"For the most part, they have what they want and need."

"How about your jolly companionship, your understanding, your presence? Do they have that?"

"My *what*?" he exclaimed. "Oh, they don't need me. They all have their own lives. My kids have more than most kids do nowadays. I haven't stinted them."

"Giving them things doesn't prove love, does it? Wouldn't an interest in what they are doing be a better way?"

"Oh, I think now they would just tell me to go mind my own business."

"Well," I said, remembering how well he understood that God was his own intelligence, "right where this Life Force in you expresses Itself as intelligence, it also expresses Itself as Love and Joy. Love is there, waiting to be expressed. Can you find the way to express it? What would be the most loving thing you might do? It will give you great joy, because joy and love are companions. A little while ago, you made a flat statement, 'I am not reaching the feeling,' and I think if you remove the word 'not' that is all you need to do. You have a sense of needing to do just that, haven't you?"

A wide smile spread over his face. "I am reaching the feeling. Thank God for intelligence!" A twinkle came into his eyes. He snapped his fingers. "I have been around men who are continually finding fault with the government, local or federal. We have discussed a good many restrictive and binding laws arguing and bickering about various ways and means to make corrections. Oh, I am not blaming them, now, at least, for I see how we've been scattering thought power."

"That's right. You formulated opinions on what came to you through the senses. Then you indulged in an incorrect reaction, and the feelings of love and joy vanished."

He rose to his feet, suddenly elated, and clapped the flat of his palm against his forehead. "Now I know what the thought which kept repeating itself to me meant! The phrase 'No man can serve both God and mammon' kept coming to me. Added to it, now and tnen, would be, 'A rich man cannot enter the Kingdom of Heaven.' I had begun to think I was doomed, but I had put on these the wrong interpretation! I had been looking at all of those unshakeable sense impressions, the outer."

"That's right; and the 'rich man' is a thought which deals solely with all the accumulated sense impressions. 'Serving mammon' is the same thing, paying attention to these impressions," I agreed.

"Well, I feel pretty good right now. But another question comes to me. If we aren't to trust what comes to us by means of the senses, how could we correct anything? We have the designing board, mathematics, the laboratory. We use the senses all the time."

"The senses confirm what you know," I answered, "also what you do not know. The little chap in school who says seven and two are eight, does not know what seven and two equal. When he has learned to count, and finds that seven and two are nine, his senses confirm it, do they not?"

He laughed, "Yes, but I don't see how seven and two can even appear to be eight! In any way."

I pointed out the window, "See those trees above the rooftops? They appear to be growing out of the tops of the buildings, but you know they are not. How do you know it? A great many things appear to us one way, when in reality they aren't like that at all. What a person thinks he sees is what he himself believes. But believing something doesn't necessarily make it true; it only seems to be true. If you believed those trees grew on the rooftops, it wouldn't make them do so.

"The Bible's statement that *anything is possible to him that believeth* means that what you find to be true of God, when believed in by you, can be brought into your experience. Obviously, if it is not true of God, nothing will be changed. For instance, the earth was once believed to be flat, but that belief didn't flattened it out, did it? That belief was due to sense impressions, and all that it accomplished was to keep the people in ignorance of what the shape of the earth really was." I saw his smile of understanding.

"What I must know is that God is love and joy as well as intelligence. I think I will do that quite easily now. I see now that I was taking a sort of prideful credit for my success, and forgetting to pass on the honors to where they rightfully belong."

Listen to Your Own Words

If you want to know what your own sense of need is, try listening to what you say—if you aren't aware of it through other means. The way your thoughts are running today show up in what you choose to discuss.

When you want others to cater to your whims, speak pleasantly to you, or help you with something, and they do not, but rather avoid you, your need is to know God as Love.

When you ponder the meaning of Divine Love, the Intelligence within you helps you to find ways to express it.

It may be that you have been only thinking of yourself, and your real need is to find a way to express this quality to others. You help them in their need. There is an old saying, "Help thy brother's boat across, and Lo! thine own shall reach the shore."

There are moments for all of us, while we are still learning to control our thoughts and emotions, when things come at us like a bang! It might be a telephone message, news in the mail, a fire in the house next door or even in our own, when it is difficult to remember how it is we are to think. Our first thought is "Oh God!" The point is, hang on to it. We seldom do. Not until we are well-trained, until we have so conditioned our minds to the awareness of Omnipresence, that we do not slip back into believing sense testimony, do we stay serene. Such practice of the right feeling should be done while there is no great sense of need.

What is God to You?

Do you know that God is always active and that His action is loving action? Do you know it in the same way that you know two and two are four? Do you know that God is the substance of all supply? God may be the activity which brings the substance to you, but He, or It, is also the Substance. Do you really know this, or do you just make a noise with your mouth? *Knowing* it is going to take some pondering, if your cupboard is bare.

Your job is to convince yourself. It is futile to go around telling others that you believe in Divine Power. Only your own serenity during a "storm" is going to convince them that you really believe. If the outer effect overwhelms you, you have not convinced yourself.

To know God is quite different from knowing *About* God. When you really know God in all the aspects, the sense of needing anything leaves.

You will not scheme and plan to get others to do what you want them to do, for you see clearly that this would be interfering with their freedom. You are aware that such action clogs the channels through which good flows to you. It brings wrong results, and is therefore a mistake.

Aid Another to Change His Wrong Belief

When you know that someone else is accepting a sense belief, and the exposure of it is a sure way of avoiding further dilemmas and faulty actions, you are not being unkind to tell him about it.

Can you safely trust your own wisdom to point out that he is taking his thought from the wrong source? To aid another in changing his belief, or to cease dramatizing his hard luck, is an act of love. Are you too afraid of evoking his displeasure?

There is a tactful way of doing this. Bring the two of you together in your mind, as though you are really speaking to yourself. As if this is your own belief you are going to change, you may say something like this:

"I see how it is that you understand it this way, because I have often done the same thing." Then, go on with your *correct* thought. Talk as if you were talking to yourself; in reality, you are.

Folks often ask, "Please tell me what I'm doing wrong, will you?"

If you tell them, and they are unwilling to take the correct procedure, they may turn away hurt and angered. When they are willing to make the adjustment, they are grateful. Not only that, but they do make the necessary change in their way of thinking and acting.

Should you blame yourself if they are hurt or angry with you? Not at all. In the God Mind *no one* is hurt.

"But I wanted George for my friend," one student said to me after such an experience.

"Do you have other friends?" I queried. "If you do, then you have no sense of need for a friend, do you?" I knew, he had many friends for he was a popular young man. "Don't you see that he is the one who did not prove he was a friend? Pay it no mind, for what you see is only on the sense level. When he learns enough, he will show his friendship."

"Oh, I get it," this chap said brightly, "I might have gotten involved in his kind of thinking if our relationship had continued. Since he is so unwilling to change his brand of thought, it might have in some way included me."

"In the God Mind there is no anger, so what could you possibly have to do with someone who refuses to give up anger thoughts?"

Take an About-Face

For all expressed contumelies and blasphemies which may come to your attention, be as polite and considerate as the mockers and scorners are not.

As you begin to act more and more as you think God might act, were God a man, you allow Him to grow in your awareness.

Occasionally someone thinks that he is disliking the person who is behaving so shamefully, but what he is disliking is the *error thought* which produces that behavior. To recognize it as only a belief, and to see that a belief can be changed, is taking an about-face. The sense of need which you are looking upon is a very large one; it requires your highest and best thought and action.

You may never know what good it has done. It may only protect you from violence, but I have known situations where it both protected me and brought the faulty behavior into alignment with good. At any rate, it is worth the best from you.

Whenever you feel miserable, dejected, morose, or confused, you have a sense of need. If you are bruised or wounded, injured or maligned, you have a sense of need. Not only when you are out of money, employment, a place to live, or adequate clothing do you have this sense of need, but you have it also when you are out of friends, when a romance disappoints you, and when you find nothing which interests you. When you moan, "No one understands me" it is a sense of need.

This sense of need comes from having most of your thought centered upon the world of effect. It comes from putting your attention too much on the delinquencies and mis-doings of everyone else. Take an about face and become the example you have been wishing others would be. No matter what specific appearance is giving you all of these negative feelings, once you begin to express the jewels within yourself that sense of need will leave you, for this is a Universal Law.

You are not being advised to join the ranks of those who go around with a long face, thinking it to be a mark of piety. condemning everything others have found pleasurable. Such as these cast a blight on all they contact, for they are denying the same God they profess to worship.

There is no sense of needing anything once you have located the little fox that has been eating away on the vine. This pleasurable experience can be yours, as soon as you perceive that you are not this funny little thing you have believed you were. Whenever you are not joyful, you will note that you have gone back to believing that you are this strange little being which causes all of your grief, irritations, and annoyances. Begin right now to recognize that this self is as ephemeral and changing as the clouds tip in the sky. It's never the same two minutes in a row. There is not one thing about that self which is not subject to change.

To those who believe themselves to be this outer self, everything appears to be out of control, and life is one long, unbroken sense of need. When business affairs are harmonious, something else is not. There is always some crisis.

Misuse of Free Will

One of the most fascinating things you can learn about yourself is that the law of your life is a law of freedom, but because you have used it in opposition to the Will of God, you have brought about a feeling of bondage. If you have been getting nowhere, it is because your attention is occupied with trivial things, personalities, and events, and future occurrences you anticipate which never quite "come off" to give you the joy they seemed to promise. These are the actions of this *self* you thought you were, which I shall call the "natural man."

The natural man always allows his senses to govern his intellect. The natural man has all kinds of knowledge, which does not in the least improve his personal life. He brings about imperfections, disharmony, and bondage.

The correct use of the will is to join it to the Will of God. I believe that there is a great deal of difference between whether you think God is within you or a Something outside of you—a Something you can only meet after you leave the body.

How could you unite with God were He something separate and apart from you? How could you know His Will today if you could not meet him until you left the physical body behind? It is true that you *do* leave behind the physical body, in thought, by ceasing to think of your body as YOU.

You have grown close to God when you have closed out the world's turmoils, troubles, discontents, and disasters, and found serenity and the feeling of peace.

Bondage of the Natural Man

A God of Love does not set aside one group and say, "These are the only ones I have an ear for," nor "These 'natural men' are my favored ones;" so if you have put a fence around your denominational group, you have closed out more than you have taken in. Teachings which make

God something unattainable unless you pay a certain amount of money to some organization come from the natural man. You cannot buy a better seat in heaven with "what is Caesar's," for heaven is like nothing known to the senses—it is not like a seat on the fifty-yard-line at a football game.

If your "generosity" is prompted by the fact that your gift is a tax deduction, you are still steeped in the senses. God is just as far off to you as some other planet!

Perhaps you believe in God, just a little bit, because you are intelligent enough to have observed that since there is a creation, there must have been a Creator to have brought it about. Perhaps you are fairly good in most respects. You might cheat a little providing you are fairly sure you won't be caught; you might claim to be an agnostic, declaring that you don't know for sure if there is a God. We know we can trust you, somewhat, for at least you aren't pretending. But if you say you believe in God, and are still intolerant, spiteful, greedy, scheming, and crafty, we know you are merely giving lip-service to cover up. It will be only a matter of time until you reap what you have sown.

The natural man never finds real joy, real love, or real wealth. Money he may have, due to his machinations, but he can never buy what he really wants.

Money is not a key to the Kingdom of God. The natural man seeks money, and regards it, not God, as power. He errs.

Better Than Your Own Will

The great essential for ridding yourself of bondage is to realize (to see with your real eyes of wisdom) that the *Will of Universal Intelligence and Divine Love* would have to be far better than what your limited little self could possibly imagine.

This is not easy for the faint-hearted, nor the cowardly, to see; so accustomed is he to leaning upon what he can touch, handle, and see with his eyes, that turning, to something completely invisible sounds like nonsense. Should you discover that you are the sort of person who thinks in this manner at times, such as when making decisions, try believing "Thy Will be done."

If you are sincere in trusting the All-Intelligence, and know that Its knowledge of all the factors involved is to be a real help to you, as well as to others, many apparent obstacles will be moved out of your way. It takes courage to abandon yourself to Infinite Will. So often, the thing you thought was right for you is the exact thing which would have only caused you more grief and trouble, so you don't get *it*, but something much better.

For some people, letting go of their personal opinions is about the hardest thing to accomplish. They are sure they know more than Infinite Wisdom has to offer. The natural man's ego is a large parcel of foolishness, for he has no knowledge that these outer effects are the consequences of his habitual thought patterns; to think he could change the effects without changing the patterns from whence they come is sheer folly.

It is a Law of the Universe, that when you conform yourself to the Will of God, a more satisfying and splendid result will take place.

Do you, right now, have the capacity to apprehend what an Intelligence which knows all and loves all might be able to give you?

It gives to you of Itself, which is loving care, guidance, and protection. In the Book of Matthew, the Sermon on the Mount tells you how you may become pure in Spirit, and thus understand the Perfect Life Force. Up to now, you have been using this in a limited and restricted way by tinkering in the world of effect, believing that you were to ask God to do things your way.

"Thy Will be done" is a thought which aligns you to the very best, in all ways. Your real need is always to learn what the Divine Will is for you.

Imagination

Don't confuse imagination with intuition; they are not the same. The imagination is one of the senses; but because it doesn't show up as an outer organ, as do the eyes and ears, most folks are unaware that it is one of the senses.

Intuition is being taught from within; it is the "still small voice." It comes from contemplation of the word "Truth." You can learn to become intuitively aware, at all times, of whatever you need to know.

In some circles, it has been taught that the imagination is the power to use, and that if you can imagine anything strongly enough, it will take place. This has come to be believed in because so many negative things, strongly imagined, do take place. Folks are heard to say, "I just knew that terrible thing was going to happen!" Such brain activities have been termed "psychism." Nevertheless, this is the wrong use of thought. The feared adversities show up as facts because there is so much feeling put into them.

We shall deal with the subjects of psychism, fortune-telling, clairvoyance, and such subjects later on. Meanwhile, be careful of how you use the imagination; the "bad" thing you imagine for someone else could just as easily happen to you.

The senses are characterized by the fact that they deal with the "pairs of opposites." The imagining powers of some often cause them to dramatize any unpleasant condition out of proportion to what it actually is. It never occurs to such individuals that they might dramatize these events in an opposite manner, stressing the good, or even expecting the good to be a final result.

Consequently, the imagination, out of control and going negatively, is the starting point for much unwarranted fear.

The "fear of God" as originally used in the Bible meant respect for *Universal Law.* "It is done unto you, as you believe," puts the responsibility upon you, and once you understand this, you will respect the Law.

You will not relinquish that sense of need until you have trained yourself to think rightly about others as well as yourself. You have what is called a "defense mechanism" by which you can justify all of your own actions. Now you must see that everyone else has this also. This allows us to live with ourselves until we have learned a little more about how to be the sort of person we can stand having around. It does not, however, eliminate our fears.

The Sense of Need Produces Fear

How is fear displayed?

1. By subterfuge, exaggeration, and avoidance.
   Ask yourself:
   a. What do I hide, and why?
   b. How do I try to build up my importance?
   c. When do I pretend?
   d. What do I avoid? Whom do I avoid?'

2. By damaging remarks about others.

   Ask yourself:
   a. In what way do *I* do what I accuse *others* of doing?
   b. Why do I see them as I do?

3. By being willing to harm anyone, or cause hurt or harm.

   Ask yourself:
   a. Am I trying to take something away from someone else?
   b. Am I envious, or jealous?
   c. Am I really thinking correctly while I have a desire to harm?

Your sense of need is showing you that you must strengthen certain character traits, is it not?

Since this can only be done by understanding that God is not a man who is beneficent, loving, and wise, and only on *your* side, but is actually a Source of Right Ideas, isn't it better to contemplate His Nature?

The ideas you now have, if you have fears, have come from outside sources: newspapers, radio, television, novels, and what your friends have told you of their experiences. Now and then, a movie or stage play has impressed you, leaving you with some belief. You have been barraged with the opinions of others, many of which you have adopted as your own. Haven't you heard political speeches which "set your teeth on edge?" Or read something in the news which upset you so much you were unable to sleep? Do you know that it is possible for a news reporter to leave out part of the facts, or worse, to combine two true facts in such a way as to arrive at a completely different meaning?

Do you know, too, that for all these things which appear to your senses as "evil," God is good? In addition, do you know that God is in charge, or are you still thinking that some man, or group of men, are in charge of your future?

One of the Biggest Boulders

Can you eliminate the feelings of discouragement and doubt? An act of courage gets discouragement out of the way. Doubt is one of the biggest boulders before your, treasures, blocking them off.

This pseudo self, the natural man, you have so long believed you were, has placed these boulders in front of your treasure. Since he is spurious, what he has placed there is equally false. Can you see how false your doubt really is? If you can, it will vanish instantly.

If it doesn't, and doubt, fear, and discouragement still remain, you have put "otherness" in the way. It isn't an accident that the first commandment is. "Thou shalt have no *other* gods before me." That outer self which you see in your mirror, together with your personality, is the "graven image" which you have been distinctly told you must not have as a god. Did you think it meant only that you must not worship a statue or a picture?

Maybe you have been condemning yourself too much, or praising yourself too much. Maybe you have been taking much personal credit for your suuccess? Maybe you have been blaming God for your failure? Or, do you "see" it? As long as you are patting yourself on the back, or on your little pointed head, you have been missing the whole point. Only God, or Spirit, is whole, good, and complete.

Admit it, you've made some errors. The fellow you're doubting is yourself, not God. You are a channel through which God has been working. When you have made room for Him to come through, He has benefited you.

Let's correct one thought right here. Much has been said about the "human" spirit. There is no such thing, for "human" means duality, and Spirit means Oneness. It is infinite, and since there is no opposite to that which is infinite, there is no "otherness."

Every now and then, someone whose name is well-known makes a statement for publication to the effect that the Bible is a book no one understands. He means he doesn't, and that's all. Many do understand it, and are delighted with their findings. If you learn to jettison such suggestions quickly, before they take root, things will go more smoothly for you.

Spotting the Difference Between the Natural Man and Self

The natural man is a bargainer, giving only in hopes of getting. The real Self gives for the joy of it, expecting nothing in return. The natural man gives to his church in order to "buy" his salvation. He reasons that he can take his gift off his income tax statement. His soul is in the same state as ever! He doesn't understand the meaning of "Make not my Father's house a marketplace"

What was Jesus talking about when he tipped over the money changers' tables and said this? Let us look at what this has to do with you.

The temple, a place of reverence and worship, had grown from a small church building to a huge place of many stalls and courtyards, with porches where the money-changers exchanged foreign coins for Roman money. There was a fixed discount on this exchange which gave them a nice living wage. During religious festival time, the temple officials, who then ruled the land, thought it a good time to collect tithes from these simple country folk. Some had no money, but had stock, sheep, cattle, or doves which they brought to sell. The priests took the best of these for themselves. When Jesus saw what was taking place, he told them this was not the way to do things.

Your Mind is "my Father's house." You are being told that you have filled it with materialistic beliefs. Jesus, your awareness of God within, tells you that you are being cheated and that you are doing it all to yourself.

This lesson of commercializing the temple applies to us all. When you first learned a little bit about the value of prayer, you had an unwanted condition which needed changing. You found that you could, by prayer, make these changes.

Like a child who has just learned how to wheedle a parent into getting his own way, you began to think of more and more "things" which the senses would enjoy. Boom! The next thing you know you are living entirely from the senses again! As you began to want more and more "ease in matter," your "system" failed to work. *Doubt* set in.

The admonishment, "Make not my Father's house a market-place," is telling you that as long as you are only interested in the bread and fishes, the *results*, nothing more is going to happen. You have returned to the natural man and taken on your sense of need, which remains until you move your attention whole-heartedly from sense to Spirit.

Two Distinctly Different Ways of Thinking

An irrepressible conflict takes place when your materialistic thoughts collide with the Great Design. This is heart-breaking to the ego which thought to build up self-interest again, to renew pride, enjoy self-aggrandizement to the utmost, and be indulged with sense effects. Unable to comprehend that he must fit into the overall Design, allowing God's will and not his own, he moans, "Oh, what's the use?"

When, or if, you reach such a place, ask yourself these questions:

1. What if my will to have more money costs me my health, or comfort, or peace of mind? Would I still want it?

2. What if my will to have success and fame costs me the love and companionship I now have? Do I still want it?

3. Is my will God's will for me? Am I willing to give up my will for that of the Greater Intelligence?

Your reasoning and sense intellect, which is your will, does not know what will give you the highest joy; but God does. It is happiness you are after. This mental means of scheming, plotting, planning or conniving is as different a way of thinking as burglary is from earning a living. While it may get you the result, it will cost more than you bargained for, and will leave you with the same faults you had before.

Hidden, Unconscious Beliefs

The idea that God is ALL, the Life Force which animates all there is, is an idea which is often argued about, particularly by those who want to be somebody. Unable to grasp how this idea would put their thinking straight, they find it offensive.

Evading it with rhetoric and claiming their right to dissent, they build around this belief others which are heavily charged with emotion. Through this self-importance they place themselves in a position where their beliefs have dominion over them, rather than their being in control of the beliefs. Because they have insisted in believing in two powers, they find that destructive beliefs keep sprouting.

The remedy for this is, as Paul said, "To die daily," which means to scuttle this self-importance and see that God is in charge.

Such persons often talk much about "positive thinking," carefully avoiding usage of the word "God". To be ashamed of believing in God is just about as ignorant an attitude as one could possibly have. It shows that one has a low opinion of oneself, as well as being ignorant of who God is, what God is, and where God is.

When your senses apprise you of such an individual, your need is to remember that the Life Force here is God. God is Life. Is someone ashamed of his life? Figure it out; it says a lot of things. Such a person represents one of your own beliefs. How will you "trade in" this belief for a true idea?

Who Are the Wicked?

Those with the wrong attitudes, who are completely taken in by the senses, are called bewitched or wicked. Those who are good people could not come under this classification, because they take their expression of justice, kindness, and consideration from God. In Daniel we find this:

NONE OF THE WICKED SHALL UNDERSTAND; BUT THEY THAT BE WISE SHALL UNDERSTAND.

(Dan. 12:10)

Everyone has some beliefs which are correct, and which motivate their actions. It is to these you turn when you wish to correct the false ones.

We might liken ourselves to little machines which are continuously making beliefs, some good, some just so-so, and some not at all good. If you have a preponderance of beliefs which are not true, understanding will come slowly.

The "how" of eliminating wrong beliefs is simple enough, but not always so easy.

A Good Beginning

Ask yourself:

1. What do I do that shows I am hanging on to my feeling of self-importance?
2. How often do I engage in something which, in itself, is really destructive?
3. Why is it that I don't have a better realization that some of my actions aren't going to be productive of greater good?

Do you ever indulge a child's whims because you want that child to "look up" to you?

Do you spend money recklessly, under certain conditions, in an effort to establish a picture of yourself as you would like to appear?

Do you follow your imagination, rather than your intuition?

If so, this is the natural man, who sees "only in part, as through a glass, darkly."

Every time you return to the antics of the natural man, you will have a new sense of need.

A Higher Conception

All that is in form, including your body and the chair upon which you sit, and all which is within range of your senses, every object and person, represents an idea. When your idea realm is perfect, that is, when you understand that as an idea, the object is perfect, whatsoever is reflected as the form must also be perfect. This is not easy to do, for your senses tell you that these forms are new, or old, or in the process of wearing out, but you must allow your mind to deal with the Perfect Idea, not the form as presented.

You are the Light. Time, such as clock or calendar time, has nothing to do with the Light which you are. The thoughts of others have nothing to do with that Light which you are. You are always free to correct the false picture in your own thought realm. If you follow the reasoning of the natural man, continuing to judge by appearances, assuming something to be true because your senses reported it, you are rejecting your opportunity. But if you can realize that all form is brought forth from ideas, and you now correct the false ideas, what has been appearing as faulty is adjusted to meet your higher conception.

All spiritual healing is done this way. God's perfect idea of you, reflected in your soul, as your soul, shows forth in the form you know as physical body. The physical, material body you see is not God's creation; God's creation is spiritual, whole, and perfect as idea. Can you close out all your sense impressions long enough to comprehend this with your mind?

The Senses Will Confirm

When you have held to the Perfect Idea, and it is established, you will have a feeling that will cause you to exclaim gratefully, "Thank you, Father."

You will not start to look for results, because this would be taking your thought back to the senses. Nor will you think, "It is going to be done." Rather, your thought will be "It is done."

With most persons, when the work has been done correctly, the attention does not return to that specific item at all. Sometimes the senses confirm the correct belief within minutes, but no matter whether it is hours or weeks, the correct concept is already working.

Forward-Going Steps

Every changed belief is a step in the right direction. Once you have had the experience of trading in a faulty belief for a true one, and noted that the senses confirm it, it is more clear to you why you must cease judging by appearances.

Your wisdom and strength of character are far more valuable to you than satisfactions gained through that which only appeals to the senses and temporary wants.

Counting your blessings and being thankful for whatever you have right now is a fine attitude, and certainly better than counting your troubles and problems, but it is not finding God. It is still being in the sense mind, unless you are able to realize that your blessings are your advanced understanding. You must train yourself to come often to the thought, *"God is my spirit, my life, my joy, my supply. God is present with me now."*

This is always your real need, even though it may appear to be knowledge of what to do about employment, or business, or a family condition. For a momentary anxiety, for all disappointments, for any disturbance, turn to your own serenity within. Claim that it is present.

If you are one who likes gaiety, thrills, and laughter, or you enjoy the tingling stimulation of playing the horse races, the stock market, or going to the gaming places at Reno and Las Vegas, you will find that as you work with this Power in you, *It* is many times more joyous and exciting than these. Not only that, but It is more lasting and beneficial. Unlike these other games, you won't risk too much and come away disheartened and angry with yourself. Also, unlike material wealth, which is soon spent, the Power grows, expands, and continues to give you greater joys. It fills every sense of need.

Trials Are Simply Exercises

In your new jubilant consciousness, you are not bogged down when something shows up as a test of your sincerity. You know that you will come out on top if you stick with it. Mistakes are only lack of understanding, or misunderstanding, and you know now how to align yourself. You remember that in the story of Creation of Genesis, the evening came before the morning; that is telling you that mistakes come before understanding. You know that Light is understanding the principle. You know that you are that Light.

Reading a book like this one is like reading a map. The map is not the transportation, but only a direction giver. When you study a map, you don't conclude that you have taken the trip. Neither will your circumstances be improved merely by reading, so don't put off your enjoyment of life any longer!

CHAPTER 8

Infinite Power Is Present

1. ONENESS. Take this lesson when you can be absolutely alone. Forget all the other people, all the events. YOU are the only one there is. Here, now, you are All.

   Speak aloud and say. *"I am. I exist. I am alive"*. Hold your attention upon this *all alone* feeling. Move your attention to the life force which is the aliveness. It is beating your heart, causing you to exhale and inhale. It knows how to digest your food, convert it into energy and new cells for bones, muscles, skin, tissues, and is completely intelligent.

2. UNION. You have just made a mental union with your own life force. This Life is God . . . your Source . . . your Father. IT is giving you Itself, and all that IT is.

   Speak aloud and say: *"God, I know you are here. You have given me intelligence, love, strength, peace, and joy."*

   You may carry this thought further to the activity of any organ of your body, or an activity in your affairs. When you do, remind yourself that you are dealing in thought with an *idea*. Any idea in the Mind which is God is already a perfect one. You know that when you consider this Idea, you are not thinking of it as it has appeared to your senses, but rather as a Perfect Idea.

3. FEELING. If you have accomplished these thoughts, you'll have a feeling, a really good feeling, in your

mind. If, at first, it seems hardly noticeable, don't be discouraged. You are just new at it. It sounds so simple and easy and your senses are used to finding everything difficult, that you are apt to be holding to the thought that this could not possibly be so easy. It means you need to relax more.

Try saying aloud, *"I am so calm, so serene and peaceful. I am really enjoying this."*

More and more similar ideas will attach themselves to this *"I am," like "God is where I am" or "I am growing more relaxed."*

Infinite Power Is Present

This is the best exercise you can take if you are worried or anxious, or if some big trouble seems to becoming in front of you. The bigger the difficulty the better this exercise works. You do not "make" it work; it is always present and always working. What the exercise does is allow you to discover this.

You are making room in your mental realm, much in the same way you might re-arrange the furniture in a room if you expected a piano to be delivered.

Back of every discordant condition being out-pictured to you, there are mixed up thoughts and emotions cluttering up your mental realm. If the room into which you intended putting your piano was too cluttered, some of the items would have to go and a space would have to be made.

That is exactly what you are doing when you take this exercise, you are *making room.* You are giving up disturbing sense impressions and allowing the peaceful ones to come in. Actually, they are already there, these peaceful ones, in the same way, the room for your piano is there. You have the room, so all you need to do is to take some things out.

If for a long time you thought you had to go to someone else, another man or woman, you should now be able to understand that *alone with God* is the better way. If you must lean, why not learn to lean on something which is not limited? You have decided to do so, haven't you? You have been working with your false beliefs, and converting them into true ideas.

Why do you need this exercise for right-feeling?

Truth Must Be Comprehended Completely

There is a parable in Luke 15:11 which begins "A certain man had two sons . . ." and this is what it is saying: you have two beliefs about yourself, and one of them, the younger, leaves home. You left "the Father's house" when you began thinking of yourself as a separated entity, on your own. You believed you were the body. Why is this belief the *younger?* This concept is the judging by appearances and since the concept comes first, before the reflection, the belief that you are the body is the "'younger son."

The belief which "stayed at home," that is, the "elder son," does not leave your Mind, which is "home." Thus, the "certain man" says to the elder son, "Son, thou art ever with me, and all that I have is thine."

When you bring this idea of the reflection, the body, back to the Father s House, back to the God Mind, and know that here it is a perfect idea, you have the feeling of this Oneness with the Father.

You are in the "Secret place of the Most High," and it is a condition of your thought, not a location.

This "Father's house" is the same as the Kingdom of God, which, in Jesus' teaching, you are told to seek first. When Jesus was asked where it was to be found, He said "The Kingdom of God is within you."

By thinking of what God must be, you are "making room" for His right ideas. If you tend to fall asleep at first, during this exercise, that is all right.

Sleep Is Nature's Way of Renewal

Rest in sleep is a letting go of problems, of the affairs of the daytime activities known only by the senses. Sometimes one's mental condition can be so disturbed that insomnia results. Anyone who is troubled by the inability to fall asleep greatly needs an instruction such as this lesson provides. His sense of strain and tension is coming from his feeling of being separated from God. He is not "abiding in the shadow of the Almighty" and this is most likely to be due to incorrect ideas of who, what and where God is.

The true knowledge of God is an actual experience, not a theory. It relaxes the thought, the muscles of the body, and elates the entire being.

Repeat the Exercise Often

Your own knowledge of the Truth that the Presence of God is right where you are, turns disturbing beliefs into vitalizing, energizing ideas. It does away with confusion because it brings a recognition of peace. It helps you to surrender hard feelings, beliefs in obstructions, and automatically eliminates anything which is false.

How Long Does It Take?

Since there is no time in Spirit, as it is always "now," it doesn't "take time" at all. The Truth is, this perfect state *already exists*. So the question is, "How long will it take you to 'see' it?" Are you aware at *all* times of your immediate Oneness with God . . . Alone?

Because your senses know of something called "time," the moment you return to sense consciousness, you begin to calculate what is to you a reasonable length of time before your new good shows up. Unless you are careful, you are apt to conclude that soon this niceness will happen, forgetting that it already exists.

Your senses live in a world of clock and calendar time and their first report to you is, "It hasn't happened yet."

Have you grown strong enough to silence them? God is your strength. Do you *know* this, or are these still just words? Do you know that you couldn't lift your arm to turn this page of this book if it weren't for the Life, which is God, that expresses Itself through your body'? Do you know that you couldn't move your eyes from one word to another if this life force were not present?

What Are Your Senses Telling You?

Do you have a belief that you cannot see well without some sort of outer aid, such as contact lenses or glasses? Are you wearing a hearing aid or using a cane to help you walk? Do you take some kind of medication?

Where have these beliefs come from? Why, from the suggestions blasting at your senses, blazing in your eyes, blaring in your ears, blighting your sense of smell and blanking out what awareness of God You might have!

No, don't blame anyone else. They are in the same boat that you are, allowing their senses to accept more and more faulty beliefs. Their need to know what it is that is fooling them into their dilemmas is just as great as your own.

A Feeling of Love

When you love another person, there is a feeling of warmth and high regard, here is admiration and esteem. No one needs to suggest that you give this person your attention; you cannot refrain from doing so.

When you love God, it is this kind of a feeling you have. It is easy to give God your attention.

Since we have told you that God is your own life force, you are apt to conclude that this means to keep thinking of yourself.

But which self is it you are going to think about? The God created, or the mental concept you have made of yourself? If it is this latter one, you will be concerned with your likes and dislikes, your own wants, your Personal opinions and self-importance.

If you are thinking of the one He created, in "His image and likeness," you are thinking of what God is, and your love is for God, not the mental concept of your senses.

BUT WE HAVE THIS TREASURE IN EARTHEN VESSELS, THAT THE EXCELLENCY OF THE POWER MAY BE OF GOD, AND NOT OF US.

(II Cor. 4: 7)

Whenever you are experiencing a lack of ability to see good everywhere, or know the meaning of perfection, it simply means that you have returned to the sense-made concept of yourself. You think of yourself as one among many others better circumstanced than yourself, or, more important, more skilled, more needed, more intelligent, and more powerful.

You have "bumped your nose" upon some belief which is incorrect, acted upon that belief and gone swirling back into sense consciousness. During such periods, you feel that you just can't read anything inspiring and grasp the meaning of it. You want to turn away and declare it all "a lot of bunk." Try reading the *23rd* or *91st Psalm,* at times like this.

Unless you are determined, you might not come out of it right away; but remember this, as long as you remain in this negative state of consciousness, you are making still more problems for yourself.

Curb the tendency to visit with another and talk over all that is bothering you. Much of the ground you have gained is lost when you resort to such a practice. It would be better to call some kindly-dispositioned person on the phone and tell them you are feeling fine and to have that person's agreement.

If you are one who has just a select little group that you love, and you can excuse them all for their misdemeanors, you will find that you dislike all others who do the same or similar things. You are like a parent, or grandparent, who dislikes all the neighbors' youngsters but never bothers with correcting the faults of his own, and fails to see that his children follow the example set down for them.

Come back again and again to realizing that whatever you see is disclosing to you one or more of your self-beliefs. If you love your child you should be able to love your neighbor's child. When this Oneness, this Union, is established within you, you'll understand how you achieve it.

Therefore, go back to the exercise at the beginning of this chapter *often*. Your unification with God will make you wise enough to take care of any situation.

If, right now, you are very much in love with someone, you are divinely blessed, for it is that feeling that is God. If you are not, at present, joyously in love with someone, see if you can recapture that feeling without putting anyone's image in front of you. Can you love the whole world as God loves it? I said, as God loves it, not as the senses see it. Everyone and everything is a perfect idea.

The Best Way to Teach

It has long been held to be a fact that the best way to instruct is to tell the student what to *do*, rather than fill the instructions with "don'ts," but it is still a good idea When to point out where the puddle is, lest you step, or fall, into it.

One of the biggest misconceptions is that once one learns that he and the Father are identical, it is quite all right for him to use this knowledge to get another person to do what he wants done. I teach a "don't" at this point, because it is the best way to say it.

1. Don't try to make anything, come from this or that person.
2. Don't lean upon anyone for your happiness or joy.

3. Don't pick a place known to your senses as being the best place for you.

4. Don't look to any organization as the source of your income, or wealth.

If something happens which seems to indicate that this person or that place is the best for you, it is correct to then know that should it be true, nothing can prevent it; but individuals have often been known to pray that some dear friend will take them on a lovely vacation, get them a better job, or supply them with some other need.

This looking to outside effects is being back on the sense plane again, and what you have done is to limit the good you desire by making it come through the channel you designated. If it was not Divine Will to send your job to you through that channel, or the vacation, or love, or whatever it was you wanted, nothing at all takes place. So you sit, disappointed, wondering why your prayer didn't work.

Teach your thoughts that your opportunities are unlimited, in all ways, for anything at all. Teach them that the possibilities for joyful experience are vast, enormous, and don't have to be confined to some small, momentary good, that is here and gone again.

All the other people you know have the Divine Right to think and choose and do as they please. You have no right to interfere by wishing they might be the channels through which your good is to flow to you. Unless God moves them to do something in your behalf, keep your mental fingers off.

Erase False Thoughts

You are relieved of all thought of clinging to persons and outer effects when you fully understand this principle. This understanding will grow as you use the exercises herein. The realm of Spirit is inexhaustible. It is not just *some* substance, it is *all* substance. It is not just some energy, it is all the energy there is. It is not *some* power, it is all power.

Become so aware of this Spirit within you which *never fails*, that you lose all sense of failure. Allow yourself to become so sure of It's presence that a temporary lack of anything no longer sends you into the doldrums. Be ashamed of being despondent. Recognize it immediately as false thoughts, and remind yourself, "I am supplied with all good."

When Others Seem to Be Leaning on You

If you are called upon often to do this or that for another, and you go against your better judgment, you are most likely not rendering them much of a service. If you think of many reasons why you do not want to go, the best one is, you shouldn't be doing for another what he is unwilling to do for himself.

This is not, however, always the case. Perhaps you enjoy the feeling of being wanted, needed, and important. If you truly enjoy it, and are not being dishonest with yourself, then we might say this was God's desire for you. But if you are only trying to make the best of it, you'd better have another look at what belief you have. All people want genuine friendship, real interest and someone to tell them they are wonderful. Can you really approve of the reasons these others have for leaning upon you? If not, remove your support. It is senseless to be offended or indignant when it is within your power to change.

Hold Nothing Against Anyone

Bless, don't blame. You bless them when you know with all your heart that the Infinite is within then as love and intelligence, and they don't require anything from you. Become busy with your own business of lifting your own consciousness, of taking care of the things you need to do.

The next time someone asks you for your assistance, take your thought first to God before you agree to run and help. Ask of Him what He would have you do. It may be that the Higher Intelligence has another plan for you.

Kindness and compassion are wonderful qualities when they are not mixed with resentment and dissatisfaction.

BE YE NOT YOKED TOGETHER WITH UNBELIEVERS; FOR WHAT FELLOWSHIP HATH RIGHTEOUSNESS WITH UN-RIGHTEOUSNESS? AND WHAT COMMUNION HATH LIGHT WITH DARKNESS?

(II Cor. 6:14)

Get back to the feeling of love, without putting some person in front of it. Ponder the meaning of the word, for it is the grandest feeling in the world. Let it expand and expand until you feel you just love everyone. See if you can't feel that you really do love all people, everywhere, and that they are also loving you back. Feel that you understand them all and you will if you think of them as God's perfect ideas.

Becoming Acquainted

Joy and delight become yours when your attention is moved away from what the senses have told you, and the feeling of love is never really lost. It is always there; it just gets buried under these impressions which come from outside. That is why the Bible tells you to "Acquaint now thyself with Him, and be at peace."

How do you become acquainted with anyone? By association, by showing an interest, and by attention. How much would you know about the other person if you did all the talking and it was all about yourself? If you are going to become acquainted with God, you will have to give attention to what He is. He will express his feelings and his ideas to you, if you be still and listen.

Are you one who has to be doing something all the time? Do you turn on the radio or television so that you won't be lonely? Do you have to be occupied every single minute doing something, keeping your brain busy? or can you take time to get acquainted?

Has this idea of getting acquainted meant to you plowing through book after book, yet never really being still to listen? Are you so eager to reach the end of this one that you have not taken time to really *do* the exercises?

Some folks think that if they just replace one kind of sense impression with another one, they have done the job. So, they stop reading the newspaper and turn on the radio.

When you make the effort to hold your thought realm still, though alert to ideas coming from the Universal, all you seek is a feeling. Don't expect a message in words; though sometimes, when you are sufficiently developed, one may come, but it will be more as an idea.

The more you do this, the more potent the thoughts will be; they will become revelations which increase your understanding. Whatever question or problem you have had in your mind will bring its own answer, as soon as you are steeped in the feeling of pure peace and love. Your thoughts are not still enough if you are regretting, worrying, reasoning, or planning. Your feeling must be *trust*.

I know that you are getting something from this, but I urge you to trust this Power *most* when you are inclined to drift away.

There always comes a time for every follower of Truth, when it see to the senses that help does not come fast enough. At such a time, someone else, steeped in his *senses*, will accuse him of being "unrealistic"—of following after a rainbow. Please be assured that you are doing no such thing. *You* are the one who is realistic, and the one who speaks so to you has merely viewed his own lack of understanding. Such as these are a long way from the Father's House. Recognize that this represents a belief of your own.

Jesus' words, "Love your enemies, bless them that curse you" (Matt. 5:39) are for your own benefit. Get back to the feeling of the Father's Love. While you allow yourself to be hurt, or worry, you are not "being still." While what comes to you via the senses can still disturb you, you are not practising enough what you know to be true. The senses will govern your emotions until you learn to govern them. It is necessary to take yourself literally by the ears and cease thinking such thoughts.

Stop fooling yourself that because you read and occasionally think good thoughts that you have rid yourself of all those sense beliefs. You may think that because you have stopped voicing them so much, that they are gone, they aren't gone until they no longer crop up to disturb you. If you have ever exclaimed, "But I wasn't thinking about anything like that!" after some shaking-up has taken place, have another look. You were thinking the kind of thoughts which were going to bring it into your experience. It may have been that someone who treated you shabbily was punished, and the punishment was justified. That thought, in your mind, is harmful to *you*, not someone else. Why? Because right there is a place where compassion has never been introduced. The "wrong" you saw was a belief, a sense belief . . . your *own*, which you never bothered to correct.

Subjective Thought Patterns

Below the threshold of conscious thought are many beliefs which neutralize, or deny, what the conscious thinking is attempting to adhere to. Arguments will rise up, as Janet's arguments did in her story in an earlier chapter.

Be prepared to meet those arguments. It is done by being so thoroughly acquainted with what God is that you can quickly silence them.

As an example, suppose you are looking for a job, and your first thought is, "God is perfect intelligence and right action and works through me to lead me to the right place."

Let's say then that you have a subconscious belief that someone you know don't like you. Let's say it began years ago when your daughter got married, and because you didn't want her to move from home, you disliked your new son-in-law. Naturally, your dislike and disapproval of him didn't bring real love and respect from him, and sometimes he found pleasure in disagreeing with your views. But you have learned not to let this bother you, and outwardly you treat him civilly. The subjective thought pattern you first held has never been completely removed. Your conscious belief is that he doesn't like you, because *you* don't really like *him*. Other similar beliefs have begun to attach themselves to this one. Because the *belief* is the pattern formed, you see a good many things about others you don't like.

This is the argument that is going on and when you say, "God is all; God is love," this belief says to you, "Except for all these I don't like." You put the Word in, then erase it. God is no respecter of persons, for the life force is within all.

Responsibility for Right Beliefs Is Yours

Since it is your mind which must accept the idea that God is Love, you can see that when you are disliking anything, your attention has moved back to what the senses see and believe. The moment you limit "the Holy One of Israel," you have limited yourself.

This is why you must always come back to this *Aloneness*, of being the only person. Then you no longer concern yourself in thought with your opinions of others, or their opinions of you.

You are thinking of your life force as spirit, and knowing that it is identical with the All Life which is God. This union is called the "Moses" experience. You discover that "I am that I am," and the Lord God is One. You remember that Moses is told to "have no other gods before me." If you think there is another person, outside of this Spirit, who has a mind, intelligence, or a power apart from God, you have made him into another "god."

What This Communion Does for You

It dissolves these subjective beliefs. It gives you a sense of peace and love and joy. It clears the way for your opportunities to be seen by you. It makes you alert and full of energy. It turns your thought away from wrong beliefs and causes you to see that whatever God wants you to do is what you want to do. You know that you get your good from an infinite supply-house, and that it is much better than borrowing it from a friend or neighbor. You say "Thank you, Father" with a great gratitude and love.

How Will Your Good Come?

It might be offered, or given, from the very person you would have asked; but then, it might come from someone you don't even know as yet. You might be led to it through an impulse to do a kind deed. It could come as a bright idea, something which you had not previously considered. It may be something that you are to do yourself, by yourself, an accomplishment only you could achieve. The ways and means are just as unlimited as their Source.

Which "Tree" Do You Eat From?

You ate for so long from the Tree of the Knowledge of Good and Evil that now you are willing to give it up and EAT, to take your sustenance from the Tree of Life.

Someone defends himself with, "Oh, but I was born with weak eyesight; it's hereditary!" This is nothing but a belief they were saddled with by others. Sure, it's a carry-over from a former existence in mortal coil! We say to those, "Get rid of it now," unless they want to see how it is to be "born blind."

Say often to yourself, "I now take my attention off all limited forms and place it upon the limitless Substance." Wealth? Can you think of any greater?

When you get the idea of something, just say "thank you." You have accepted it, and it has to show forth on the sense level. Often it comes instantly, but in some cases other events must make way for it. No matter, it is on its way, because it exists.

Now is always a brand new moment, unsullied and perfect. Learn to keep it so. You don't have to fill now with past beliefs you know to be lies. You are ONE WITH GOD.

CHAPTER 9

A New Starting Point

Having better acquainted yourself with your Creator, you can now comprehend that you are a new starting point for His creative activity. You understand that you do possess all the requirements necessary for beginning, and that you can begin right here and now.

A hundred years ago, an inventor could bring forth a new idea and net a fortune. He received the idea, saw its possibilities, and enjoyed his search for the ways and means of bringing it forth.

Today, inventions are on a larger scale and many men work on one idea. Each mechanical part of an aircraft, for instance, has to be synchronized to fit in with the entire assembly.

Teamwork Is Necessary

The keynote is teamwork. By catching on to what teamwork means, we are able to see what the overall design is a little better.

Engineers and inventive, creative people are often commissioned to work out a completely new idea. Each individual who works on the project knows what his specific goal is. Those higher up know that if an idea can be thought of, there is also a way to work it out. Science, which is just a word meaning "present knowledge," keeps advancing just because of this "teamwork."

When this is missing in an organization, it could well he because something happened to the idea of loyalty. Viewpoints of what the goal is become divided, and complex situations develop.

When two partners disagree, one wanting only to make a fine product and the other to make money by cheapening the product, that business is already on the rocks. While they argue, someone else will produce the good product which will but them out of business.

A Divided Viewpoint

There must be this same kind of teamwork that goes on among the employees of a large successful organization, among your own beliefs.

No such teamwork is attainable while you have a divided viewpoint, or fail to know what your goal is. It is up to you to decide who is to be the authority for what thoughts you entertain. You must become the "boss" over your thoughts. If every letter, phone-call, or news item can sway your emotions this way and that, your viewpoint is divided.

You may not, in your present circumstances, do everything just the way you want to, or have all things to your liking, but you can *think* as you please.

You Are the Boss

At all times, you are in charge of what you hang on to in your thought realm. It is within your domain to correct any thought which you do not wish to think of as true. It may be your current experience to be hearing "bad" things but you can realize that it is only your ears, one of your senses, which deliver this report. You can know none of it is true of God. You have been given the freedom to express yourself, just the same as these others have, so why not express what you think? Do you have the courage of your convictions? Or aren't they convictions yet? Unless you can express them, you aren't sure.

Take an about-face; look in the opposite direction . . . at what is TRUE; not at a present fact which is changing constantly, and is never the same two minutes in a row.

Do You "Chicken Out"?

It is your sense thoughts which cause you to feel you dare not voice a comment. It is these sense thoughts about the objective world that is the wrong starting point, so you must remember that *you* have a *new* starting point. You are a place where the creative wisdom expresses itself. If you stop it down so that it can't be heard, you are a poor boss. "First, to thine own self be true," is good advice.

If you think you don't know what to say, begin changing that belief by telling yourself that you are always saying the right things, the helpful things.

Why wouldn't you know the right things to say if you really know who you are?

You are a starting point for this creativity, which must express itself by means of you. It already walks you, lives you, beats your heart. Let it expand into greater expression through your voice and your smile, as well as your thought.

In the Charge of Angels

Thoughts of the Truth are "angels" which bless and protect. When you witness an accident, however minor, remind yourself that there are no accidents in spirit. You'd be surprised to know how often persons involved in collisions have been uninjured simply because some one nearby knew enough about the law to make that statement with conviction.

If you see a fire, or hear fire engines clanging away, think, "There are no fires in spirit." The damage done will be negligible, if you have believed it.

When someone seems to be ill or ailing, think, "There is no illness in spirit," and refuse to accept the evidence presented to your senses.

There are no broken bones, nor germs in spirit. All such things are of the sense pseudo-mind, appearing only because believed in. Because it is a law that every belief produces an effect exactly matching, we can see how "man has made many inventions" and became his own worst enemy.

Next time you are face to face with someone who is voicing an untruth, speak up. His life and your life are the same life. You are correcting one of your own beliefs. You are moving away the boulders in front of your "jewels."

You have these senses as a sort of measuring rod, by which you can tell how you are doing. The more joy and love and peace you have known by means of your senses, the stronger is your knowledge of your relationship with the Infinite. The point is to remember *not* to look outside of yourself for the good you wish to experience by means of your senses.

What You Now Discover

From this new starting point you can look and see meanings which were veiled to your comprehension before. How often did you crucify (cross out) the still, small voice of Truth, for the testimony of the senses? When did you "deny" your Savior, the Divine Love within, which says to you, "Lo, I am with you always?"

Your new apprehension discloses to you how often you mistakenly ran to another man or woman for help, advice, legal aid, or some kind of knowledge, when you might have turned within, to the altogether lovely and beneficent Power?

With your new awareness you grasp the fact that you never were so weak as when you thought strength and wisdom came from the little human self. You now see how ineffectual a mere academic education really is, for it only solves part of your problems. You always bumped up against a place where it wasn't quite enough.

Where your eyes observe disorder, your mind observes that Order is Heaven's Law. Where your ears hear discord, your mind knows Harmony is the Law.

At your new starting point, you have put God, not yourself, first. You demand teamwork among all your beliefs by knowing first of all that you have made them, and that you are going to make all the wrong ones over. As long as you remain at your mental concept of yourself, you will be inclined to put yourself and your own desires first, and see things only from your senses. This is why you learn to put God first, and listen to what He would do by means of you.

A clarifying example is the story of Mabel R. and her young niece, Marilyn, who was a young divorcee with a two year old baby.

Mabel had a long face the day I met her, and in reply to my greeting, she said, "Oh, nothing very exciting is happening; mostly I'm worried about Marilyn. A girl her age should have a lot more fun than she's having."

Knowing Mabel to be a student of Truth, I was surprised that she didn't instantly change her own viewpoint, so I made a couple of statements reminding her to direct her thought to God, Universal Wisdom, Love, and Joy.

"I know all that" she waved a weary hand. "I'd like to see her having some fun."

"You know everyone's life shows up as his own state of consciousness, Mabel. Why don't you teach her?"

"Too young," she tossed off my suggestion. "She needs to live a little first. She's such a gay little bug, likes to dance and kick up her heels."

"Live first?" I asked. "I think you know the concept must come before the reflection. Maybe you'd better change your own belief about her, and what you see there." I went on my way, knowing Wisdom was always present.

Well, Mabel changed her belief at sense level, by buying Marilyn some new clothes and baby-sitting for her so that she could go out and "kick up her heels." There was an automobile crack-up and the girl landed in the hospital with a broken leg.

When I saw Mabel again, she lamented, "When I would do good, I seemed to have done evil."

A good desire, formed at sense level, had produced its usual outcome of additional problems.

I pointed out to her that the belief was what she should have changed. It turned out that the girl was unhappy because of her broken marriage; she had decided it was her own fault, and had a subconscious desire to punish herself.

Nevertheless, during her laid-up period, Mabel found the time and opportunity to teach her and talk with her.

"Aunt Mabel," Marilyn asked, "Why didn't you tell me about these things before? I've always wondered about such things, but I didn't think I knew anyone smart enough to answer my questions. And you were right here all the time!"

In due time the little family was re-united and living happily together. So Wisdom always was present, everywhere.

Remain Calm

If you have teamwork between your beliefs, you will not find it difficult to remain calm and serene when others panic. You can stay unhypnotized by appearances, no matter how frantic and panicky those around you become.

Now that you know the difference between acting from a sense belief, at appearance level, and really arguing it through to knowledge of present wisdom, you should be able to prevent the hypnotic action of the senses from overwhelming you.

When you concur with another's criticisms and fault-findings, you will find it difficult to remain calm. This is something you must watch all the time.

A material interpretation of the Bible will not, and never has, set anyone free from false beliefs. Until you have the spiritual interpretation, you will not remain calm while other's are panicked and frantic, and remain unhypnotized by the senses' reports.

The sky overhead and the earth you walk on are beheld by the senses. They are not the "heaven and earth" God created, told to you in Genesis 1:1.

The "god" you formerly thought you believed in might also have been only of the senses, if you thought there was a flesh and blood "son." This may be confusing to you because Jesus speaks of his flesh and blood, and you have been told you must believe that Jesus came in the flesh. This, also, is the sense level interpretation of the Gospel. The "second coming" is symbolic of Man's evolved state of understanding his union with the Father.

Now that it is becoming more clear to you why this union, though already established, must be recognized by you, you are able to have teamwork among your beliefs. Perhaps this answered a question as to why some of your prayers have not been answered. Is there a sense-made belief in a power apart from the Infinite Power, which blocks, or acts as a dam?

You can remain calm when you know there is no other power, and God works only for good.

Help to Others

You give but little when all you offer is material aid. So many give such aid with the thought that the recipient is lacking in intelligence, strength, or some other, quality. It is characteristic of humans to view such "charity" with suspicion. They are prone to ask, "What motivates this apparent generosity?" Viewed with mistrust, the kind act is warped out of shape and is not a boon but a bondage.

The thought which put one in a position where he required outside help, if not changed by showing him ways in which he could help himself, is still there.

Whether it is a nation accepting foreign aid, or an individual, the principle is the same. Since nations are made up of individuals. It is essential to happiness that each person be a growing, expanding, more productive entity. A person who does nothing is like a rusting mechanism, soon incapable of working at all. All must understand that Spirit is the starting point, and each know that this life force is in himself and all others.

A good many persons like to think of it being in themselves but fail to recognize that it is in all others and everywhere present. The way to do it is to contemplate what God *is*, not the *appearance* of what God is not. Then, you will have changed your viewpoint.

To give wisely and lovingly is an art you learn gradually. You change from giving just what you have no further use for, and calling that your generosity, to finding ways to fill a need. You find ways to help those who have special skills, or want to learn a skill, to express and be of service to others. You begin to praise and encourage a good idea another has by putting your own shoulder to his wheel, in whatever way you know.

I have a letter from a woman who says she is praying that God will touch the hearts of people to help her and her family in their great hour of need.

God is always doing this. God also touches those who think they are in great need with ideas which they may follow, themselves, to fill those needs. So much depends upon the idea they have of the Universal Intelligence.

The Mist of the Senses

Have you been mystified (mist-ified) trying to find a "god" you called not see with your eyes, or hear with your ears. Have you really thought that by looking up to the sky, you were thinking to heaven? How long have you searched with your eyes for a sign of the "second coming," thinking to see a man float down to earth? Perhaps, while in church, you have thought yourself to be in the Presence of God? You were, You are always in the Presence of God, even when your beliefs have made it seem otherwise.

Do you know that "King Herod" is the symbol for your sense beliefs? It is the word, or key idea, which represents the thought that you are something separated and apart. It is the one which gives the instructions to all the other beliefs for such a long time, and allows the crossing out of this beautiful and lovely Self. How long will you crucify your Christ? This thought is the one that keeps telling you that you live in a world of billions of other entities, most of them downright evil.

You have many beliefs which God didn't create, but you have used God's life force to bring them into being. Shall you continue to believe in their reality, these foolish things which only harass and torment you and take you into all sorts of ill-smelling places? Shall you continue to look outside for help, when you can see yourself as a new starting point for the Creator to express what He is? You are becoming more and more aware that you are not this weak little ineffectual thing that is only a mental concept formed by your senses, and you understand that *you* are that Son you have hoped would come. *You* are the Perfect Pattern, the Idea God created.

What You Already Are

Are you, or YOU, the Son? Do you "get" what I am saying to YOU? How much do you become what you already are? Have you ever heard of an actor who played a certain role so long that he thought he was the character he played? Have you "payed the piper" enough now? You have played the role of being what your sense beliefs kept telling you that you are. Are you ready to be God's Idea? You *are* that; can you realize it?

Look at it this way: when you learned the multiplication table, did you add anything to the principle of mathematics? Didn't you, rather, learn something that was of use to you? Nothing at all happened to the multiplication table, nor did you "use up" all the numbers, so that they couldn't be used by another. You simply became aware of certain undeniable facts.

It has often been said that everyone believes in the same God, no matter what religious denomination he professes to follow. In one way this is so, in another it is not. Since every man's idea of God differs, some degree of true awareness is always present.

Your idea of what God is in some way matches your concept of yourself. You will not think God is just if you are not always just, nor will you think God is loving and kind when you are not.

What have been taught? More to the point, what have you accepted, as really true, of that which you have been taught?

Are you jolly, cheerful, willing to help? Are you expressing the best you can, all the time? Are you an inspiration to those around you, causing them to want to emulate your behavior? Does something which you are cause others to be a little better? Do others seem to behave better when you are around? Do they dress more neatly for you? Do they make any effort to be as kind and thoughtful as you do? My, there's a great difference between following a leader and being one, isn't there?

What kind of Power do you believe in? Do you see how you must first *be* it, and let your light so shine? Ah, it is glorious when you discover that you are that Divine Love, that Infinite Intelligence, and that there is no need to adjust anything in the world of affects.

A Higher Viewpoint Does the Work

You know better than to attempt to "adjust" the multiplication table to suit yourself; you simply learn it and make use of it. If you make an error in multiplying, that error is "unreal" as far as the multiplication table is concerned. Your sense-belief errors are just as unreal to Divine Wisdom. Suppose you do not "know" the multiplication table? How chaotic would your figuring be? It is no different when you don't "know" God.

A good many people are in this same spot, where religious concepts are concerned. They follow a leader who gives them his opinions, many of which are at the sense-concept level. These people think their leader knows because he wars against evil, wears the clerical garb, and was graduated from a certain seminary. They are completely unaware that they follow a sense concept of religion by so doing. We might liken it to learning the multiplication table from someone who only bows there is such a thing. I do not say that every religious teacher knows no more than that, but I can say with impunity that much teaching is done at sense level.

At your new starting point, you are seeking to find out for yourself. If you were taught, as a child, that Adam and Eve were the first humans to be created on earth, and followed that up with the next question, "Who did Cain and Abel marry, when there were no other women on earth?," possibly it was never explained to you that this was purely an analogy.

Now, your higher viewpoint shows you that the writer was teaching a cosmic lesson, that when you live solely from the senses, the offspring you will have will join with other effects God did not create, and one kind of thought will cancel out another. You comprehend what it is that "casts you out" of the Garden of Perfection.

Ridiculous Absurdities

Sunday-school teachers all over the country have been telling Bible stories with no more idea of the meaning of them than if they were telling "Jack and the Beanstalk."

Children have been told that *they* killed a man named Jesus, who loved them. They have grown to adulthood fearing a "god" who would "burn them in hell," if they failed to follow the dictates of their church.

Some have been taught that they could rely upon their dreams of the night, because the Bible mentions such things as dream prophesies.

Many have been taught that the devil has more power than God. What rubbish!

The "Wisdom" of Man

The very fact that Man's teachings postulate two opposites, a heaven of golden streets and pearly gates and a fire and brimstone hell, proves it has been made up by the carnal mind! And the carnal mind is enmity to God.

The world's greatest thinkers have declared that they believed in the individual's continuance as consciousness, but they admit they can find no proof. Now and then, one not recognized as such a "great" thinker has some experience which convinces him; he sees a vision of one who has passed on, or receives a message. With what does he see and hear those who are no longer in the flesh? Those who know only by means of their senses cannot grasp this, for the "wisdom of man is foolishness to God."

Legends Have Been Passed Down

Locations have been marked as the actual historical sites where Scriptural events took place. Grave clothes have been photographed as the ones worn by the Savior. Out of an era noted for its vice, error and corruption, when brutal injustices were rampant, legends were conceived and passed down as gospel truth. Is it any wonder that such warped and twisted mentalities came forth with a teaching filled with duality, the pairs of opposites? The original meaning, "respect of God" became translated "fear of God," implying that the Creator could do terrible things to you.

The sad part is that many of these same ideas are still being passed on, and fear of God rather than love of God keeps many in bondage to a false ideology. Out of this ignorance another incorrect viewpoint arises—that God's Son was a man who accomplished great miracles, taught a beautiful truth of life, and was not saved from an ignominious death, but was nailed to a cross. Then, as if this did not insult your intelligence enough, you are asked to believe that He came forth in a finer body, which scarcely resembled the former one, and he was not recognized.

There is even one teaching which holds that this "finer body" then separated into billions of atoms, which you can take into your body, when and if you ever learn how.

Do you see that these are *all sense concepts*? The early theologians who doctored up the manuscripts, adding a word here and there, or removing one, in an effort to make the text "reasonable" must have been pretty confused boys. Our present Bible is replete with faulty translations and mistranslations, but strangely enough the TRUTH remains, and can be seen.

The story of Jesus, who became the Christ, is not an historical event which took place nearly two thousand years ago, but is a story about YOU. In an esoteric way, it is stating facts which had their beginning long before the beginning of calendar time. A thought did attain this state of consciousness, and it is named Jesus, the Christ, the only Son. Oh, yes, all the landmarks are real, the Jordan is a real river, but its meaning cannot be perceived by senses.

When the Apostle Paul says to you in Romans 3:23 "For all have sinned and come short of the glory of God" he is speaking of the Jews and the Gentiles. You have thought these referred to classifications of people, races, and creeds. Yet, if you have ever read the Scripture with your Real Mind, instead of with your already-formed beliefs, you know that you have been told clearly what is a Jew and what is a Gentile.

You Gain Perception

A "Jew" is a *belief* which comes from the heart of you, not a person of a certain type or class.

FOR HE IS NOT A JEW, WHICH IS ONE OUTWARDLY; NEITHER CIRCUMCISION, WHICH IS OUTWARD IN THE FLESH.

BUT HE IS A JEW, WHICH IS ONE INWARDLY; AND CIRCUMCISION OF THE HEART, IN THE SPIRIT, NOT IN THE LETTER, WHOSE PRAISE IS NOT OF MEN, BUT OF GOD.

(Romans 2:28-29)

A "Jew" is a belief which knows the law.

A "Gentile" is a *sense belief* which knows nothing of the law.

Paul tells you that ". . . when Gentiles which have not the law, do by nature things contained in the law, these, having not the law are a law unto themselves: "

You are being told that when you have a sense, belief, even though it *is* that, if it is a good one, a help to all and showing harm to none, it is of the Law of God.

He tells you that all of your beliefs have come short of the glory of God, that your beliefs have been in error, not you.

As you travel from sense to soul, to Spirit, many more wonderful things will be revealed to your mental awareness. It is said so beautifully in the Book of Romans, and now that I have given you the key, you can read it for yourself.

You have your starting point, and can see how a *name* in Bible language signifies an idea. Adam, is your first concept of yourself as body. Christ, or the "last Adam," is your final understanding, when you reach it, of just who you are! Every step of the way is outlined for you. You are at this starting point of changing over all your beliefs, and particularly those which are "Gentiles," and do not know the law.

Now that you see how sense beliefs have played their part in giving incorrect interpretations, it is clear to you what you must adhere to. It makes it clear, too, why there are so many religious denominations, and sometimes misunderstandings between them.

FOR I AM GOD AND NOT MAN; THE HOLY ONE IN THE MIDST OF THEE.

(Hosea 11:9)

CHAPTER 10

Beyond the Senses

Reaching this lesson, you are no longer asking the question. "How do I do this?" for you have been practising what is given in each lesson. Only by doing something do you learn the "how." Every word in this book is telling you *how*, for it is changing your viewpoint; but unless you practise the exercises yourself, the sense beliefs which have become anchored will continue to function in your experience.

Close your eyes right now, for a full minute.

Think: *"The intelligence I have is God. My own life and intelligence is God. This Perfect Life Essence is what I really am."*

Were you able to do this for a full minute without letting thoughts of the senses come in? If you did, you most likely had a feeling of gratitude and a calm, poised mental state.

If you were unable to keep thoughts of events, and what you must do next, in abeyance for even a sixty second period, you have not been reversing the negative things known by means of the senses as you go along. Throughout the day, you must learn to do this, for many negative things show up, and unless you are alert, you are allowing more negative impressions to join with those already present.

You know what is meant by thoughts which come from the senses: anything you have seen, heard, felt by touching, smelled, or tasted; anything at all in the world of form, called the relative world.

Thoughts such as, "Where shall I look for a job? Why

131

is this pain in my body? Should I call John, or Mary? I'm going to go buy that house. I should turn up the heat and close that window. I'm getting hungry," are all thoughts which come from the senses. Every one of them must go, so that you give your full attention to what God is. You can do it for a full minute; you can do it for a full hour!

You enter in awareness of your own completeness, as you withdraw your attention from the relative world. Every time you do this, you benefit. When you do, you are connecting yourself with all the energy, all the wisdom, all the good, in much the same fashion as you connect an electrical appliance to the plug on the wall. There is just this difference, that you are already "plugged in" by the fact that you live at all, but when you turn your attention to the nature of this source, contemplate its presence within you, you draw from it what It is.

This All-Creative Power is never a failure. Where your attention *is* has much to do with your personal success or failure. A thought of failure is a false belief; it comes from what the senses have perceived. It is not always easy to turn away from a wrong manifestation which today stares you in the face, and know that it is not true or real.

Attract Your Success

The Divine Principle works for you by working through you. The Light, or enlightenment, is greater than darkness, for Light overcomes the darkness, it is never the other way around. You enlightened awareness is comprised of:

1. There is a God. God is Life . . . MY OWN LIFE.

2. This LIFE is mine, and is MY MIND.

3. This MIND is the Mind of God.

Where is the mental attitude that denies that all God is must be present?

You do know that the Spirit of this Mind which is God, must be present at all times and all places, don't you?

Is there some doubt about this still remaining? Are you limiting the possibility of the willingness of the Divine Principle to work?

Then you aren't believing that God is Love.

Why not?

Could it be because you are not loving, kind, and understanding? Is it because you intentionally block another's progress by your opinions, which you now know are formed at sense level? How can you get what you want, and what is important to you, while you cannot see that God is the Great Givingness? What do you have to give other than correct and true ideas? Nothing at all; for the world of effect is continually changing. You can give a man a meal and he will be hungry again in a few hours.

Give him a true thought and he'll find ways to get his own meals. You can awaken his skill, talent, ability, strength, and righteousness so that he never knows lack, or want, again. Know that his life force is no different than your own, and let your compassion fill what the senses call a "need." Even though his present understanding is meager, he will feel gratitude for the love you express.

Touch the Feeling of Love

You have found this union with the Presence of God, now you are doing the same thing again, but going a little deeper into it. Romantic human love is just a sample of what Divine Love is like. If you can combine this with parental love for the tiny infant, the mother-love, which is ever alert to giving care, you are drawing closer. Divine Love is caring for all in the same manner. It is a recognition that everyone's life is precious to Him.

Will you have to move some boulders out of the way? Whom do you hate? Maybe there is one whom you don't particularly care for, or someone who has hurt you?

Take time right now to see that this is a belief which came from what you saw, heard, etc. *Change* the belief.

How? By noting that it came while you thought of yourself as a physical body, a personality which was your mental image, that any belief coming from this pseudo-self is just as false as that self is, and by remembering that you are the Perfect Idea which God created, that cannot be hurt or harmed, nor feared.

Let yourself feel the peace and love and ease that comes from this knowledge. This feeling is the Spirit.

Make sure you realize that spirit is not an invisible body, for a body would indicate a limitation. If you have thought of God as an invisible body, stop it, for visible, or invisible it presents a picture of something contained within something else. It spells limitation. Such thoughts bring you back to the relative plane.

Allow this spiritual feeling to expand itself; it will if you keep your thoughts on feeling. You are now doing what is called, "thinking in your heart." You can arrive at an unspeakable feeling of joy and bliss, if you are willing to take the time to do so.

A World of Difference

THESE THINGS HAVE I SPOKEN UNTO YOU, THAT MY JOY MIGHT REMAIN IN YOU, AND THAT YOUR JOY MIGHT BE FULL.

(John 15:11)

Pure joy invigorates you when you pray correctly. The physical senses ask for something of the senses: homes, jobs, health of body, a loved one, or some "thing." You are told that the thoughts of the head receive nothing because they only want to consume it with lusts.

What a difference there is in asking that you be given right ideas, so that such outer things are forthcoming.

You are altering your viewpoint of life from the way the sense man sees it to the way of Impersonal Love. If you think you have to have a reason to love someone, that they be "nice," you have missed the whole point. You *are* loving them when you recognize the life force in them as nothing but God's life. You don't have to invite them to your home, for this is sense level again, and here, always, you are free to choose what beliefs you will entertain.

The Inner Self

Your own unlimited potential is the wholeness of spirit. Having this feeling of love for all, in a quite impersonal way, brings the accompaniment of joy, the feeling of success of actually possessing all the characteristics of God.

It is a feeling that says to you, "God loves me and cares for me. He has given me everything, it is within me right now. Everything is present here and now."

This inner self is the Divine Pattern and every time you turn away from the outer effects to feel it within you, you are dissolving some mortal belief. You are dropping some lie, some untruth, which has blocked your expression and experience of good.

Outside Sources of Possible Good

It may occur to you that some particular person, or an organization, is to be the outer means through which the Spirit is going to bring you good, and you may be right, but don't depend upon it. Keep remembering that it is God who works through all. You and the other will both benefit; otherwise, it could be a one-way affair.

Your senses are strong for quite a while, but the time does come when you can really Know from within, no matter what or how the senses may deny.

If you hold to the Truth, you will not try to hold a thought that some individual will change his way of thinking to yours, nor attempt to "sell" him by clever speech. You by knowing the Divine Will has already taken care of everything, have brought yourself around to a place of acceptance, and it matters only that *that will* is carried out.

Then, what you see in the outer world of effect will be far better than anything you could have tried by the force of your mental means to accomplish.

This is not to say that you may not have good ideas which can be carried out, nor that you are just to sit and dream. You must move from prayer to performance, for it is from God that you get these good ideas.

For instance, you will know the difference between backing a project that retards or prevents progress, and one which promotes it.

Your Senses Are Going Through a Training Process

You not only take the substance of life from an invisible something called feeling, but you also take ideas from the same source. You are making beliefs now much serve you; yes, they act as servants to you.

Your first "good servant" must be this thought:

"God, being my life, and what and where I Am, is in charge; therefore this 'I' of me is in charge."

In charge of what? The affairs known by means of the senses?

"God is Spirit, and Spirit is feeling. I have created the belief that I am in charge of my feelings."

Knowing this, you can make another belief, such as, *"God is always a Success; therefore I am a success."*

If there is something you have been striving to accomplish, but the senses have been barraged with negatives and failure looms, do the exercises as given in these lessons. The barricades and barriers will not just go down, they will vanish completely! The world is full of people who not only want what you have to give them, but will help you to see that they get it. The Spirit doeth the work.

The only thing you have to fight is discouragement, and courage is your best weapon. Know God is your courage, and it is always present.

The moment you observe anything with your senses which removes your feeling of a good present, here and now, take your thought to a higher viewpoint.

When violence, or anger, is what you observe, take your thought to Peace. *Think* what it means. If it is disorderliness, think of Perfect Order. God is Balance and Order. If it is injustice, think of Divine Justice. If it is carelessness, or inconsideration, think of Divine Intelligence as being universal.

When people are reported to be in a warring state of mind, know this is not so, but merely a negative use of mind power. If it is hatred in any of its varying degrees, think of Perfect Love, in all people at all times. These are all beliefs which you, now, do not have to accept. If it is thought alone which makes all these reports, a higher thought can change it; and it is only the way in which ignorance is displayed. Take the thought of Intelligence as being in all and through all, and watch these events fall apart. We are all training our senses to see and experiences better world.

Contradictory Beliefs

You may have to work hard on some of these beliefs, but once you understand just how you are to go about it, the evidence will prove that this method is correct. I repeat it over and over because so many ask repeatedly, *"How do I do it?"* even after they've been told exactly how to do it.

Discover the Real You

Do you still think that you are born of human parentage? This is what being "conceived in sin" means. Since a sin is a mistake, you are mistaken if you think your mom and dad "created" you. It only seems so to the senses. A physical man and woman have no more power to create life, in the true sense, than you have to create a tomato from holding out your hand and saying "abracadabra." Argue it, if you must, but you'll never find what you are looking for, until you stop arguing and see that only God is the Creator, and there is no other.

God alone is your "Father-Mother." What does this do to your present concept of physical parents? What does it do to you, if *you* are a parent? Doesn't it help you to see that you are only a channel through which Life worked, or Nature "worked?"

Do you see how it relieves you of becoming possessive, domineering, or dictatorial? Doesn't it stop you from looking at faults and shortcomings and force you into realizing that Divine Life is everywhere?

I hear you ask, "But, what about the act of creation, of conception, that brings about the birth of the tiny infant?"

A natural law! A seed is planted and it grows. YOU, the REAL SELF, yes, your God-Self, the Spirit, does it. You, the *human* entity, had nothing to do with the formulation of the babe.

When you sow a seed, and a plant forms as a result, you had nothing to do with the making of the form for it does its own growing. It may have been needful for you to provide the proper conditions, such as watering, and so your intelligence provided the knowledge, but you had nothing to do with its actual growing process. So is it with the infant. "Something" took over, and did the formulating, and that "Something" is the Father, of you, me, the infant, and the plant.

Someone also always says, "But I look like my dad. I have the same tendencies, the same weaknesses. I also have talents my mother has."

The senses again, with their many beliefs.

Learn to Know You Inherit Only From God

"Weak eyesight runs in our family," alibis the one who has never learned to think for himself.

If you are guilty of "inheriting" any of such things, aren't you about ready for your real Inheritance?

The senses will continue to confirm whatever you insist upon believing. They are already out-picturing to you everything which you have accepted as being true.

You have freedom of choice, but wouldn't you like to be free from all that is making such a mess of your life, if that is the way you now see it?

Shall you continue to be heir to all the wrongs your predecessors believed in? Shall you go right on believing in all the lacks, the wrongs, and the evils, or do you really wish to be convinced that God is your Father, the loving Father who created you as His Perfect Idea? You have already made up your mind, but now do you see how much work you must do on these beliefs?

From God, you have inherited only Good, and it is eternally yours; but you must believe it, and know it. Why do you have to know it with your conscious mind? If it is already true, why must you keep moving wrong beliefs out of the way? Because as long as you believe in your human heritage, you are making the biggest mistake of all. You are denying your birthright.

Suppose there was in some bank fifty million dollars in your name—but you don't know about it. There it is, yours, and no one ever told you. Of course, you couldn't even *try* to spend it. Well, not believing in your birthright is even worse. Not knowing your Real Self, you cannot possibly enjoy anything of the Father's house.

Is God, not some *man*, YOUR Father, and the only source of your life, strength, love, intelligence, joy, and wealth?

Divine Love Is Not Divided

Within you, as your life, is also Truth. There is no opposite to that which is All. There is no opposite to Love, no hate, dislike, mistrust, fear, or deception. When you know God as Truth, if there is anyone attempting to deceive you, that deception will be brought to light in time to protect you and your activities. Intentional dishonesty will be exposed before it can do any damage. No damage can be done when you have taken your Inheritance.

Keep recalling to your attention that God is the Life within all, as you think of God as Divine Love. The word, Love, translated from the Greek by the early scholars, meant "consideration," not sexual expression, as it so often is taken to mean today, nor family affection and friendship; just being considerate.

You express consideration for all to benefit and you shall benefit. Every time you are considerate of others' rights, others' good, you are expressing Divine Love.

What if you encounter others who are not considerate, while you are? What should you do? Pray first, then you will know that your actions will be wise. Their rights stop at the exact point where yours begin. You have every right to protect yourself against imposition. Of course, imposition is a sense belief, which you begin to change right away. When you pray, you are given the right idea with which to meet the issue on the sense plane. All man-made laws tend to follow the Divine Law, and have had to be made to keep those ignorant of Divine Law under control. Some individuals learn consideration the hard way, and breaking a law on the sense level shows they do not understand the spiritual level. Thus, your prayers.

You are not obliged to associate with such as these, but you are under an obligation to yourself to pray for them, for every one of them represents some sense belief; maybe not your own, but those of others who are in some way connected with you. You live in a race consciousness, filled with all manner of silly beliefs, ignorance, and inharmonies, and you have to train yourself to not take on any of these beliefs.

Never pretend a friendship you do not feel, for this is hypocrisy. You gain nothing and lose much. Keep things on the sense level as calm and poised as you can, and as truthful. Preserve the core of what awareness of your God-Self you now have by avoiding insincerity or posing. You *can* do it without hating, without fault-finding, without even an explanation.

Break No Laws

You are in the process of learning that all troubles, inharmonies, sicknesses, and ailments are the result of a broken law, a broken *spiritual* law.

Just as there are punishments and fines made when man-made laws are broken, so are there reminders and punishments for breaking a spiritual law.

Someone laments, "But we didn't even know there *were* such laws!"

Who hindered you from learning about them? There has always been a clergy of some kind, willing and ready to help you as best they could. They have known about the laws. Why did you read the movie magazines and the sport pages, the novels and the news, when there is always a Bible to read?

But, now you see your mistake. You are rectifying them. You are even happy and interested in doing so. You want to do it right. Do you know why? Probably someone prayed for you!

Oh, yes, there are many ahead of you who have already learned what to think, and when to pray. There are many who have seen in you some one of their own wrong beliefs.

How to Pray for Another

You are called upon to pray whenever you see or hear anything of a disturbing nature. No matter what it is—health, wealth, or happiness which seems to be missing—it is a call to prayer. Mean, surly, snarling or grouchy persons are also a call to prayer. Stupid, dull and foolish ones are also reminding you to pray.

Recognize that what you see is a sense belief. You remove your thought from it, and begin to think of just what God is. "God's Love and Intelligence is right there where that Life is showing," is the thought.

Suppose the person is ill, or in pain, then you do not think of him as a person, but only a thought, a belief. It is his belief, not yours. Don't make it yours. No one is sick. If you get sympathetic over the sickness and the pain, you've done it wrong. Your job of praying will be harder. Do this correctly; before you even go to see the person, know that no one is suffering. No one believes in sickness, illness, pain, where you are. YOU don't believe, because you know YOU are the Spirit. Only on the sense level does this seem to be a fact, and it is a fact on the sense level, and comes from a belief. You are changing that belief for him. To do so you must realize that he is also one of your beliefs, not as a sick person, but as a healthy one.

You can, of course, do this without even going to see the person, but if you are strong enough in your faith in God, do go and talk to him about things in which he is interested. Take his mind off his body. God will do the rest. If it bogs you down to see one who is ailing, send flowers and your good wishes, and do your praying at home. You'll do nothing to help either of you by joining him in his faulty concepts.

Stop fearing to speak up when you know something to say which will change the trend of another's thinking. No long tirade or lecture is necessary. Sometimes as simple a statement as "I'm sure God is in charge," or "This, too, shall pass," may be the thought which will work wonders.

Make Yourself Some Good Servant Thoughts

Make this belief for yourself: "I always know the right thing to say."

Have you ever said to yourself and others, "Oh, good heavens, I'm always saying the wrong thing?"

Have you thought, "All through my childhood, I was so often silenced or argued with, that now I'm afraid to speak out, even if I know I'm right," and kept that with you, even though there were times when your good ideas might have saved the day?

Or have you believed, "I don't know too much about this, so I'd better not say anything?"

If this is the case with you, make a new belief to replace those thoughts. Tell yourself over and over that you are always saying just the right thing. Tell yourself that you speak so that others understand what you mean. If you have caught yourself saying, now and then, "Oh that's not what I meant," learn to say what you *do* mean. Know that you *can.* Think before you speak. If what you want to say to someone seems hard to say, write it out first, then you can have a good idea of how it is going to sound.

Clumsy speech comes from muddled thinking. You can speak in such a way that others feel you say the right thing.

You might think that, too, that others do understand you. Those I know do understand me," or "I speak in such a way that I do get my ideas across."

Consider the making of your thoughts the, most important factor in our life. Train yourself to feel the way you wish to feel, then you'll make thoughts that serve you well.

If your own thinking is muddled, what you read that is true may often seem incoherent, vague, and fuzzy. Then make yourself this thought servant:

"I am understanding this, now. I do comprehend."

Right Thoughts Cancel Wrong Ones

Not only is God your individual life and intelligence, but He is also Universal Intelligence. Condition yourself to thinking that all things are working together for greater good.

At the sense level, your politicians and news reporters would have you believe that everything is working together for greater "bad." Many take these reports quite seriously, building greater fears and hatreds. When the candidate of their choice is not elected, they slump into morose and unhealthy mental-states, declare the elections are "rigged," and fail to understand that this wrong thought can become externalized.

You can wipe out any picture of an undesirable condition with the knowledge that the Spirit of God is forever present as everyone's intelligence and love, and thus see harmony come out of any chaos.

It has already been made clear why you must consciously know this. You use this power every minute you think, and you cannot afford to think negatively. Can you imagine how this world would appear if everyone understood this?

You Do Not Have to Wait

It does not matter what others are doing, or neglecting to do. You can begin the practise of right thinking, keep it up consistently, and change for the better all that pertains to you and your experience.

An outstanding instruction of the Bible is, *"Physician, heal thyself."* Even the most sincere miss the significance of *"Work out your own salvation."* When one neglects to take a new viewpoint from a spiritual level, he is apt to regard himself as perfect and all others as faulty.

To guard against this, go back often to the first part of this chapter and work with the idea of being alone, with God.

Get into a habit of calling upon this Great Intelligence which you meet through your own individualized intelligence. Get out of the habit of acting in haste and regretting the action. Take time to consider what the most intelligent action on your part might be. If you play chess you know that the first move you see is not always the one to make. Think of all possible outcomes to each possible action, then do what is most efficient and most worthy.

Know that the Spirit, which is Universal, is guiding everything and everyone. If something happens which appears to be contrary to this, it is only coming from some sense belief, which will be moved out of the way if you hold to the right thought, *"All things are working together for good."* The person, or group, which seemed to stand in your way, will either alter their decision or be moved out of the way for something better to take place. You may benefit in an even more effective way, but only if you *know* the Spirit is Universal. The Spirit is guiding everything and everyone to a favorable result.

Recognize Your Advantages

You are understanding more and more how important it is to keep the state of your own feelings peaceful and joyous. This true joy is not obtained by running around grabbing everything you want, or by doing as you please. Those who interpret it this way, regret it. It is an inner joy, dependent not at all upon others, or any outward activity. This is not to say that others, or special activities. will not be present; but rather that you are joyous even when they are not. YOU are happy all the time.

With this *feeling*, you can easily think pleasant thoughts, and these thoughts will externalize.

You have been apprised of what you should do, *how* to think and feel. You have been told *how* to find union, *how* to become acquainted with God, *how* to move away from sense impressions.

Have you ever tried to teach a small child to tie his shoelaces or button his jacket? You tell him how, then you let him try it. *He* must perform the action.

Have you taught anyone to play an instrument or drive an automobile? Do they learn by reading a book, or listening to what you say? No. They learn by performance. You advance in the same way. Important ideas for you to hold to have been put in first person, present tense, so that even as you read, you are the one saying and thinking them. Make them your own so that you *remember* them when outer appearances shuttle your thought off in another direction.

Whenever you are troubled about anything, it is because you are breaking some law; not Man's law, not that which legislative bodies pass, but a Universal Law. The remedy is to get another viewpoint. Your goal is emancipation from inharmony, from belief in lack of good. You attain it by considering what God must have to be, and what your relationship to Him has to be.

CHAPTER 11

The Problem Maker

Work Out Your Own Salvation

Your childhood experiences have had a great deal to do with how you react to events today. This is where you "work out your salvation."

Each state of progress in faith is a proportion which bears a title. *"The book of the generation of Jesus Christ, the son of David, the son of Abraham* (Matt. 1:1), tells you that you have been changing your viewpoint by comprehension of the God within.

The title of "Abraham," as well as his earlier one "Abram", belongs to you. Abram means human faith, the kind of faith the senses know. Abram (you) left the Chaldees (sense and brain reasoning) and went forth into Canaan (the discovery that thought comes from an invisible, unlimited source). It is a new "land" to you: Abram's "wife" (reflection) was called Sarai, and Sarai was barren. You were not able to prove that what you thought had any power.

You returned to the sense world of visible objects (Egypt), but you did not stay long. You strive to become aware that your Mind is invisible and unlimited. But, still thinking of yourself as physical mankind, you are unable to conceive what is meant by a "spirit" or a "spiritual idea." You take refuge in compromise, and fail to bring forth any really constructive ideas.

You have learned that it is possible to "find" God, but "working out your own salvation" will take time, effort, and determination. You have many thinking habits yet to be changed. Child training is a good way.

How Do You Teach?

You are not inclined to teach a child whom you truly love anything you know will be harmful. But are there things you *don't* know which you are quite unintentionally teaching, by *example*? Everyone should consider well what he says and does in front of a small child, for the child is more apt to do what he sees done, than to follow good advice. The one who realizes this is careful to correct his own careless habits and be pleasant and polite, thus avoiding setting a bad example.

Many of your own faulty concepts were implanted when you were a child, and have become deeply rooted. If there are children around you, you can rid yourself of your own as you set the proper example for the youngster.

Years ago, I sat in a room with a young mother who told the story of her own childbirth pains in front of her three-year-old daughter. The child burst into tears, for she had been able to follow the story and know that she was the baby who had caused her mother so much pain. Many years later, we learned the effect this belief, never properly corrected, had when as a young lady, that girl said, "I don't ever want any children!"

Her sense of guilt was not easy to move. It had its effect in many things she did, and would not go.

Let us mention some of the things both parents and grandparents do in the rearing of children, in the hope that some of your own misconceptions might be unveiled to you. Even if you are not a parent, there are children, at least once in a while, in your world. How can you be an influence for good to them? We are living in a world today where many young mothers believe that they have to hold down a job while someone else acts as baby-sitter. Such women have a rich and worthwhile opportunity, if they but realize it.

What you teach another, you are in a sense teaching yourself, for every place that you see life you are seeing a belief of your own.

The parents of an unwed, expectant mother viewed their daughter's condition with horrified disapproval. I learned that they both held down jobs, and had done so for a good many years, and that they belonged to a number of organizations and clubs. They had not neglected their civic duties, nor their church, but they had certainly neglected their child!

This girl did not know God was her Father-Mother, she thought her parents were. Had she known, she would have been somehow apprised of what the consequences of her search for love and affection might turn out to be.

"We kept close tab on her," I was told. "Keeping tab" was just what they meant, too, and that was *all* they had done.

The parents wondered whether they should insist upon this boy marrying their daughter, have an illegal abortion, or let the baby be born and rear it themselves.

Just because a biological law has taken its toll by no means says that this boy and girl are ready for the problems of married life. To insist that they marry is not only another short-sighted arrangement, but is often disastrous to all three, unless some degree of understanding is arrived at. An abortion is not the correct answer. All this sense-level figuring simply brings additional problems.

Let us switch to the young man and woman who know how to intelligently view their life ahead, far in advance of the wedding ceremony. They know there will be adjustments in personality habits and in financial affairs. They have the knowledge of how to prevent childbirth until they are ready for parenthood. They know that to court it before they are ready is like jumping in the ocean without knowing how to swim.

The school of thought which says we must take no precautions against child-birth is strictly of the sense-level. There would be much less crime in the world, on the sense-level, if people took the time to properly rear their children, and be wise enough to plan their families.

Rules of conduct come from the Divine Mind, and embrace honesty, courtesy, and cleanliness as a beginning. The child should know how those rules benefit him. No matter how young a child can spot inconsistency. He will watch you to see if *you* do what you tell *him* to do.

Punishment for Disobedience

Every child is glad to know that his parents will not permit an infraction of their rules. While punishment may be distasteful at the time, it should not be disregarded, for this gives the child a feeling that someone cares, and that the rule is important.

Parents make a grave error, when, thinking to give the feeling of security, they pass up the need for some kind of restriction. To say to a child that he cannot have his dessert unless he eats all of his dinner, and then give it to him anyway, is to cause him to disbelieve any other cautions you might make that he should follow.

The custody of a child to rear is a precious right, and every parent and grandparent should be able to know that this seeming "soft-heartedness" is nothing but "soft-headedness."

However strange it may seem, a child do not resent a restriction or punishment when he has been made to understand that what he is told to do is for his own good, for his safety and protection.

Never threaten a child with any sort of penalty unless you are prepared to carry it out. If he loses faith in what you tell him, he isn't going to believe anything you say. Later, when you tell him not to play with the matches, he is liable to burn the house down.

The Value of Praise

A child, just as an adult, wants favorable attention, but not unless he has done something to deserve it. Praise him when he has done nothing to warrant the praise and he thinks you are a fool. But you *can* look for what you may sincerely praise, can't you?

You will, of course, discipline yourself to be unmoved by pouting looks, tears, or other emotional displays, when you know the chastisement is bending the twig in the right direction. You will gently guide the young mind in the right direction, to that which is pleasant and interesting.

You Witness Many of Your Own Beliefs

If you are training your children to be courteous, you will have to avail *yourself* of all the rules of proper conduct. There may be things which you do not know, because of never having been taught. You may have some discourteous habits, of which you are quite unaware, like borrowing things which you have been too short-sighted to buy for yourself, or bothering others when they are busy.

Children have a way of showing up many of our beliefs which need changing. If your child tells lies possibly you had better have a good look at what you are doing.

The small ones are seldom tactful. They are often interested only in being entertained. Few really want to accomplish anything. Many do not like to share their good. Some like to make trades in which only they benefit.

When a child's generosity is exploited, what do you say?

How often do you praise a child's good manners? Do you take time to comment favorably on his prompt response when you call, and thank him? Have you expressed pleasure for the quickness of executing some task?

Children listen for these compliments, just the same as adults do.

Imparting Instruction

A child must understand why there is a taboo, or ban, on some activity. When the reason is not clear, he is apt to do *just that* in order to learn why he should not. His inquiring mind 'must be satisfied. When a child knows he follows your instruction for his own best good, he is willing to comply.

Not only does this require your ability to communicate your ideas, but also calls forth from you a thoughtfulness of what needs he might have. When you attempt to communicate an idea to a very young child, do you use words beyond his comprehension? Many adults do this and then wonder why they have disobedience.

Hurried instructions about what not to do, as you rush out the door, may well turn out to be just a suggestion as to what to "play" next. As the woman found out whose six-year-old son was given a toy saw as a gift, when she called to him, "Don't saw the handle off my umbrella!"

Knowing How to Correct

When you are looking at quarrelsome, unruly, and disobedient children, you are being given a picture of your own belief which must be trained. You are not being unkind to a child when you refuse to allow him to harm himself, and neither are you being unkind to yourself by insisting that you have better beliefs.

You can look back upon your own childhood and note how you first became afraid of germs, diseases, bullies, and reciting in class.

If you have learned the importance of being selective about what you think, you know how to teach the little ones, without implanting foolish fears.

You are quick to discern that raucous shouting and screaming at children brings about an opposite effect from the one you wish. While it may arrest their attention, for the moment, you know they will imitate you in their play, just as you have imitated someone who set that example. You know now that both environment and heredity are of the senses, but that within you, and all, is the Perfect, Pure Intelligence.

In Your Midst

There is Perfect Faith within, which beautiful gem

glimmers out from between these boulders of sense beliefs, and shines through the crevices.

You have moments when you grasp the fact that you are really quite wonderful, even though not always appreciated. No matter what you have done, or failed to do, or what has been done to you, you can now view your treasures with an eye to expressing them more fully.

You are able to see that all human life is a series of states of consciousness. You see blossoming and blooming, age and decay. Beliefs change, and when they change for the worse you see or hear of epidemics, calamities, and wars. When you discover the Real Truth about yourself, these false beliefs come tumbling down as though shaken by an earthquake.

Aware now that you must always think from a higher viewpoint, and first change the thought, you know that as long as you believe anything *is* as it appears to the senses, your attention is in the wrong place.

God is Mind, the Real Mind of YOU, the Essence of Life. And, your name (nature) is changed to Abraham. Abraham is spiritual faith. Your concept of self (Abraham's wife) has a new nature, too. It is Sarah, who is no longer "barren." She is to have a "son." Abraham is to be the father of "nations." Do you see that this means "constructive ideas"? You will find this account in the Book of Genesis.

The Cloak You Wear

Your body exists within your own mental realm. A mind out-of-ease is a body without ease, or dis-eased. The physical body as you now view it is the product of the human, or divided, thought, which believes in both good and evil, and is subject to all manner of accidents, hurts, and ailments.

Have you been striving to keep your body safe and healthy, while letting anything and everything go on in your thought? How foolish! What a waste of time to take exercise, vitamin tablets, and health foods, while you allow fear and selfishness and anger to make the climate right for germs! And, how silly to believe in germs, when you might believe in God!

The quality of thought, called Abraham, and its reflection, Sarah, is your awareness that everything is a Word, and that a Word is a thought.

A Difference Between Idea and Opinion

If it seems to you that I am arbitrarily announcing something for which there is no proof, let me remind you that this is something you can prove to your own satisfaction. The proper names used in, the Scriptures, as well as places and events, stand for qualities of thought and ideas. Opinions come from sense-beliefs. Real Ideas are the "children" of God, and they include Abraham, Isaac, Israel, David, and Solomon, as well as Moses and Jesus. These qualities are already within you as Key Ideas, and they, too, have many "children."

As long as you identify yourself with the carnal mind of the senses, believing in both good and evil, your concept of self is as one person among billions; you are not thinking in your heart, but in your head.

With your senses, you are always looking at your beliefs. When what you perceive is distasteful or troublesome in any way, it is a belief you have made and which YOU can change. Judging by appearances is "The Problem Maker." If you are able to see that you've been doing this most of your life, you can also understand how some belief you are currently faced with can be handled.

When persons you have known move away, or are otherwise removed from your experience, should you grieve? If all they represented to you was love, and they never presented themselves as a problem, that love will wear another body. If they represented nothing but a problem, one which you seemingly could not solve, don't you see that their absence is the solving of that problem, as far as you are concerned?

The Image and Likeness of Your Beliefs

All of your environment and the people within it objectify your, beliefs. Some of them do come from your "heart," from your faith, and the degree of your belief in God. Many come from movies and novels, as well as news and conversation. The ones which come from your own past experience are the ones most difficult to dislodge, for they seem most real. They, too, have had "children." or offspring.

You have been taught that the brain thinks, when actually it only records impressions. It is like a radio which appears to be playing the music you hear. The Thinker is the Mind, or Life, the *real* YOU. Just as you understand that the radio isn't playing the music, or being the voice you hear, but that it is coming from a broadcasting station where choices are made by a program manager, YOU, as the thinker, can make choices as to what you believe.

The Creative Medium

One of the early philosophers, Plotinus, said, *"Nature is the great No Thing, yet It is not exactly nothing, because it is It's business to receive the impressions of Spirit."* We might put it this way, *"No effect makes itself, a thinker takes the undifferentiated substance, which becomes to him, for him, according to the nature of his thought."*

The Truth about everything walks over the waves of error and silences the storms by revealing Itself.

Control of Human Opinions

We have all heard about, or read about, someone who passed on in conditions of sordid poverty, who left a fortune in money hidden near-by. If you think it the height of folly to die in discomfort and hardship when there was something at hand to prevent it, how foolish are you to hold to opinions formed by the senses?

A miser is one who will not use what he has for himself, nor circulate it to benefit others. When you do not express your beliefs to others who need to hear them, it is because you fear. Such fear is caused by your human opinions. It leans on the staff of hardened belief in personality. You see your personality, and the personality of others. This is not Oneness!

When you try to believe in the corruptible mortal and the incorruptible Perfection, at the *same time*, you are hopelessly buried in enigmas.

You, and you alone, have given your beliefs power to think that you are an individual person, so many years of age, living in the conditions you now find yourself in.

Haven't you already discovered that a great many of your own opinions have been proved to be greatly in error? Did you ever buy stock in something, hoping to become wealthy, only to be disappointed?

You didn't listen to the Wisdom within, but you did listen to your human reasoning, trusting to something called "luck."

If you hold a grudge against anyone, or indulge in any sort of back-biting, if you dissect others and gossip about them, ridicule what are to you their short-comings, the problem-maker is still with you.

If you think, "Due to present conditions, I cannot express as I wish," you are making a problem.

Does the future scare you? Do you worry about your family, and friends, or your business? The problem-maker is at work.

You have no other choice but to discipline such thoughts. You will have to force them out. Until all the false education is annihilated and all this is seen to be but negative mental attitudes, you will continue to fashion problems.

Seek a New Mood

Prayer makes you withdraw from the objective world and the evidence of your senses. All the faculties and activities of the mind are stilled. You think: *"The Father and I are One, but the Father is greater than I,"* and you realize that this Life Principle appears as the individual YOU.

The Passover symbolizes the expansion which takes place now; and when you have fully disciplined all of these beliefs, it is called, *"the day of Pentecost"* (Acts 2:1-4). The "tongues of fire" symbolize Love, and you feel the pleasant new mood, or the Holy (whole I) Spirit. The text says that "they were all filled with the Holy Ghost and began to speak with other tongues," which does *not* mean that you will speak another language, heard by ears. If you have been ill, you—having *that* awareness·—speak in the tongue of sickness, telling about your pains and discomfort. As you realize your Oneness, you speak in the tongue of health. When all your false beliefs are gone, you speak in the tongue of love and joy and abundant good.

What a world of difference there is in this meaning than in the one which holds that some ancient language, long forgotten, would be spoken!

Many Have Been Puzzled

Students of comparative religions have sometimes been confused by the discovery that all Sacred Books give forth the same ideas. Buddah and Zoroaster were both supposed to have been born of a virgin. From the Talmud we have:

OUR GOD IS A LIVING GOD. HIS POWER FILLS THE UNIVERSE . . . HE FORMED THEE, WITH HIS SPIRIT THOU BREATHEST.

From Taoism:

MAN HAS A REAL EXISTENCE, BUT IT HAS NOTHING TO DO WITH PLACE; HE HAS CONTINUANCE, BUT IT HAS NOTHING TO DO WITH BEGINNING OR END.

These pre-Christian doctrines led many to believe that Christianity was organised by the Roman Emperor Constantine, borrowing, its ethics from Judea and its ritual from Asia Minor.

The sacred book of the Mohammedans, the Koran, says this:

THE LORD OF THE WORLDS HE HATH CREATED ME AND GUIDETH ME: HE; GIVETH FOOD AND DRINK AND WHEN I AM SICK HE HEALETH ME.

The teachings of Buddha say:

THEREFORE IT IS CLEAR THAT IGNORANCE CAN BE REMOVED BY WISDOM.

The Upanishads of India say:

THE ONE GOD WHO IS CONCEALED IN ALL BEINGS, WHO IS THE INNER SOUL OF ALL BEINGS, THE RULER OF ALL ACTIONS . . . AS FAR AS THE MIND EXTENDS, SO FAR EXTENDS, HEAVEN.

The Bhagavad-Gita of India tells us:

HE WHO IS HAPPY WITHIN HIM, WHO REJOICETH WITHIN HIM, IS ILLUMINATED WITHIN, BECOMES ETERNAL.

Taoism, believed to have been written and taught by Lao-Tze, a Chinese philosopher, older than Confucius, possibly around 600 B. C. has this to say:

THE FARTHER ONE GOES OUT FROM HIMSELF, THE LESS HE KNOWS. WHAT IS HEAVENLY IS INTERNAL: WHAT IS HUMAN IS EXTERNAL. IF YOU KNOW THE OPERATION OF WHAT IS HEAVENLY . . . YOU WILL HAVE YOUR ROOT IN WHAT IS HEAVENLY.

The Zend-Avesta of Ancient Persia, says this:

THE WORD OF FALSEHOOD SMITES, BUT THE WORD OF TRUTH SMITES IT.

There is nothing to be puzzled about once you see that the enliglitened of all ages have taught the same ideas. Only those steeped in material effect and the physical senses are arguing about the historicity of the Christian Bible.

No Other Gods

Go into the privacy of your own mind, which the Bible calls "the closet," and ask your Lord within to give you the Secret Doctrine.

All the "mist"-ery, the clouds of mortal belief, leave as the sun—your Son—shines. The light will dissolve the mist.

That thing called "discontent" that comes when you have a divided allegiance, will go when you cease having a "god" of your senses, something you desperately want that you don't know how to get.

You Look Too Far Away

You know you never find anything unless you look for it where it is. When you look outside of your Self, you are looking too far away.

A woman who wanted to rid herself of some of her faulty beliefs went to another woman who claimed an ability to look into past incarnations, former existences, so that she could better be able to see what she had done wrong. They called these *Karmic errors.* Well, they had an exciting time, supposedly reviewing the many characters she had played on the stage of life. Did it help this woman to find her Real Self? No, it just made she false seem more real!

There are others who want to know their future, by means of fortune-telling, astrology, numerology, and even spiritualism. They are all interesting as subjects, and those who seek knowledge by any of these means seldom realize that what they are doing is assuming there *is* an Intelligence that *does* know. What they fail to see is that they already have that knowledge. It is within themselves.

The old Darwinian argument as to whether or not Man descended from the apes is amusing when one looks at the phraseology, for "to descend" is to go lower. This is like all other such reasoning from the standpoint of the senses, so it is no wonder it winds up in argument.

Wrong Reactions Are Problem Makers

The tendency to get all steamed up about injustice is a jimdandy way to do the next thing the wrong way. You haven't always known how to control your reactions, and when you react negatively in anger and temper, your thought is more than just discontent.

The sort of thinking which balefully blames another, condemns outer conditions, sees stupidity, and hates unfairness, must be jettisoned. This is not easy to do because injustice is something which riles everyone.

Correct the Feeling

"What man meant for evil, God means for good." You are being shown, clearly and accurately, just where your own wrong belief is, and what it is about.

You believe in *injustice.*

"But I try never to be unfair!" you exclaim.

Aren't you being unfair and unjust when you are willing to blame someone else, who is also a place where God's life is expressed?

"Yes, but . . .," you protest.

What are you going to do about it, write a letter to the President, or your Congressman?

God is bigger, greater, more powerful than them. Why not go to the top? Or don't you think God is the "top?"

What is "to blame" for this injustice?

What else could it be but lack of intelligence—in other words, ignorance? Where would you get more intelligence to fill this empty place called "ignorance?" You would have to look for it where it comes from, wouldn't you? You would not think of preventing others from learning how to have more intelligence, and thereby exercising, justice, when such would also benefit you. On the contrary, it gives you great joy to know that you do know how to call forth Divine Justice, and make room for intelligent action.

Ignorance Is Always to Blame

Consider a four-year-old child who has been told he must not leave the yard, or the sidewalk in front of his own house. He is willing to obey this, but along comes a small puppy with which he begins to play. The puppy runs and he follows; the puppy grabs hold of the child's coat with his teeth and the little fellow tries to free himself, moving away from the area. So wrapped up in the puppy's antics, the child is not aware of moving away, and soon he is around the corner on another street. His mother looks out, fails to see him, and begins to make a frantic search. When she finds him, she spanks him for disobeying her. He has a punishment he doesn't understand. Was he to blame?

You say the puppy was to blame? No. The child's ignorance of the puppy's nature was to blame.

Likewise, you as an adult, have places of great ignorance when you live solely from sense testimony, and you reap similar punishment for what you do not know.

Have you ever loaned money to someone and not been repaid? Weren't you ignorant of that person's habits and character?

Have you ever been caught in the rain without rain-coat or umbrella? What was to blame? The weather? Wasn't it your ignorance of the fact that it was going to rain?

Years ago, I watched a baby who was at the crawling age, who had picked up a hairpin and inserted it into an electrical wall socket. No one in the room knew what he had in his hand, nor what he was going to do with it. He was a good baby, but ignorance of what that action was going to do did not exonerate him from the effect he experienced. The shock knocked him several feet into the center of the room and gave him great respect for that funny little thing on the wall.

It is possible to disregard man-made laws and not get caught at it, thereby getting no penalty; but when in ignorance of God's laws you make the wrong use of *them*, there is a penalty.

Man's Understanding Unfolds

Man is evolving and his comprehension of Universal Laws appears to be somewhat limited. Man's use of the Law of Mind is a personal, individual action. As long as his thought is in accord with the Universal Harmony, the Law is set in motion for good. Thus, when anyone intends harm to another, he is ultimately harming himself.

Since the action of the Law of Mind is as automatic as any other Law of Nature, it behooves Man to know what it is and understand how to correctly apply it. He learns gradually that the mental cause and the outer condition are identical.

If you can comprehend that when your individual will power is in opposition to the Universal Will, or God's Will, you have shut yourself off from your Source of Power, you will learn to follow the stream of Life back to Its Source, and bring your thoughts and purposes into alignment with Original Good. In this way you cease making further problems.

Mulling Over Hurts

Without vilifying another, try to understand exactly why your feelings have been hurt. What thought and emotion did you hold which should have been altered? Did you try to hurt another? Did you pass unfair judgment? Did you really know all the facts?

Remembering that hurts do not necessarily come back to us from the same person we so unfairly judged, we are aware that we specialized this Law of Mind quite unconsciously, and It returned to us the same sort of hurt. It is quite easy to produce discord instead of harmony, but that is not what we wish to do.

Every hurt is a blessing, for because of the hurt we determine to formulate thoughts and ideas that will benefit all mankind.

Vindictiveness, that feeling of needing to even up the score, is one of your greatest problem-makers. You indulge it to your own sorrow. Try instead to understand why someone acts as he does. It might become clear to you that you might have done the same thing had the conditions been reversed, and you were the one having the experience you now criticize.

You have no choice but to use this creative power, but you *do* have a choice as to *how* you use it.

Block another's right to the expression of good, and you have blocked your own.

Haste Is a Problem Maker

Time, when you understand what it is, will expand to meet your needs. When there is order in your mind, your activities are organized, and there is no need for haste. That feeling of urgency which precipitates rash and thoughtless actions, comes from confused thinking. Haste breeds recklessness, causes forgetfulness, and poses further problems.

Learn to do first things, first. Some housewives fad to make themselves and their homes presentable the first thing in the morning, and so are embarrassed when unexpected callers arrive. Of course, no one should ever be an unexpected visitor. In a day when there are various facilities by which we can pay others the courtesy of announcing our intended visit, or better yet, waiting for an invitation, we need not make ourselves into a problem for others.

Businesses often limp along because first things are not recognized, and thus not done. On a purely relative scale, the customers' needs and wants are overlooked.

When you have learned to do first things, first, there is no need for haste, because what is important has been taken care of. You no longer squander your energies upon what is of little or no consequence. You have learned to avoid the need for haste when you have stopped wasting your time chatting on the telephone about something better left unsaid. You leave grievances, sicknesses, worries, and troubles out of your conversation, and find that you have time for all the constructive happy things you want to do.

Tactfully Change the Subject

When you find yourself in the company of those inclined to speak in such negative fashion, simply remember that Divine Love dissolves instantly all that is untrue.

Having assumed the responsibility for your own thinking, knowing that all you think, say, and do, is important to you, you can free yourself from a, good many unpleasant experiences by refusing to accept as true any gossip you hear.

See how adept you can become at changing the subject to a more desirable one. If you can say so sincerely, tell the one who speaks of past illness how much better he is looking. Recall to mind that Divine Love governs you in all human relationships, and you will know how to change the subject so that no more of the same is forthcoming in your presence.

If you feel inclined to offer a helpful thought, such as encouragement or praise, do so, but avoid feeling the coldly critical indifference to one who appears to be dogmatically opinionated about his own views. In the Truth, there is no resistance. Everyone is seeking to better his lot in some way, so your mental task is to know that this person is *finding* the right way. It doesn't have to be through you, so don't argue.

It is unnecessary to call anyone's attention to his preference to speak derogatorily of others, as long as you know you are able to look past his opinion to the Truth of God. Those who have made derisive gossip a habit will drop out of your environment.

You Don't Call the Wrong Thing "Right"

You meet these kind of people because you still believe they exist. When you have convinced yourself that there are no such people, you won't be meeting them any more.

You have beard the saying, "Take time to be holy." It means. "Take time to think of yourself as whole." As you more and more think of God's Presence as perfect life existing in all things everywhere, you are following a command, "Be ye perfect, even as your Father in Heaven is perfect."

You are not calling the "wrong thing" RIGHT, but are looking past what the senses have told you—the sense belief you have formed—right into the heart of Truth. To no longer have unpleasant reactions is freedom in-deed!

We Blame None

Are we blaming your parents, teachers, and associates for the fears and selfishnesses which have been educated into you? No, we are only pointing out how you came to have them, showing you how you have been growing in understanding during every moment of time. All learn in the same manner. It is possible to see through all human errors to the Infinite Good. It matters not *now* how long you have had unwarranted fears, been without case, suffered the distress of lack, been unloved, or unappreciated; now YOU can change it all.

Eliminate the Problem Maker

Right now, for this moment, you can seek the Kingdom, where ignorance is dissipated. Within the Kingdom, there are no people, conditions, or things, to disturb you. The Kingdom is nothing but Love, Joy, Power, Peace, Intelligence, and Truth. This is "the Mount," and it is a *feeling*.

Here, you *know* that you never had any Father but God. YOU *know* that All that God has, or is, is yours. There is no ignorance here, no lies here, no weakness here, no human opinions here, no false beliefs or hurts, and nothing to cause fear.

Your recognition of God's Presence as your own livingness has become real to you. There is no need for haste, for everything is *now*; there is no confusion, for Perfect Order is present.

Teach by Being

The little child, the teenager, the neighbour, and the business associate, everyone you meet, will be taught by what you are BEING.

You will BE . . . calm, peaceful, loving; you will BE intelligence itself. That's what you ARE, but you can't BE it, until you *know* you ARE it.

The voice of Wisdom directs your speech. "I will walk and talk in thee." From your BEING, you'll speak with authority, but it will not be the aggressive, tyrannical speech of a dictator; it will be kindly wisdom, instantly recognized and obeyed. It will not be academic knowledge from the elevation of a human personality, nor from moral goodness," but rather a simple right answer which takes care of the need of the moment.

For yourself, you see instantly which faulty belief had brought about what you called your "problem," and with True Knowledge you can wipe it off your slate of sense perception.

What the Four Gospels Teach About Problem-Makers

Have you as you read the four Gospels, wondered why there are four accounts of the teachings, so similar in many passages, yet differing in an overall picture?

I have told you that the first Adam mentioned is your own first concept of yourself, as natural man, the physical body. In Matthew, you find the concept that Jesus (the I AM) is born of woman—of a virgin, to be sure, but nevertheless, the female being. Yet, in the first chapter of Matthew, you are given all the generations from Abraham to David. Abraham is your spiritual faith, but David means the Source of Pure Thought. There are fourteen steps to awareness and these are made clear to you, the reader, also. From this Book of Matthew, you learn first to "repent," that is, to change your viewpoint. Recognizing your Self, for the first time, you are then led into the *"wilderness"* to be *"tempted of the devil* (your senses)."

You might spend quite a little time in this state of consciousness. Your senses begin to tempt you with all sorts of suggestions; "Why, just look, I can get anything I want this way."

Scarcely aware that your attention has turned again to the senses, you find that you often must recall to mind that, *"the angels have charge over you, lest at any time thou shalt dash thy foot against a stone."*

Your inner Lord begins to teach you, saying, *"Repent; for the Kingdom of Heaven is at hand."*

Do you quickly see that it is saying, *"Change your viewpoint? Stop looking at the outer things and consider the vast, unlimited goodness of God, the Infinite intelligence that knows all that can be known."*

The Book of Matthew is saying to you, *"Which is the greater, the gold, or the temple that sanctifieth the gold?"*

What concerns you, the body and personality? Or the Real Self?

You've heard about the goose that lays the golden eggs. Would you care what became of the golden egg, as long as you were still in possession of the goose?

So, in Matthew, you find much instruction which you can follow. The Sermon on the Mount, the Lord's Prayer, and all the stories lead you to see that you are to *"call no man your Father upon this earth, for one is your Father, which is in heaven."* Again, you are told not to look here nor there, for the Kingdom for it does not come with *observation.*

Doesn't that say plainly enough that you will not "see" it with your eyes? Why look up at the sky?"

The Gospel of Mark

Here, the human viewpoint is being adjusted to the reader's perception. Perhaps you honor God with your lips, but your heart is far from the real Truth?

How many believe that they are following their Lord because they don't smoke, drink alcohol, or gamble?

THERE IS NOTHING FROM WITHOUT A MAN, THAT ENTERING INTO HIM CAN DEFILE HIM; BUT THE THINGS WHICH COME OUT OF HIM, THOSE ARE THEY THAT DEFILE THE MAN.

(Mark 7:15)

Isn't this telling you that evil thoughts are your problem-makers? Many who avoid *doing* what they think of as "evil," are *thinking* about evil all of the time!

The Gospel of Luke

In this one, you are told how to become aware of spiritual concepts, those jewels which are already within you.

Mary (Pure Spirit), and Joseph (Divine Love), have given rise to your awareness of God within. This "virgin" substance, unused as yet, with no thought impressed upon it, gives birth to your understanding of Divine Love.

The parable of the Prodigal Son is telling you that you live amidst eternal good. It makes clear that the Divine urge is always pushing you toward your goal of greater good. It is telling you that as you turn to God, God turns to you, with all His blessings.

The Gospel of John

When you have reached the place in your growth where you no longer look for *external* help, this Gospel has meaning for you. Your periods of spiritual enlightenment have grown longer, and you are understanding that the revelation of your "Sonship" must come from within, that it never comes from the intellect or the senses.

HE WAS IN THE WORLD AND THE WORLD WAS MADE BY HIM, AND THE WORLD KNEW HIM NOT.

BUT AS MANY AS RECEIVED HIM, TO THEM GAVE THE POWER TO BECOME THE SONS OF GOD, TO THEM THAT BELIEVE ON HIS NAME.

(John 1:10,12)

Every word, every true idea, is already established in you. As you read this Gospel. It becomes increasingly clear why the "promises" of God are laws. You have what you need to sustain constructive ideas, but any good quality, not expressed, grows weak.

This Gospel tells you how you can continue to grow strong, until your own Sonship is an *ability*. In the teaching of Jesus, you are not told there is anything wrong with the appearance, but rather not to form any judgment according to those outer impressions.

Judging From What Appears

One of your biggest problem-makers is a tendency to

judge from the standpoint of the appearances. Not fully realizing that what does appear comes from your own beliefs, you lean to doing just what Jesus admonished you *not* to do, and go right on judging the appearances.

He didn't say the appearances were faulty, but that there was another side to them. Since there is nothing in the world of objects which has only one side, should you not look at the whole, rather than the part? Your distress comes about from being ignorant of the whole.

You have the mental capacity, the ability, to comprehend, but if your training has been so used to looking for faults and flaws, that these are all you see, an effort will have to be made to train your attention so that you can always be happy and successful.

When there is much that you dislike and disdain, you will find it difficult to find love, real love, the kind you want, for it can only be expressed *to* you in the degree that *you* can express it.

Divorced persons are often in this predicament. They want love, believe they are able to express it, (and they are), but they keep their attention too long on what they have disliked.

Marrying for the Wrong Reasons

Marriage for financial security, social position, or fear of loneliness, are not good reasons for joining lives together. Some marry only for sexual needs, not understanding that the chemistry of two bodies coming together was all they had, and that respect for one another is a vital necessity.

Admiration and respect belong to real love, and if these are missing, it is likely that each will regret the union.

What should you do if you are already involved in such a mistake? The husband or wife which you think is far from being suitable can be seen to be just what you need for your own character growth. The imperfections you see in this mate are merely your own beliefs being reflected. It may not be easy to see where these originated, but if you will continue to identify yourself with your Source, and by that I mean thinging *"I and the Father are one,"* you will see less and less evidence of these beliefs.

Beliefs are often changed by removing oneself from the outer evidence, but unless one knows that he is changing a belief, and puts wholeness into his mind, he may be no better off than he was before.

Character Weaknesses Make Problems

It is a character weakness to lean upon any outer thing, or person, for joy. Alcoholics have a character weakness. Because they do not entirely approve of themselves as they are, they attempt an escape. There is nothing harmful in wine, whiskey, or any alcoholic beverages, except when they are used unwisely, as a crutch.

Most of the things theologians have called "sins"— smoking, gambling, drinking-are done to excess because they are believed to be joy—givers. The error is not in the act, but in the kind of thinking which causes the act. Running to the pill-box is just as much of a character weakness as becoming a gambler, an alcoholic, or a chain-smoker.

We are not saying that good medical advice should be shunned, just be sure it is good advice. Again, you "render unto Caesar what is Caesar's," and use your intelligence. If a potion or pill helps you, take it, but try to find what kind of a belief is the cause of discomfort.

It is not what goes into your mouth that damages you the most, but rather what you are saying. What comes out of your mouth is what you are believing.

A woman who claimed to have read many books on the science of the mind and its workings said in front of a whole group of people, "My husband always gets colds in the month of November, and is sick through all the holidays." And she called herself a *student*?

You must always use the Law of Mind on yourself. Make yourself think rightly. Once it is clear to you that every belief is the gimmick which produces some kind of an effect, a great many mysteries will be cleared away.

Breaking Up the Ridiculous Beliefs

Understanding that prayer is but a tuning in to your own greater intelligence, a deeper feeling of peace and love will break up the ridiculous identification with all the "bad things." You understand that this is not some kind of trick of manipulating the intellect, or a way in which something you can't see is prevailed upon to "heaveho" and jump to gladly do your bidding, but you can instruct those foolish thoughts to "be still."

The action you indulge as result of what you see and hear—the emotion you allow to govern you—the thoughts you persist in entertaining: all of these must come under your control, if they have been negative.

Be sure you know God is Infinite, not finite, and you will not be muddled with a belief in two powers. The so called "bad luck" of number thirteen, and the black cat crossing your path, are no less stupid than your belief in insecurity or sickness.

Curb *all* tendencies to react negatively.

CHAPTER 12

The Secret of Greater Love

You have been practising what is given in the lessons to the best of your ability, and are somewhat aware that your Light is already shining. Joy flourishes and grows when it is rooted and grounded in Love, and you are more certain that Love is the power. This joy is one that no man taken from thee.

It is shining through you even though you may not, as yet, be fully aware of it at all times. There is something new, different, and sparkling about you as you practise-making yourself think correctly.

You are aware that God has written His Law in your inward parts, and you know that this Law of Love is already established within you. It has become ever easier to turn away from the negative things presented to your senses, and see with your mind the wholeness which is a cosmic fact about your life.

You have been able to observe how selfishness and greed, the striving for place and station, recognition and reward, have brought restlessness and competition. You have noticed that the same attitude among races and nations have brought war. You are aware that you have been taught competition, taking sides, and resentment against others. You have noticed that "fighting for peace" is *man's* "wisdom", which is "*foolishness in the eyes of God*," and you have turned within to find Peace and Greater Love.

Perfect Love Casts Out Fear

You are now able to understand yourself better, and know that it is only when you fear, something that you are inclined to argue, quarrel, or fight.

Now that you know what it is that causes you to lose your temper and resort angrily—that it is nothing but a belief which carries out such action—you have been successful in making new beliefs, or "good servants." You have seen that it was simply a place in your belief realm where Love had never been introduced . . . a place of fear.

You have noticed how incorrect thoughts brought up unpleasant emotions, which hurt only you, and have constantly moved your mental attention to, "*In the beginning, God.*" You know that the "beginning" is always *now*. You know God is that Perfect Love and that It is Omnipresent. It is in all places, working for the highest good of all.

Your Abilities Expand

Be not discouraged if at first there seem to be quite a few beliefs which are causing you to have to "work like a beaver." You have accepted the findings of the senses as being "true" for quite some time, and have believed others who based their claims upon the testimony of *their* senses.

You are entirely capable, for you have asked for the Light, to see the way, and your prayers give you strength and courage to remain serene and fair. All that is happening is that you are faced with the opportunity to expand your abilities.

When the going seems to be rough, place your attention upon this Greater Love, the Perfect Love which is giving you of what It is. This gives you the understanding of others, which has been, up to now, lacking in you. Your intellect has not always correctly interpreted what the eyes see, but your Mind, which is Wholeness (God), takes in the intellectual powers, giving them strength and know-how, and enables you to be understanding.

The most effective time to work with your new awareness of power is the exact moment when you first begin to feel offended, troubled, or in any way disturbed by what you have seen or heard.

Knowing, *then*, that the Spirit of you is God, who is Perfect Love and Understanding, the TRUE IDEA will unfold itself right where the material belief has been enthroned. You have then made yourself a "new Servant" . . . a right belief.

"Look Unto Me and Be Saved"

The "me" you are to look at is your own spirit. In doing so, you know there is only one Spirit, and that you and your Father are One.

Of course, you are not going to *feel* this spirit if you keep wondering whether someone else is doing "wrong," or continuing to think that you are being treated badly. Your "household" would then be divided. Neither will you arrive at the proper feeling if you are still considering, what that "strange pain" is, and wondering if it is anything serious.

Your attention must move back of all these effects, to Pure Being. "*Be still, and know . . . that I am God,*" is to be done gently, easily. It is a feeling that there is nothing around you, outside of you, at all. You literally move from one state of consciousness to a completely different awareness. You "float in space."

You move into a *new* feeling that is marvellous! You feel joyous to have the opportunity to do so. The so called "troublesome event" is seen to be merely a stepping stone for you, a way in which you will discover a greater good. It is your moment to touch Divine Love, to experience Divine Consideration, and really know that *nothing* is impossible to Spirit.

It is something like being in freezing cold and then coming into comfortable warmth and protection. It is something like having a wonderful friend who loves you deeply and will do anything for you. It is something like being given a cold, refreshing drink when you are hot and thirsty. Yet, it is more than all of these, for it meets *whatever* your need is.

While you bask in this new feeling, like you would in warm sunshine and fresh clear air, you are letting go of all that has distressed you. The finite self you thought you were is merging with Infinite Spirit. You can trust It. It cannot be other than It's own nature, which is all good. It is the Source of all illumination, all knowledge, all love and joy. You have touched the moving Principle of Life and you *know* that all the forms of things and objects are but symbols of *ideas.* You understand that when you have the *idea*, you have the substance out of which shall come its form, on the relative plane.

You know you are God's Idea. You know that the awareness of Life announces Itself as *"I Am"* and you understand why this is so. You comprehend that the Spirit is imperishable, powerful, and indeed, All-mighty. Your own treasures are no longer something you read about, but are known, cherished, and appreciated.

Outer Conditions Change

Now you really enjoy being a source of good for another. You, too can speak with authority.

There is an ancient adage, "What thou see-est, that thou beest." What you give, you give to yourself, and what you withhold, you withhold from yourself.

When you give, you will give wisely, whether it be instruction or a meal. There will be no self-thoughts in the way, such as, "I'll do it, but I can't afford it."

If you are one who, in the past, only "gave" because you could take it off your income tax, you now will clearly see why such action was so one-sided, and why *you* never benefited from your "gift."

If you have ever lost faith in persons to whom you have given help, and who failed to repay you or feel gratitude, you now understand why.

FEAR NOT; I HAVE CALLED THEE BY THY NAME: THOU ART MINE. WHEN THOU PASSEST THROUGH THE WATERS, I WILL BE WITH THEE.

(Isaiah 43:1, 2)

"The waters" are all those sense beliefs, and Greater Love is with you as you pass through them on your way to victory.

You will never lose if you will stand fast and do the loving thing. When it is not clear to you just what the loving thing might be, drop the whole situation out of your mind and think of what God is. It will come to you whether you are trying to save another from continuing in his mistake, or from the effects he reaps due to his own ignorance.

Change the belief you are seeing reflected about the individuals who appear to need help, by *knowing* God's intelligence is right there. In ways you cannot see now, the bread cast upon the waters will and must come back to bless you. Look to God, not persons in the flesh, for gratitude. Gratitude is a quality of God; when you feel grateful, fully and completely, you will not see anyone who is not.

GREATER LOVE is knowing the Omnipresent Infinite so extremely well, that what appears can be fully disregarded. While your senses may observe an appearance of some lack, you *know* that it is not true. Your knowledge then, must be expressed. A reluctance to speak the Truth is nothing more than admitting that one doesn't really believe it. It is exactly the same as saying "God isn't All, in All and for All." It simply means that you must do more work on your beliefs.

Let me give you an example of how Greater Love works.

One day, while I was getting ready for a radio broadcast, a frantic husband telephoned me to say that his wife had injured herself and was bleeding to death. He had called me, instead of a doctor, because due to some past experience she had a fear of doctors and hospitals. Although she had not been one of my students, she had long been reading books of an inspirational nature, attempting to rid herself of these fears. One of her fears had to do with going where there were groups of people, but I had been invited to their home upon several occasions, so they weren't complete strangers to me.

The panic in his voice roused me into action, as I realized I must stop off at their home on my way to my "live" radio broadcast. I had just telephoned for a taxicab when the thought came to me, "Why allow yourself to be stampeded into being as hypnotized by appearances as they are?"

"Of course!" I thought. "Nothing is 'wrong' in the mind which is God. There is no 'time' to God, since all is NOW. Neither was there any person to hurt, or be hurt." God was present as this woman's life, I knew, and therefore all the Power there was had to be present.

The cab came and off we went, but there was a train-crossing, and we had to wait for a long, long freight train. It was as if everything of the senses was contriving to convince me that I, of myself, was going to "do nothing" anyway. But I knew this couple, and was sure that until they saw my physical body, they would be hard put to believe that anything was being done. Their belief in God was entirely of the senses.

While I sat there, waiting for the freight train to pass, I thought, "Why am I going at all? Since I know God is there, and already active, I do not need to make the trip at all. Am I only going to satisfy their senses?"

The still, small Voice replied to my question, "Thou are a witness. Where your eyes observe disorder, you know Order is there; where your ears hear panic, you know my Peace; where there is fear, you bring Greater Love."

The last car moved across the tracks and we moved forward.

When I walked into the bedroom where her husband had carried her, this frail little thing lay white-faced and frightened. They told me quickly what had happened. This young woman, who had never done any heavy work in her life, much less any heavy lifting, had done a wash during her menstrual period. She had attempted to carry a basketful of wet clothes.

I sat down beside her and took her hand in mine, saying, "There's nothing to fear, and nothing to sustain fear. There is only God's Great Love. Be at peace."

The clutching of her hand relaxed, and she smiled wanly as I went on, "The Intelligence which created this pattern of your body is present and knows how to put all things in order, and has done so, right now. Every organ and activity is perfect right this minute."

These words were necessary for both this woman and her husband, for both believed "something had gone wrong."

We sat in silence then, while I knew that nothing had happened, for there is no discordant activity in spirit and the Divine Spirit was all that was real. As I sat there I knew that her belief was entirely untrue, and thus dissolved.

Several minutes passed before she said, "Oh, the pain is stopping. It has stopped hurting so bad."

I smiled and thought, "There is no reluctance to give up this faulty experience. She willingly lets go of it."

Suddenly she said, "Oh! That awful gushing has stoped too. Oh, I'm so thankful."

Aloud, I said, "Thank you, Father. I knew that before I called, I was answered."

Magic? No, Magic is supposed to be a "secret power." Nothing is a secret in the sense that you can't know about it; it is "secret" only when you *don't* know.

A miracle? No. A miracle, or what is called a miracle, is simply the operation of a law, seldom known and therefore not used. Nothing unusual about it; it always functions when it is known and used.

The Use of Intelligence Already Present

Had this woman used the intelligence she already had, she would have realized that she had not developed sufficient muscle strength to attempt to lift a large basket of heavy wet clothes.

We might also ask: "Did she resent the fact of having to do this wash? Resentment shuts of the flow of intelligence.

Greater Love is always present, only needing to be recognized. God made you out of Himself. What did you think you were made of? When you are able to see yourself as the perfect Spiritual Essence, you are at the Source of Ideas, and space and time vanish.

"Greater Love tath no man. . ." You have a lifelong habit of thinking that you are of mankind, or human. Changing your viewpoint of yourself is not easy to do, and you cannot do it by yourself. You have to turn to the Father.

You must learn to "Let this mind be in you, which is also in Christ Jesus." (Phil. 2:5)

What Kind of Problems Can You Solve?

You, as a human person, don't solve any of them. If it seems that you do, let me ask you if it isn't rather your intelligence that finds the solution?

I once walked into a kitchen which was literally taken over by a swarm of ants, and when I suggested to the lady of the house that we pray about them, she retorted, "Oh, I wouldn't bother God with that!"

Since ants, or any pest, are symbolic of irritations, how better would you get rid of them? A spray may do away with the ants, but what are you going to use to rid yourself of your irritations? They will show up tomorrow in a different guise. Prayer will remove both the ants and the irritations.

God is not a man we wheedle into doing something for us, as this lady seemed to think.

As complex and vast as the operations of Universal Laws are, whatever you know now about them opens the way for you to know more. Anything and everything you need to know is available to you. The requirement is that you go to the Source of these Ideas.

A Well-Designed Plan

In the successful business world, there is good government which functions according to a definite system of order. Greater Love reveals what this Divine Order is. When you want to know more about Divine Order, you will have to remove disorder from your present thinking.

Lack of order, or lack of good—in fact, a lack of anything—simply means that these which appear to be missing are not being expressed. They are there, within, so actually it is a lie to say they don't exist, isn't it?

Can you begin to express them? Can you make yourself into a jolly, congenial, generous person? Would you be able to see the advantage in being an honest, trustworthy, and dependable individual? It is wonderful how many others like that you meet as soon as you express those qualities yourself.

As an example of this, a gaunt-looking man with lusterless eyes came into my office one day, to ask if I thought I could prevent his going to jail. He had spent many sleepless nights, he said, as he wearily told me his story.

"I'd been pretty full of suspicion about my partner," he began; "I got to thinking that he was cheating me. I'd known him to pull a few fast ones on others, and decided that he wasn't above it.

"So I was determined to out-smart him. I know that what I've done is illegal, and now, at last, I'm about to be caught. At first, I had a lot of satisfaction thinking I was out-witting him, but now all I feel is shame. I'm more ashamed of having become the sort of person I hate, and being justifiably jailed, than anything, but I just don't know how to set things right. It's gone too far."

Never Too Late

"Are you telling me," I asked, "that you are willing to set things right, as you say?"

"Oh Gosh, yes," he said quickly. "It's not so much that I'm afraid to go to jail. Understand?"

"Yes, I understand. But you would set things right, if you knew how?" I could see he meant it.

"Some people I know have been attending your classes, and . . . well, from what they have said, I sort of got the idea to come up. One of the fellows has been trying to cheer me up, but, of course, he doesn't know what my trouble is. I heard them talk about right and wrong prayer, but I don't quite understand it. I've said, 'God, help me.' but so far nothing has changed."

"Yes, it has. You're here. Not only that, " I added, "but you have expressed the desire to do things right.

That is the important thing."

"Well, when I could see I was going to get caught anyway, thought I might as well tell you, and if you couldn't do anything about it, it wouldn't make things any worse than they were already."

"Were you discouraged about anything before you began to have these feelings of suspicion about your partner?" I inquired.

"Discouraged?" He stared into space, thinking. Then, quickly, "Oh, yes, business hadn't been good. I felt it was his fault. At first, when I thought up this way to get even, I felt real cocky, real smart. But did that discouragement have anything to do with what I did?"

"Could be," I smiled. "The cure for feeling discouraged is to perform an act of courage. The way you chose wasn't the wisest way, for it began as revenge. It would take a great deal more courage to go to your partner now and tell him the whole story, wouldn't it?"

He rubbed his chin and nodded. "Is that what I have to do?"

"Do you feel that you have that much courage? Is this something you can bring yourself to do? Admit what you have done, and why, and also to offer to make things right?"

He drew a long breath. "Nobody likes to admit he's been a skunk. I will say that in the last few weeks, I've considered it."

"Well," I said after a moment, "whenever any of us do anything which gives us a better feeling about ourselves, we are well on our way out of whatever the difficulty is."

We talked a little about what religious background he'd had, and it was pretty slim. His mother had talked to him some about God and Jesus, and taught him the Lord's Prayer, but he hadn't been inside of a church since he'd grown up, and only infrequently as a child.

He was surprised to learn that the Bible was about Universal Laws, and why we learned what they were and how to use them. When I explained to him that honesty and non-violence was the easier way, he found he was able to smile.

"I sure learned that one the hard way. It's kind of peculiar; most of my life I have just sort of naturally gone along that way." He shrugged. "Guess everyone has to make some mistakes, eh? I've got a nice wife, though, and a kid. I knew this would hurt her and the boy terribly, and it just made me hate myself all the more."

"I know that whatever the spirit moves you to do will be the right away, so I'll continue to pray for you. Just remember that your opinion of yourself must be a good one . . . this is fundamental."

In a few days I heard from him again. He had found the strength to sit down calmly with his partner and tell him the whole story. The partner was more understanding than he'd anticipated, and everything worked out for the good of all. He agreed to take a cut in his own salary until the deficit was made up, and both learned what not to do.

Guideposts

Troubles are often just guideposts. Every trial is a lesson showing the importance of right thinking and intelligent action. Vindictiveness, that "now-I'll-get-even" thought, is not just harmful to the other person, the one to whom your action is directed, but doubly dangerous to the one who indulges it. If I stress this point a great deal, it is only to make you aware of the constructive use of your mind. These actions may have become unconscious thought patterns, upon which you may act without counting the cost.

No matter how Stubbornly the negative condition be fronting you hangs on, nothing can interfere with the eventual coming forth of good. Neither you nor anyone else is big enough to stop the Power which is God.

To Perceive With Clarity

When you doubt your capacity to understand, it is because you are leaning upon some material "prop." These are often other persons, or some organization; sometimes, it is a sum of money or a business enterprise. Greater Love will show you what you have been using for a "crutch."

Many individuals are ignorant of these facts, and, believing that things happen by chance, they think they are at the mercy of others, when actually all that is taking place is coming from the subjective realm of their own thought, attracting or repelling, according to their own thought patterns.

If your good ideas, or services to be rendered, are refused at one place, it does not mean that *you* are repelling that good. It simply indicates that there is another place more worthy, from which you and they will benefit in an even greater degree.

Never belittle your own understanding; you are being led, guided, and helped at all times; intelligence is replacing ignorance, and you are never limited by any existing conditions.

Spirit is like a fluid, which takes the form of anything it is poured into. It "makes things" out of what It is. It never leaves you, but you can leave It only in thought, when you consider It's opposites.

The End of the World

Spirit has no boundaries, and therefore no "end." The appearance world is not to be destroyed, but to be understood. It "comes to an end" as a power when you understand that what you have been judging by is appearance. This is the only "end of the world" there can ever be.

The "rapture" the Bible talks about is the feeling you have when at last you discover this. The nature of the world of appearance is entirely dependent upon who you believe yourself to be. As long as you believe that you "have a mind" in a mortal body, all that you see is distorted and confused. When you begin to understand that YOU are the Mind, and that the physical body is a concept within that Mind, you are able to see how it is that all you see in the world of effect is also in your mind.

How to Apply What You Know

1. Practise relaxation by removing attention from an effects.

2. Have a fervent desire to entertain only constructive ideas.

3. Stop looking for results. They cannot be prevented from showing forth, when you think aright. As long as you keep looking for them, you are subtly telling yourself that they don't exist.

4. Search within your mind for a new idea. Do this, by holding your thoughts still. The idea is already there, and will come to conscious thought.

As you withdraw your attention from the existing conditions and consider the treasure of Greater Love, You know what is meant by *"All that the Father hath, is mine."* It is like a white light that shines through your former thought patterns, taken from the relative of the *"pairs of opposites."* You see the foolishness of what has been believed with such clarity that it makes you laugh with joy. You have found the intimate, personal Source from which you may draw all inspiration!

The "world" believes in many individual minds, but YOU know what the Mind Principle is. You see One Mind, the Spirit of Life, moving through all. YOU know that in It, there are no obstructions, no stupid actions, blocks, conflicts, or confusions. In *Psalms* 75:3, where you read, *"The Earth and the inhabitants thereof are dissolved,"* you know it doesn't mean they are all going up in smoke or fire, or nuclear bombs. Yet, what about the Japanese cities which were bombed? Wasn't it your sense mind which knew about that? Haven't we said that all in the world of appearances is temporary? You have burned a log of wood in your fireplace, haven't you? The imprisoned energy in the log was freed, as heat and warmth. Nothing "happened" to Spirit. Wherever the spirit of life is, it is eternal.

Why should the experience called "death" fill you with such distaste if you really believe it is a movement toward God, the All Good?

How Do You "Commit Adultery"?

When you attempt to mix sense impressions with the Truth, you are committing adultery. It has come to mean, to the world, being disloyal to one's spouse in a sexual way. Because of the mistaken concept of the nature of God, social and moral "laws" were put forth by the sense beliefs of Man. If you willingly cooperate with these, it is to your advantage, as far as the sense plane is concerned.

The unsocial, and unmoral, which we designate as, *"criminals,"* are those who have not been aware of their True Identity. It was the social and moral agencies which classified Jesus as a criminal and executed him. Doesn't this tell you anything? He, who said to Magdalene, *"Neither do I condemn thee. Go, and sin no more,"* asked YOU to *"follow him."*

Evil may have a relative existence, but it has no substantive existence. The Treasure within you, pure, whole, and complete, cannot be united with the reflections outside. The seventh Commandment says to YOU that they cannot be "mixed," or adulterated. Thoughts brought into existence by means of sense evidence are temporary, and have nothing to do with Divine Order.

The Great Commandment is *"Thou shalt love the Lord thy God with all thy heart, and with all thy soul, and with all thy mind,"* and the second is like unto it, *"Thou shalt love thy neighbor as thyself."* You cannot do this if you think of yourself as a separate entity and intellect. What you have done to another, you have just done to yourself.

You Have "Created"

Cease attaching importance to those things perceived by means of the senses only, for you are bringing about many things by visualization; that is, making pictures in your thought. These are the "graven images" you are instructed in the second Commandment *not* to make.

This is the committing of adultery, which you will not do when you are following the Great Commandment. No man (thought) can serve two masters.

To divide your thought between what the senses have seen and heard and the Perfect, is the "Kingdom divided against itself" which shall fall.

When you are really following the first Commandment, these other things *cannot be done.*

If you are one who feels he has broken all the commandments and there is no hope for you, let me say, YOU never broke any; "beliefs" broke them.

You exclaim, "But didn't I make those beliefs?"

Your false concept of who you are made them.

Today, you *know* who you are.

What Greater Love Does

By clearing the debris away, we find it is pleasant to be alone, to have time to think. There is no longer that impulse to have to have something going on every minute, to be with others, to be entertained, amused, or catered to.

It gives you time to spend in constructive effort, doing something you truly enjoy. There is no longer the half pleasure derived from this fruitless search among result and effect, but a full enjoyable interest. You do not have less fun and joy; you have more. You have it all the time, and not just in fleeting moments. Whatever is Required to perpetuate this feeling of wholeness shows up, as if by magic, at exactly the right time.

Greater Love has also produced many helpers for you, such as a new friend, or a teacher who will help you through the darker places, while your beliefs are changing. These come in many fields and are called by many different names, such as teacher, counsellor, practitioner, minister, priest, or rabbi. Remember only that the Great Teacher is within you, and that you are not to "lean" on these others, expecting them to do for you what must be done by *you*. Some of these charge fees for the time they allot you; others have a system of "love offering," which means that you give as you expect to receive. Naturally, if you expect but little, you'll give but little. They, who so trust God's beneficence, often depend for their sole support upon these "love offerings." It is interesting to them to see how God balances accounts.

Some persons will lay a little more than they feel they can afford in the basket. Others will first look to see what the average offering is, and do likewise. Some will surreptitiously drop in a dime or a quarter, and there are those who "get to talking or looking at books" and forget all about it.

How does such a teacher, being dependent upon the contents of what falls into the basket, remain "in business," pay his own rent, buy his food and clothing? Because he has the awareness of this Greater Love. He has learned how to trust the invisible supply. Demand and supply are two ends of the same stick. This he knows and trusts. He does not form judgment about these niggardly "givers," even though he is often quite well aware of who they are. Even though he knows their understanding would unfold faster and they would have fewer problems were they to express greater generosity, he keeps his attention upon the Perfect Life force which they represent.

By so doing, his own supply comes to him through other channels, and he is often made fabulous gifts. Should he stoop to condemnation, he might have an embarrassing lapse between the demand and supply. He has to know so well that everyone has a right to think and act as he sees fit, no matter if that one's thought and actions are wrong, so that he can stand free of his sense impression.

Counsellors and practitioners have told me that they have actually had persons steal money out of these baskets set out for love offerings. A well-known lecturer on the subject of Mind Science said that he had known about an usher, who always offered his services when this lecturer spoke before thousands, as one "with sticky fingers."

If you are one who wonders why something wasn't done to stop this, you have missed the point. Those who engage in such practises always punish themselves.

Not "getting caught" is not escape from the results. The lesson must be learned. Something bigger demands it. The motion of any belief through the mind creates, or causes, an emotion. When the belief is incorrect, and it has moved into an action, the emotion which follows will be like it, equally wrong, *disturbing*. It will continue to disturb, and this is the punishment the person feels. It may take various faces—pain, loss, or lack of some wanted good.

Everything in the world of matter that you hang on to, lock up, or fight over, is nothing but the reflection of a belief, or an idea. Hold on to the idea of your Greater Good, Divine Love and see it everywhere, and it will not matter if someone runs off with some article.

What Belongs to You?

You might think that what you bought and paid for, or what has been given to you as a gift, belongs to you. Have you ever "lost" anything? Where was it lost? Just to your senses, wasn't it? You can still think about it, can't you? To your senses it had shape and form, but what did this object represent? Beauty? Some kind of service? What was its function? Did it represent harmony, or love, or peace?

How to Think About Loss or Theft

The object represented an idea. It is God's Idea. (Give it back to God.) You and the Father (God) are ONE, aren't you? You have the idea which that object represented. The *idea* isn't lost or stolen. Don't forget that the Life of everyone else is God, too, even if "thief" seems to be a word in your consciousness. There are no thieves, just the God Life.

A student of mine had his cash register taken from his service station one night. He reported it to the police, and then followed with this method of thinking.

The cash register was found the next day in a vacant lot, broken open, the money gone. There were no clues. The sum of money was not large and the repairs to the equipment not too costly, but this businessman continued to work with this thought. Several weeks passed.

One evening at this man's home, the doorbell rang. He opened the door to three persons, a young man and his mother and father.

The young man thrust out an envelope and said. "Here is the money I owe you, which I took from your cash register when I and some other fellows stole it."

"Come in, come in, please," this student said pleasantly. He led them into his living room and invited them to be seated. "This is real nice, for your sakes as well as mine."

The parents introduced themselves, adding, "Jim has always been a good boy, but when he was unable to sleep nights, we knew something serious was bothering him, so we finally got him to talk."

"It was like this," the young fellow explained, "we guys were always kidding each other, daring one or the other of us to do something. As I think back on it, I guess we just got carried away with our bravado. You know, you see a lot of things in movies and TV and you wonder if you could do the same."

"I understand," said the service-station owner. "It began as a lark and a test of bravery. Did any of you really need the money?"

"Well, I guess we thought we did," the boy said, looking

over at his mother. "Mom was after me to get a job, when school was out. Oh, I don't blame her! A big kid like me ought to be able to earn something, and I had tried. I only knew of a few places to look. I'd watched the newspaper ads . . . about all I knew to do. We fellows got to talking it over and decided that if the older folks didn't know enough to help us a little bit, they deserved having us be a little crazy."

"Just trying to prove that you knew how to do something?" their host smiled.

"We were looking for places that we might suggest to Jim that he go," the mother put in, "for despite all the things one can see that need doing, it seems there is no one planning to get them done, that is, organizing and supervising, so that these young people can learn."

"Well, that's not entirely true, Mama," put in her husband, "what we should say is that there aren't enough of them doing it. Lots of folks don't like to hire these young people, haven't patience with them."

"I've got a job now," Jim said, "and that money there is the whole amount of what we took from your till. We guys split it between us, but I'm paying it all back, because neither of them can. One of them has since stolen a car and was caught, and the other is sick in the hospital. Gee! Whoever said crime doesn't pay is sure right."

Obeying the Feeling Within

The young man who obeyed the inner feeling and told his parents what troubled him, found that he had the support of his parents.

What happened when this student stayed with prayer? It reached everyone connected with the act. Eventually, the other two boys were reached through Jim and my student and brought into understanding of better ways of gain than by means of theft.

As your own awareness of Unlimited Spirit expands, you awaken, or "touch" the Divine Center in others. Anyone connected with a wrong action which concerns you, is stimulated from his own Divine Center to make corrections and amend his ways.

Everyone's desire for more good, whether it be for good employment, more money, better friends, a nicer home, a more stately existence, or a more loving mate, is only the desire to express what each feels he has inside. Your prayer, recognizing the Divine within all living things, helps you as well as these others toward that attainment.

Other Blessings of Greater Love

You are protected from many small annoyances. You cannot be involved in the schemes of those who think only from the standpoint of their senses. Those, who would use you only for favors you might grant, stand in awe of you. Others can say all manner of things against you, slander you, revile you, and defame you, but everything they attempt to do will somehow turn into an advantage for you.

As long as you reverence the Life itself, represented by the forms of these who so behave, you are "blessing" them who so revile and persecute you.

Some years ago, when we were shopping for a good used car, we found one that seemed to be just about right. Before we could say that we would take it, the salesman slammed down the hood, exclaiming, "You don't want this car!"

We were astonished, as I'm sure he must have been too, at having been so activated by the Spirit. Things about this car which didn't show were known to Divine Mind. Shortly after we found the right one, which proved to be an excellent buy.

The rewards of this attainment of consciousness cannot

be compared to the advantages of any other effort. No material wealth or power compares to the understanding of how to commit everyone to the care of his own Divine Spirit.

The person who practises this knowledge has an irresistible charm and dignity which is intriguing to all. He knows that Infinite Intelligence is active in every detail of his life, always establishing order and harmony. He knows better than to turn his attention away, for even a moment, from the Indwelling Spirit, to think that the action of another person can stop the Power which is God.

Even when danger, at sense level, appears, you cannot be harmed or hurt when you have placed your reliance upon God's Greater Love for you.

CHAPTER 13

ESP, Dreams, and Reincarnation

There have been many unusual effects, which have been chronicled and documented, and these trail back as far as we have written records. They include the study of dream meanings, the sending and receiving of mental messages, palmistry, astrology, numerology, in fact any kind of "divination" as to what the future holds.

The Fascination of the Strange

Psi phenomena, parapsychology, the seeing of apparitions. experiencing poltergeist activity, telekinesis (the moving of objects without using physical means), clairvoyance and clairaudience, have become sciences. The principle objective of any science is the pursuit of the unknown, and this field, while experienced by many, has not been understood.

None of these unusual effects are without cause, and they all do occur. Invisible influences have a captivating lure for a great many, who study the mystical and occult. Since a mystic is just one gifted with spiritual insight, all are potentially so endowed. That all have not experienced some form of the unusual, by no means says that all are not going to.

If you scoff at this, it is because you fear, and if you fear, it is because you do not understand. There is nothing to fear. An understanding of anything eliminates fear of it.

The words Extra Sensory Perception (ESP) imply that the physical senses have in some way become extended. Actually, it is the understanding, when expanded, which brings in greater awareness.

195

The Doctrine of Reincarnation

It is helpful to have some knowledge of this doctrine, for the literal, sense impressions of certain Bible texts have confused many, just as have the theory of spiritualistic phenomena.

This doctrine holds that re-birth affords an opportunity for continued development and a final understanding of eternal life. It does *not* hold that you are reborn as any other form of life, such as an animal or bird.

I say that it is helpful to know what this doctrine is, but you can find no help at all in discovering who you were, or what you have done in a former embodiment. I will not say you cannot remember, (some have), but I will say that it is unlikely. You do carry over any skills you have learned, and all advancement you have made. How else can "born geniuses" be explained? How is one born crippled, blind, or deaf, unless it is so that he now has a chance to learn what he previously refused? How else would he be given a change to amend his faulty beliefs, his incorrect conclusions? One who has been born mute has a belief that he cannot articulate the sounds of what he is thinking. Change his belief, and Lo, be speaks!

Mind-Reading and Hypnosis

The knowledge of hypnosis has been valuable in that it discloses how the function of thought operates. When the conscious control of thought power is relinquished to the hypnotist, he is able to direct the action of the body through his own suggestions.

This has been a valuable contribution to understanding the importance of our own conscious thinking, but who wants to be under the spell of another's thought, when he can take control of his own?

No one can be "under the spell" of another unless he first gives his consent by believing that he is. If he thinks he is, and can recognize that he is so doing, all he needs to do is to remind himself that he does not have to think he is being influenced by anyone else. He can change that belief.

Many persons are rather subtly "hypnotized" by the suggestions which come from others. "You're sitting in a draft; you'll catch cold." Or, "You will probably feel terrible tomorrow," are two examples.

Mental telepathy, or reading another's thought, is a mystery that was cleared by the science of hypnosis. In most cases, it is possible to read what goes on in another's mental realm by what is clearly visible. His posture, gestures, and breathing, and often his actual choice of words, will disclose whether or not he is telling a lie. But that is not mind-reading, which is an actual mind-to-mind communication.

First, there must be a thought to express. Some persons are not thinking, in the true sense, for all that is going on in their mental realm is a hodge-podge of pictures of past events.

Second, there must be an emotional factor present, to make vibrations. Love, admiration, or respect is the emotional current. Communication is frequently done where this regard is mutual; it can also be done when you are strongly aware of Divine Love.

Such communication is common among those who love one another. Mothers have often been led to leave for home earlier than they intended, when some member of the family needed them; some have even heard "calls."

During a war, a young man was about to lead his platoon into a field peppered with mines. It was too dark for him to see, but as he took a step forward, he heard his mother's voice cry out to him to stop. She was thousands of miles away, across an ocean. None of the other men heard it, but he ordered a halt, and waited until the first rays of dawn enabled him to see what lay ahead.

This same mother awakened herself out of a sleep by her scream, and spent the rest of the night in prayer. When her son was safely returned home, and they checked stories, their experiences were on the same date.

Whenever you think of someone, that person is thinking. about you. If you will hold your thought still, you can "pick up" that thought. It is possible to "listen in" on anything that pertains to you. By checking on these mental impressions, you can learn all you want to know about what others think of you. They may not always he complimentary, for you may learn they are discussing your faults. If so, you can use that information by amending those shortcomings. On the other hand, you may decide that mind-reading could never become popular, because you do learn some disturbing things, such as who is not a real friend. If someone plans to rob or cheat you, you can know it ahead of time and offset his plans, by recognizing that this is a belief which you can change.

Great love, or empathy, between others always establishes this communication line. All persons are telepathic when the proper conditions are provided, for this is Nature's way of progressing the soul.

Some are frightened by the thought that they might not have any privacy but when you ask them what they need the privacy for, you find you have uncovered an unsavory fact. They are either doing, or intend to do, something of which they are ashamed. Sometimes, they try to ward it off by saying. "Oh, I don't believe all that!" There are those in the world today already expert in this ability.

Some persons spend a lot of time telling themselves that doing what they want to do is perfectly all right, since it is hurting no one else. Yet, if what they are doing hurts *them* in any way, damages their own self-opinion, how are they going to rationalize this out of the way? It is natural that they would be annoyed to think there is anyone with the ability to ferret out their secret sins. This action they try to hide is actually a belief they should be rid of, for their own greater happiness.

What the Dream State Is

All the knowledge you possess, all you have developed in character and abilities, all your likes and dislikes, plus your potential, comprise what is known as your soul. This is an active "thought-body," continually functioning.

When we speak of the body, we usually think of the body of flesh, the physical form, but the soul is also a body, possessing finer, more rapid vibrations, therefore not visible to mortal sight.

The soul takes its energy from the Spirit, which is Life, so we shall call the thought-body the Soul-Spirit of you.

The brain is a receptive organ which receives all the impressions brought to it from the physical senses. It accepts all of these just like an adding-machine registers all the figures which are struck.

If you "make a mistake," toss in a wrong figure, it will be up to you to discover it, and make the correction, for the machine neither knows nor cares. In the same way, when you have given the thought-body a wrong conclusion, it is up to You to make the necessary correction.

We have been erroneously informed that the brain thinks. It does nothing of the sort; it merely catalogues information fed into it. Thinking is done in another place entirely, and your brain is no more intuitive than your adding machine.

During what we call "sleep," only the conscious side of your mind, or Soul-Spirit. is inactive. Nothing more is being put in; your "adding machine" is at rest. The Spirit begins to clear away the debris, to strengthen you for the new day; but some of these incorrect impressions you hang on to, for they attach themselves to others of similar nature. Some of these seep up to the surface of conscious thought, and as they pass the limen into pictures of things and events, they are colored, garbled, mixed up, so that rarely do they present to you a clear understanding.

Many people say they never dream, but this isn't true, of course, because the Soul-Spirit is never wholly inactive. What they mean is that they don't remember. Why they don't recall can be attributed to a great many things. It could be anything from being completely at peace with one's self, to a refusal to look at one's faults; if one is unable to see room for improvement, the will shuts off any helpful impressions.

Others dream only in symbols, and have so grown that they are able to interpret the meanings of these. Still others are aware of "travelling," and often see events far ahead of their appearance in the relative world.

No, a dream book will not help you. *Prayer* will. Perhaps you are now about to comprehend what a "prophetic dream" is? It is possible to know what is likely to take place due to what thoughts you've entertained.

Looking Into the Future

When you go to another seeking to know what the future holds in store for you, you are admitting that you do realize that there is a Power and a Wisdom which knows all things. Why not look for it within yourself? What any psychic can get for you, will be according to his or her ability to read the beliefs in your thought-body. This is done, not by reading what you are thinking at that moment, but by being sensitive enough to feel the vibrations emanating from you.

Any good psychologist can help you to see how these beliefs you hold come to be, but you will still have the job of changing them. Often just showing you how foolish it is to hold on to some old grievance is enough. No matter what the science, or art, of the so-called fortune-teller may be called—palmistry, card-reading, crystal-ball, numerology, or astrology—not one of them is going to correct your weak spots, nor develop your talents. Palmistry and astrology can show you your tendencies, numerology can point out your weak places, but all any form of psychism is going to do for you is show you what the marvels of the mind are. They will thrill you and entertain you, but don't forget, if you get "bad news" your "reader" is only taking it from your own beliefs.

Clairvoyance and Clairaudience

While these words mean clear-seeing and clear-hearing, they do not imply any connection with the three-dimensional sight and hearing. The physical senses have not in any way been extended, even though persons often speak of them as "extended senses."

Spiritism

The question is often asked if one might, with impunity, engage the aid of one no longer in the flesh. Interpreting the word "spiritual" to mean one who has discarded his physical form, some have held to this as the proper way to have God's help. Why should you need to, when all the Wisdom is also within Your Soul-spirit? How would you grow and eventually be your Perfect Self in Expression if someone else, visible or invisible, was always doing it for you?

Another question often brought up is whether or not evil" spirits can enter the body of one who is in the flesh. No, they cannot enter the body, they can enter the mental realm by being believed in. That is why anger and hatred must be avoided like the plague; they come from incorrect beliefs, which logically follow from a misuse of thought. That is why you are told to "forgive your adversary quickly."

As it becomes increasingly clear to you that all the people, alive, dead, good, or bad, are but your own thoughts, out-pictured to you, some being composites of varying beliefs, you will see why at any time, all you need change is your own viewpoint.

If appearances were true, then God would not be all-powerful, nor the energy, substance, and intelligence of all life.

Apparitions and Poltergeists

Seeing a "ghost" or an apparition, is real enough to those who have experienced such phenomena; so is a case of measles to those who have witnessed them.

A poltergeist is said to be a mischievous soul-spirit, not necessarily malicious, who has learned how to make his presence known.

It is the function of the senses to confirm whatever is believed in, so it behooves the individual to make a careful selection of what to him is reasonably beneficial.

I am *not* saying there are no such things as *apparition* and *poltergeist.*

Bearing in mind that there is no counterfeit without a REAL after which it is patterned, you should be able to see the difference between a true idea and a false belief, as far as this subject is concerned. The phrase "evil spirit" is a misnomer, first of all, because "spirit" is God, and all good. There is no such thing as an "evil" spirit, but there is such a thing as a *belief* in evil, which might behave as if it were a separate entity.

The reference made to "evil spirits" in the Bible has come about through the translations, when the word translated as "spirit" meant the *substance* of thought. We might say in regard to this "casting out of evil spirits," that you are being told that when you learn the Cosmic Law you *are no longer plagued* by false beliefs.

Communication With Those Not in the Flesh

Because the soul of Man is his individual use Spirit, and Spirit is eternal, when he passes from the physical form he is *not* eliminated. It is quite possible to communicate with him. There is nothing more strange and weird about this than there is in using the telephone. Nothing is impossible. That everyone does not know how to accomplish this by no means proves it cannot be done. At present, I don't know how to play a violin or fly an airplane, but you would certainly raise your eyebrows if I said both were impossible.

Communication is done not by voice, but by thought, and is done far more often than most folks realize. It may even sound like a voice, to the one hearing.

The pressure of hands is a common feeling to those attuned to the world of soul-spirits. Folks all over the world, throughout the ages, have told stories of, having been pushed out of the path of some danger by unseen hands.

A true clairvoyant is capable of mentally observing not only who is performing such services, but she can often see events in advance of their taking place in the objective world.

Trance-Mediumship

A trance-medium is simply one who has learned how to disengage his attention from the relative world, and by causing to cease for a time any voluntary movement, allows utterance of ideas and beliefs.

This is not a weird act, as uninformed persons are inclined to think. It is a telepathic action, mind to mind, and the medium tunes in to specific vibrations. He is always faced with the possibility of reading only the thought—realm of the questioner, or "sitter" as they are called. A trance-medium is frequently both clairaudient and clairvoyant, and exercises these abilities in a perfectly normal state, that is, awake and moving.

The value of the trance state is to make a mental connection with an instructor, a real being who has already mastered what you are just learning how to accomplish. The first Soul-spirit to come to the one in trance is called a "doorkeeper, and that one's function is to keep out the vibrations of race beliefs. A trance-medium has so disciplined his thinking that he calls forth this "helper." This is usually a gay and happy voice, which impinges upon the vocal cords of the medium, by means of breath, in much the same way that one might pluck the strings of a harp. This one gives instruction preparatory to the real instructor who might not make his, or her, presence known for quite some time after the "doorkeeper" has begun to "speak through."

Once the "doorkeeper" is known to the medium, it is possible for the medium to move beyond the thought-realm of the sitter, and thus reach the vibrations of the one the sitter wishes to hear from. Now, this is not done willy-nilly, any more than if you took a trip to Chicago, to visit anyone and neglected to notify them of your coming. However, the fact that you are led to go to a trance-medium, *may* be due to the drawing power of the person who has something to say to you, therefore that one would be instantly available. Attending a seance purely out of curiosity could leave you with a feeling of disappointment, or a large-sized doubt.

Should you want to go to a trance-medium, use prayer first, think of one or two you want to hear from, knowing they still *do* exist.

It seems to be difficult for some persons to know that the physical body is just like an overcoat, or a vehiclen worn for earth expression. If this seems "scarey" you, remember you never feared this person in the flesh, and you have no real reason to entertain fear now.

The trance-medium is proof of this ability which is also in you. The medium can establish for you the conviction that there is no death, according to its common connotation.

Your Guardian Angel

Because you have often found yourself in situations which were hard to bear, you may have questioned the possibility of having such a thing as a "guardian angel." There may be those around you on the physical plane, who, considering you inept, look after you, doing all manner of things which you should have learned to do for yourself. If so, your helper has little to do until you begin to show some aptitude, and a willingness to learn.

Every one of these advanced Soul-spirit functions as an instructor; they do nothing *for* you which should be done *by* you.

If you go to any card-reader, astrologist, psychic or medium hoping to get someone else to do something which you should be learning to do for yourself, you are like the child who wants someone else to do his homework for him.

The trials and ordeals you encounter in life are character-testing, and character-forming. You are not permitted to peek and see what the next test of your faith and understanding may be, any more than a good school teacher would supply the students with a list of the answers to the examination questions before the examination.

You smile at the immature reasoning of the little fellow who tries to trick another into doing his arithmetic problems for him, for you know it is he who needs to learn to comprehend. Yet, if you are looking for someone, visible or invisible, to give you the answers and solve your problems, you are guilty of the same kind of reasoning.

You must learn to live so that you *merit* easier examinations, and this is only done by mastering the art of thinking.

Telekinesis and Psychometry

Transporting objects without using physical means is caused by mental energy. Telekinetic energy is somewhat of a mystery, but it is a law, and has been accomplished by a few. Its basic requirement is absolute integrity. It cannot be violated, nor used for a wrong purpose. Only on the terms of its own nature is this Intelligent Power consigned to the individual.

Psychometry is the ability to handle an object and feet the mental atmosphere surrounding it. This is part of clairvoyant ability.

All Unusual Effects Must Have a Cause

Beginning from a correct premise that energy is Spirit, and Spirit is everywhere, we realize that mental energy is thought, and *what* we think about is a voluntary action.

Experimentation has proved that creative Mind follows the patterns which are given to it. This faculty of Mind does not analyze or reject any voluntary thought. It is its nature to accept and creatively produce in the world of effect all beliefs impressed upon it.

You do not create the energy you are using, it is all ready present as Life, but the thought-pictures of ages past, that is anything in the nature of effect, can be and often is, picked up by this faculty of Mind. It projects these images with mathematical certainty. Some of these beliefs which are projected are untrue, but like poverty, or illness, they seem to be true as an experience.

The higher the type of intelligence in the individual, the less limited it is, as to the effects it can produce.

What you are believing when you feel the presence of a guardian angel, instructor, or guide, is that you have reached the place in your mind where you have control. Let's put it this way; you have created a belief that helpful guidance is at hand. As soon as You have established this belief, you know instruction from within must follow.

Hitting the Control Center

It would be a mistake for there to be anything which

would circumvent one's own growth and development! So this inner awareness, which is an unseen servant, belongs to you. To think of these instructors as "other people" is apt to cause you to lean upon them.

To lean upon another, in the flesh or out of it is still a mental action to be avoided. The teaching you receive must be seen to be coming from the *belief* which you now have, if you are to benefit.

Having conscious control over your own viewpoint you begin to understand your part in the creative order. Your individual growth consists of an awareness of your increasing abilities to govern your own life and environment. You understand that it is done by conscious, voluntary thought.

The limitless Intelligence passes into you, and through you into expression. Now you can discern the difference between unusual happenings which are merely the results of beliefs, and which are the results of spiritual laws, which you are now privileged to learn.

From the Sense Standpoint

You have seen your reflection in a mirror, or a still pool, and you can find yourself in a group photograph quite easily, because you have long believed the body is YOU. When you become aware of a guardian angel or instructor, you do not "see" anyone. (I'm not referring to a clairvoyant.) It is with your mind that you know. In the same way that you are aware of "personality," which is not so much as what you see, but something you feel, you feel a presence. Your senses will indicate no change, to you, at first, but they will affirm this knowledge by drawing you to persons and places where your understanding can be further enhanced.

Remembering that what has gone into your thought-realm by means of your senses is similar to punching the keys of an adding machine, and once a total is taken and the machine is cleared, you get a glimpse of what you must do.

Several things can happen which will temporarily cause you to "forget" all the past. Hypnosis, giving over control of your conscious mind to another can cause forgetfulness, so can a hit on the head which renders you unconscious. So can something called amnesia. There are drugs by the score, which can induce everything from sleep and lethargic tranquility, to ecstatic delight, none of which will bring you one with closer to perfect living.

On the other hand, you can become so interested in something that you forget yourself entirely, for the time being. In this, you find the feeling of joy. When it is a constructive accomplishment, your joy is increased.

The Progress of Spirit

Evolution is producing beings who realize that they are part of the creative order, the overall design. In the past, instead of getting the meanings of the Bible with the Mind, the senses formed pictures of people, lands, and events, but today, despite ridiculous superstitions and mis-information, we arrive at a realization of our relationship to the Whole.

The progress of Spirit is more powerful than an earthquake, and has a greater wash than a tidal wave, but all it destroys is *error*. None of Man's plotting and scheming can stop its action.

Every idle word that men shall speak, they shall give account thereof . . . for by thy words thou shalt be justified, and by thy words thou shalt be condemned.

As you begin to appreciate that every word is a thought, and every thought a word, you know that every complaint and doubt acts as a barrier, only making your way filled with weariness and difficulties which need not be. Life wasn't meant to be arduous, and there is only one person to "work on". . . yourself.

◆ ◆ ◆ ◆ ◆

CHAPTER 14

The Second Coming

There has long been a lively dispute between theologians, students of ancient languages, and the public, as to Bible meanings. Biblical students, archaeologists, and professors whose studies render them capable of translating Greek and Hebrew, or cuneiform tablets, have spent much time and energy trying to satisfy themselves that there actually were such historical figures as are spoken of in the Bible. Much travel has gone into the search for exact sites, relics, or writings that would bolster the faith they profess to have.

The Dead Sea Scrolls

In 1947, when the Dead Sea Scrolls were found near Qumran, in jars packed in away in a cave, fresh and exciting possibilities set the Christian world aquiver. By 1952, close to four hundred manuscripts were found in that area. What was proved by this discovery? That the Bible was true?

A basic and easily observable fact appears to have been overlooked, namely that a people must have preceded present time and had literary forms by which they expressed themselves. Naturally, the places in which they lived would be mentioned! Why should it help anyone to believe in God, by proving that there was a "Jerusalem" two thousand years ago?

Mis-Translations Are Mis-Interpretations

In order to extract the meaning from the wording, one must learn to go beyond the pictures which the senses are inclined to make. That this was not done by some of the translators is evident.

Language professors have been helpful in disclosing how a meaning is altered by the earlier choices of words to represent the original. We shall take up this subject later and show you how many misconceptions began. We need not ferret out every mis-translation, nor learn the Greek and Hebrew languages of ancient time. We only need to do a little thinking.

The reason for disputes among the various denominations rises from this same cause. For instance, a commonly known one is the disagreement between sprinkling or immersion in regard to Baptism. When "water" in Bible language means thought or belief, how will a choice between a bath or a shower have anything to do with whether or not you are properly "saved?"

Let us consider also, the meaning of the Lord's Prayer, which was given as a pattern of thought. It was not intended to be something you mouthed along with the rest of your church congregation, or said over and over when you were in trouble. Clergymen are often heard to say, "Let us *repeat* the Lord's Prayer," and that is all that is done. It is repeated. You can teach a parakeet to say it, but he doesn't know the meaning of it any more than you do if all you do is say the words.

Unless you know the meaning of it, you might as well say, "Twinkle, twinkle, little star." It is a thought pattern. So let us look at what it means.

In the first place, it is called, the *Lord's* Prayer, not Man's prayer. You don't know a thing about YOUR Lord, while you still believe it is a "Somebody Else."

A Correct Thought Pattern

It begins with "Our Father." Who is the "Father," the Creator? Some personage a long way off? No, you are turning your attention to that creative part of your mind, mentioned in the last chapter. It is the basic part of you, your

Life Force, your Source. Did you forget that in Jesus' teaching, you have this: *"The father and I are one, but the Father is greater than I?"*

No, no, don't go back to your formerly entertained sense interpretation that Jesus was another man who lived long ago. Just follow the prayer and the meaning will disclose itself.

"Which art in heaven" comes next, and you are recalling that *"The Kingdom of Heaven is within you."* It is something that you realize, become aware of—a perfection at the center of your being.

You are turning your attention to the source of all your Belief, that which gave them energy to be.

Next we have, *"Hallowed be thy name."* Where *"name"* is used in the Bible it always means *"nature."* In the beautiful Aramaic language, it says, *"Perfect is thy nature."* Wouldn't you revere the perfect?

It goes on to say that this one and only Kingdom (power) reflects in earth (manifestation) as it is in heaven (concept), and that this Source gives us our daily bread (supply of life substance), and forgives us, accordingly, for our mistakes, *as*—to the exact degree—we forgive others.

What happens when you have forgotten someone? Isn't it that you understand him? And isn't this understanding the use of intelligence? Intelligence is an aspect of God, and as you have it, you *use* it. Not to forgive is simply admitting that you are still ignorant in that area of your thinking.

The pattern goes on to say that when you turn to the Source, It never leads you into evil, temptation, or any lack of good, but rather delivers you from such, because of It's nature, which is power and glory.

You are recognizing a pattern of perfect ideas already implanted within you by Life, or God.

FOR I AM GOD, AND NOT MAN; THE HOLY ONE IN THE MIDST OF THEE.

(Hosea 11:9)

"Call No Man on Earth Your Father"

To what degree do you obey this bit of instruction? Many good persons who believe they are following Bible teachings sincerely, have overlooked this in many ways. "*Call no man on earth your father, for one is your father which is in heaven,*" is your way to a firm foundation in understanding.

So many of the real meanings of the Bible have become diffused by the sense impressions which come from the words which make pictures of people and events.

You can also see how the passage of time has changed the meaning of the word as a semantic symbol when you consider any popular slang expressions. "Hot" and "cool" have come to represent things other than temperature.

Let us look at just one word, used in Scripture, the meaning of which, due to popular useage, has a different connotation than it had when it went into the Bible. "*Suffer* little children to come unto me." "Suffer" has come to mean to endure pain. In the Bible it connotes *permit*. You can follow that through and see that your "sufferings" are your own permittings, if you like.

Without linguistic science, you have had to lean upon commentaries, but how are you to be sure that what has been told to you in this manner is correct? By finding the "*Secret Place of the Most High.*"

What is Meant by Secret?

Anything concealed from sight, and kept private, is "secret," so since thoughts about people and events put expressions on your face, that kind of thinking could hardly be termed "secret." The secret place is just that, because the senses cannot locate it, a surgeon's scalpel cannot touch it; not even an X-ray will divulge its whereabouts.

It is knowing, by means of an inner feeling. The Lord's Prayer will help you find it; or the 23rd Psalm, 91st Psalm, as well as many other passages. You will find the one which appeals to you, and discover the inseparable unity between God and yourself. The "Secret Place" is the Kingdom, and is never external, but always within.

Your expansion of consciousness is a never-ending process, which begins with understanding that you will be transformed by the renewing of your mind. Finding the Secret Place enables you to "separate the wheat from the chaff," and you know when something you read or hear is true or false. From here you formulate ideas, not from the evidence supplied to the senses, but from the knowledge that you are in harmony with the Divine Nature.

The Carnal Nature

When you contrast this feeling of inner security with life as lived only from the senses, where you know only your body and material surroundings, you can easily see why "carnal consciousness" is the "enmity." When you live in harmony with the Spirit at the center of your being, everything you do prospers. The carnal mind jumps to conclusions at that thought. A way to get prosperous or rich, it assumes. What it really means is that everything you do works out for good. You may not become a moneyed tycoon for years, or possibly not in this lifetime. Or, being rich may be one of the tests you must go through, to see if you know how to wisely use what has been given to you.

Because the carnal nature is much more cognizant of evils than it is of good, it is this carnal, or sense-awareness, which gives you most of your troubles. There was a time when card-playing and dancing were considered to be infractions of God's laws. The sincere people who believed this did not realize how they slipped back and forth from their awareness of the Kingdom, to *sense* consciousness.

I bring it up because you may not realize for some time how often, you do the same thing. A trained mind can see an idea from a word description, but no training is necessary to see an object. Therefore training your mind requires much repetition.

The Bible uses symbols to develop an underlying thought, or idea, and the Second Coming of Christ is symbolic of Man's evolved state of comprehension. You can stop looking at the sky.

God created the Perfect Pattern, His Son, which, when you find it, represents the Second Coming.

When someone says, "God created all there is, the whole world," and in the next breath he includes that which is to him evil, or something he fears, he has merely slipped back into carnal consciousness.

If "evil" could be said to have a cause, that cause could only be a place where God is not known, not recognized. You might be as good as you know how to be, in all ways, and still have an area of your mental realm untouched by the awareness of God's Presence. Naturally, then, this would enable you to know of some place where there is no good, where it is outside of you, within the periphery of your senses. You would see it, or hear about it. Are you able to know that it is *not* true? This is what you are called upon to do.

When you no longer name any part of this wonderful, cosmic life, as wicked, wrong, or bad, you can be sure, that the Christ is here, where you are.

All Conditions Are the Result of Thought

Just as long as the world, to you, seems full of people who do careless, brutal, or stupid things, your mind will not be in peace. Neither will you prosper. You must relate everything your thought touches back to the idea that the Presence of Perfect Life is there. In this way, you will not work up wrong emotions and continue to create unpleasant experiences for yourself.

An inventor knows that any object his gaze rests upon is the out-picturing of an idea that is designed to "do something." Let us say that he is presented with a problem of filling a need for a specific instrument to function in a certain way, which no known instrument can do. All he knows about this idea is the action it is supposed to perform. He has to start with only the idea.

Now, let us think of you. You, too, began as only an idea. The action you are to perform is to perfectly express all that this idea represents.

Your body was designed by the Great Designer to self-sustaining, in all ways. Within it is the greatest chemical laboratory ever made. All you ever need is within you— intelligence. love, strength, and an unlimited supply of Substance, or Life Itself. This same pattern is the pattern of every other body you have ever seen, or ever will see. You understand that this pattern is not yours alone.

Because everyone is in a different degree of awareness of this, each one experiences conditions which correspond to how *he* thinks, about himself and about others.

Progress is inevitable, but you will live more happily if you can recognize the Divine Pattern as the life of all. A cause is known only by the effect it produces, and when the attention is upon a perfect cause, the effect produced tends to show perfection.

Supreme excellence is infinite, immeasurable, and indefinitely extensive, so there is no fixed state of perfection that would be the *end* of anything. Expression is also infinite. *"In my Father's house, there are many mansions,"* helps you to understand this.

One of Jesus' most significant sayings is, *"My Kingdom is not of this world,"* (the realm of the senses). Neither is yours.

How about the chair upon which you sit? It has no conscious life. It did not create itself. It's beginning was in the mind of man. Someone recognized a need and found a way to fulfill it. Whether the need is for a chair, a skyscraper, a Jet airplane, a serum, or a freeway, someone saw a need and found a way to fill it. How? By going within and tapping the Source of Ideas.

Man Follows His God

Whenever you tap the Source for an idea, and you produce something in the world of effect, you fill someone's need, and your own. Every business enterprise is designed to fill a need. Every object and article was first only an idea. When you are able to turn everything back to the idea stage, you can see how all that your sense know about are simply ideas and beliefs. You learn what the creative plan is.

What must you do? Return to the "Father's House," find the Secret Place of the Most High, and seek the Kingdom of God, or Heaven.

Not only is it unpleasant to entertain feelings of hatred or beliefs in evil, but it is unnatural and that is why it so distasteful and unproductive. It should be warning enough to anyone that when he feels unhappy, uncomfortable, or lacking any good, that he has just returned to sense level, and is taking his thoughts from the "serpent," not from God. God never makes you feel that way. Nasty tempers and sarcastic remarks delay the good one might experience a good deal sooner, since the dominant attitude of mind is what produces the nature of the next experience.

An Admission of Guilt

Whenever there is harassment, confusion, or complication, these feelings come from something, or someone, disliked. While dislike is a mild form of hatred, it can be recognized as a wrong thought. Such thoughts promote varying degrees of anger.

The feeling of anger is an admission of your own guilt.

"Guilt about what?" you exclaim, "knowing" full well that the disturbing conditions were brought about by another. Your "knowledge" is incorrect.

You wouldn't see them at all if you had changed your belief. That is why anger is an admission of guilt. Now, if you will consider this calmly, you will understand with your intelligence that some thought you have long held caused you to act in certain ways, and that your own action brought you into this situation.

One-Sided Sight

When you have not met a situation, or done the right thing, it is always due to seeing it one-sidedly . . . from your side. Seeing things from only one side, your side, may be regarded as unfair. Being capable of seeing another's viewpoint is an art the quick-tempered have not mastered, and since anger only lights the fuse for another problem, there is much good pushed away.

The inability to see another's viewpoint is the most prevalent reason for the individual's quarrels and the nation's wars.

Insight Is Foresight

A simple example might be the frustrated young mother who has scampering youngsters tracking mud on her clean floor. Failing to consider the consequences, she screams out her dismay, while a cool-headed parent has a carefully planned training procedure.

One young mother put a change of shoes on her screened-in porch, and locked the kitchen door until the change had been made. Another provided a rag and a brush, and was happily pleased when her small boys took an ever-increasing interest in neat footgear. These mothers saw both sides of the situation, and helped their children to do the same.

It is interesting to note that when one shuts off the expression of love by indulging anger and hatred, much of what he considered worthwhile goes out of his life.

All Are at Different Stages

Everyone of us must go through this moving from the concept of Adam to Christ. You were told of your creation as a Divine Idea in the first words of the Bible. This is the first coming into being. But your first awareness of this is your consciousness of being a physical form, the first Adam.

By no means is the man you see in the mirror, if your gender is male, the man God created. Nor does *"male and female created He them"* mean the men and women you know and pass on the street. These are what your senses see, and they come in different colors— black, white, red, and yellow. This is what Adam knows.

All Biblical names carry symbolical significance, so the Second Coming of Christ, symbolizes your evolved state of knowing your union with your Creator.

This has been taking place in each individual life, over eons of time, in every country and clime. The *anti-Christ* is the purely intellectual concept of the Law. What you need to realize is that the human brain and senses are not the Source of Ideas. The Power which is God is in the "heart," which means a combination of spiritual qualities, not a material organism.

When you are not exhibiting, or expressing these qualities, you are one that Christ is talking to in the book of Mark.

HOWBEIT IN VAIN DO THEY WORSHIP ME, TEACHING FOR DOCTRINES THE COMMANDMENTS OF MEN.

THIS PEOPLE HONORETH ME WITH THEIR LIPS BUT THEIR HEART IS FAR FROM ME.

FOR FROM WITHIN, OUT OF THE HEART OF MEN, PROCEED EVIL THOUGHTS . . .

(Mark 7:6,7,21)

Knowledge of Your Union

God is all power, whether you have realized it or not, but if you believe there is any human mind capable malpractise, you have just contradicted the Principle.

The Bible is not directed to a group of people, but to your own thoughts and beliefs. If you will remember that your viewpoint is dependent upon who you believe you really are, you can know instantly whether you are viewing from the senses or from Divinity. Are *you* Adam or Christ?

As Adam, you will think of Jesus, who became the Christ, as another person. Oh! wonderful indeed, but one who lived long ago, and is said to some day return. Supposing such an event were to take place, in just what way would it make you into a better person? Would it convince you that his teachings were true, and that it was about time you followed them? Don't you think you are following them to the best of your ability? *Are* you?

Your emancipation from every lack of good depends entirely upon your willingness to give up the conviction that you are that first Adam, the physical man.

CEASE YE FROM MAN, WHOSE BREATH IS IN HIS NOSTRILS; FOR WHEREIN IS HE TO BE ACCOUNTED OF?

(Isa. 2:22)

I AM COME THAT THEY MIGHT HAVE LIFE, AND THAT THEY MIGHT HAVE IT MORE ABUNDANTLY.

(John 10:10)

Your second step is to take a new basis for your belief about yourself, by knowing that you are this original Perfect Pattern, the Son of God.

You now know that you are reflecting the glory of God, and that He cares for you. To the exact degree that you care to let Him express Himself as what He is, through you, you become aware of your Sonship. You know that when you do not choose to express intelligence, understanding, generosity, tolerance, or kindness, you are just lessening the aperture through which good flows to you.

You know you are to ignore others' short-comings and mistakes and look for something to praise. You know you are to strive for sincerity, because pretense gets you nowhere. Everyone carries a "loadstone" and knows when you are only affecting an attitude you do not feel in your heart.

Ask yourself often, "Which mind am I in right now? Am I dulling my spiritual understanding by looking too long and hard at effects and by looking for results? Or am I really aware of being that Son, who said, 'Neither do I condemn thee?' Am I taking my ideas from the Source, or am I out here on the surface, just doing what I think best for me and mine? Do I look at past errors with regret, or am I keeping my attention on the Fountain of perfect Life?"

CHAPTER 15

The Joyous You

You Give Up Nothing of Value

The joyous YOU is lovely beyond all compare; the essence of all beauty, harmony, and quality. It is more radiant than the most fabulous sunrise, and more helpful than anything outside of the body.

You never have to relinquish anything of any value in order to recognize your own Divine Spirit. In Sanskrit, the word "man" means the power to think. There material, physical steps by which to reach this awareness of your real Self, which is made in the image and likeness of God, it is done through your power to think.

. . . AND YOUR HEART SHALL REJOICE, AND YOUR JOY NO MAN TAKETH FROM YOU.

(John 16 : 22)

Your Thought Is Your Key to Life

Exalt all things to Spirit and they are in existence already! Never say that things must come from this or that place or person. Say they are already in existence.

Rid yourself of fear. If you fear animals of any kind, wild or domesticated, think: *"I won't hurt them, or cause them harm, therefore I have no belief that any of God's creatures are dangerous."* When you think of all that lives in the right way, and do to them as you desire to be done unto, you'll have no more fear. Some folks fear flying things, insects or birds, and this is only because they hold on to a belief that harm can come from them. Since you are so much more intelligent than these, why hug to you a belief which is

221

useless? For fears of age, infirmity or weakness, just remember you are the Divine Spirit, connected with *all* Spirit. Your anatomy has nothing to do with the Perfect Self God created. You are receiving "daily bread, the pure substance of Life, right from the Source. To know this is to have no concern for your chronological age, and will eliminate any kind of weakness you may be temporarily experiencing.

The Spirit NEVER fails. If you have had fear of failure, due to previous experiences, pay it no attention. Turn your thought to this Joyous YOU, which never fails, because it cannot. It is not in It's nature.

Say often to yourself: "Patience and perseverance and confidence are established in me." This removes haste. carelessness, oversight, and negligence.

Say often to yourself: *"I have comprehension, understanding, wisdom and good judgment."* This will abolish indiscretion, confusion and indecisiveness.

Say often to yourself: *"I am always serene, compassionate, and at peace with myself."* This does away with irritability, intolerance, and nervousness.

Call Forth Joy

If you have been identifying yourself with defeat, despair, or despondency, know that joy is within you and needs no human trick to bring it forth. Joy is not contingent upon any outer happening. It seems to be, but until you touch the right button, so to speak, there is no possible way for you to have it in the outer unless you make way for it.

No one needs to be surfeited by luxury to find joy. Other persons' behavior or actions do not have to effect your happiness. They only seem to be a cause of your joy or sorrow.

Look at it this way: when you were six years old, there was such a thing as the multiplication table, but as yet, you did not know this. Joy already exists, in the same way.

Today, you know that the concept of multiplying has always been the same. It doesn't shift or change as the boundaries of countries do, or as the rules of spelling and grammar have, despite lexicons and grammarians. The laws of the Universe are just as unchanging and exact as the multiplication table. You memorized the table, and learned how to use it. You can learn how to use Joy, also.

When you were very young, did you ever multiply incorrectly, and come up with the wrong answer? Sure you did! But did that in any way affect the tables? No, *it* remained the same, didn't it? The multiplication table was in no way "responsible" for your error. It was totally unconcerned about your mistake. In this respect the Law of Mind is like the table, remaining the same Perfect Principle, while *you* are free to make mistakes.

From the moment you clearly understood how to multiply you made fewer mistakes, or perhaps none at all. Perhaps, sometimes when you are hasty or careless, you unthinkingly put down an incorrect result, such as making two plus two equal five. You know that did not come from the multiplication table, when you finally discover it. You know it is simply *your* mistake.

What I am saying, in another way, is that God did not create evil, mistakes, sin, nor sinners, any more than the multiplication table created the two plus two equaling five. Neither is sorrow given to you by Deity. You have been given joy; shall you use it by expressing it?

God created the idea of what is, not what isn't. Despair, despondency and sorrow is what *isn't*, or what happens when joy is not being expressed.

How the Senses Argue Back

"What have I to be joyous about? I've just lost the one most important to me!" This cry does not come from the inner you, it comes from the senses which try to dominate your emotions.

"But I have lost everything, money, home, and positions!"
All of these are things known by means of your senses.

"The doctor said there is no known cure for my ailment!"
Your body, as well as your doctor's, is known by means of
your senses. What he says to you is your own belief, coming
back into your ears.

Who turns the earth on its orbit? Who causes the sun
to shine? Who created the idea of Body?

How to Cease the Argument

Cease centering the attention upon what the sense
serpent has to say to you. No matter how the exterior
conditions appear to the senses, you know you are Pure
Energy and Substance and that this means nothing else but
abundant peace, love, intelligence, and joy.

This jewel of joy is a feeling of authority. No, not over
others, but over what you think. The world of appearances
no longer terrorizes you, for you have taken dominion over
the senses.

Outer Things Change Quickly

Once you have learned to allow no difficulty to scare
you, and have recognized that it was only presented as the
results of some old sense belief, you have the intelligence
to solve the problem, whatever its nature.

Complaining or sorrowful persons are no longer in the
orbit your daily affairs, or if so, remain on the Periphery.
When there is no longer any belief in your own mental realm
to be out-pictured as such as *they*, or as they *seem* to be,
you'll be surrounded by happy, healthy, interesting people.

In the same way, any cancerous condition is healed.
When the false belief, which is a tangled and knotty group
of emotional thoughts, filled with regrets, recriminations,
intolerance, and a great deal of self-pity, is dissolved, the
mistake is corrected. Then, there is no longer any outer
manifestation or evidence of it.

Poverty, another mistake, also goes out the window. when the Joyous YOU is found. There is no lack of anything good, when the Kingdom is being "abided" in. Because this quality of Joy is always present, most of us are touching it now and then despite what sense beliefs we may at times entertain.

False growths of any kind, from warts to tumors, disappear by being passed freely and easily out of the body when the understanding of Spirit is clear. They are brought about in the first place by misunderstanding, maladjustments, and depressing feelings. The cause of any kind of bodily disturbance is *never* in the body itself; that is, it doesn't begin in the body, no matter what you've the mental and emotional been *told*. It begins *always* in in the mental and emotional realm.

You Are Identical in Nature With God

The Joyous YOU is the spirit, which is a *feeling*. When you observe another's joy, you are seeing the effect, with the senses to be sure, of your own and that one's spirit. A quality of FIRST CAUSE, of God, is always something felt, then expressed.

It has long been observed that we are often able to perceive more truth than we are inclined to apply. Too many students of this subject can "talk up a storm" as far as what they've read is concerned, but fail to practise it when they need it the most. Even though they may tell another that a smile through tears is the prettiest kind of a smile, when their own world of effect displays a scene of disturbance, they quickly forget just what the correct application is.

Perhaps you have noticed that I keep lapping back over what has been said, adding something more to it each time? This is to cause you to become so aware of what you *must* do, and how to apply what you are learning that in such times you do not forget how available the help is. It is always "at hand."

Your Own Conduct Most Important

How you act shows how you feel and what you really believe. It takes persistence to crowd out the often unruly sense thoughts, which clamor to tell you the wrong things.

Your family and your friends and acquaintances are not going to be impressed with what you have to tell them about what you have read, but they will be impressed if you are always serene, fair, compassionate, and undisturbed by appearances. To fail to perform an act of mercy, or display friendship, when an opportunity is presented, is to let yourself as well as the other person down. You then misrepresent yourself, for, being identical with the nature of God, you have always more than enough love and joy and understanding to give. You can always help when you are called upon, but only if you *know* it, by *knowing* who you really are.

Until you know this, your conduct may well be contradicting what you are preaching. If these others listen to you with a tongue-in-cheek attitude, as though they wondered when you plan to start practising what you are preaching, this is what is being disclosed to them:

1. You are putting yourself and your wants above everyone elses'. You have *self*, not God.
2. You appear to be in a state of mental unrest.
3. You interrupt others before they are through speaking.
4. You change the subject frequently, and ask questions without waiting for answers.
5. You have a know-it-all attitude, which, unfortunately, only proves that you do *not* know.
6. You have not put *God* first, but the mortal *self*-you still believe yourself to be a judge and jury.
7. You present an appearance of one whose sole desire is to get greater good, rather than give, or express, it.

8. You are showing the mask of personality, made up of all your likes and dislikes, false beliefs, and misconceptions.

When I say YOU are not a sinner, I am talking about the Real YOU, the Idea God created, not this personality, no matter how charming it might be at times. This YOU looks past the faulty make-believe selves of others, recognizes that each person has beliefs about himself which are not true, even though they manifest themselves temporarily.

As long as you have feelings of displeasure, or hurt feelings, you have not made the acquaintance of the Joyous YOU.

You can tell when your thought comes from this self-made personality mask, because this is what you do:

1. You fear pain, poverty, and death.
2. You discuss ailments, sorrows, and disasters—your own mostly, but also those of others.
3. You engage in argument.

In short, you have played havoc with the multiplication table! What is absent is true humility.

A Humble Attitude

Many have thought that to become humble is to permit others to impose upon them. Humility is recognition that without God's Life, Love and Intelligence, you would be nothing. You wouldn't even BE! You glorify *God*, not *yourself*.

No, I am not contradicting myself, even though I have pointed out that you must do things in a way which will cause you to like yourself better. That was the first step.

The next step is to understand that all the good you do, comes, from God, within. You take no personal credit.

Without humility, you will not have an open mind. Without humility, you are apt to think that there is nothing more for you to learn. Without humility, you are inclined to set yourself apart from others, as a separate entity, and dull your own understanding.

If at any time all you see is the faults of others, work with your thoughts until you have a clearer conception of God's Spirit being in all, as all.

THE KINGDOM OF GOD IS LIKE UNTO A TREASURE HID IN A FIELD; THAT WHICH WHEN A MAN HATH FOUND, HE HIDETH, AND FOR JOY THEREOF GOETH AND SELLETH ALL THAT HE HATH, AND BUYETH THAT FIELD.

(Matt. 13:45, 46)

When you "sell" anything, you have gotten rid of it; it is out of your possession. Once you have experienced the feeling of the Kingdom in even a small way, your greatest desire is to rid yourself of all those beliefs which block the passage of greater good to you.

You will not boast and brag about what you can do, or have done, because you know that of yourself, you do nothing. Even though it is "the Father" which brings forth the good, and *is* that good, you do not sit idly, waiting. You have work to do, too. You have to move the boulders of sense beliefs out of the way.

It will not be necessary for you to tell anyone how wonderful you are, or how good your intentions, for all can see, feel, and know it as you show yourself as this new concept, in all ways. There is a wide gap between *believing* in God and *knowing* God.

Until you comprehend that this Joyous YOU is not only your real self, but the real self of others, you are going to be inclined toward being conscious of other's wrongs. As long as you still see something in other's behavior to correct, your "mirror" is showing you a wrong belief, which you still entertain.

Since the Joyous YOU is in dominion, and has authority, you already have the power to change the belief.

Affirm Your Dominion

Only the personality asks foolish questions. This mask has set itself up as "something", and only when it discovers it is nothing, does the Real Self, peaceful, joyous, and loving, show forth. Only as Its intelligence appears increasingly does individuality take the place of personality.

The word "individual" means not divided, not separated from his source. He is undivided from his good, because he knows he is backed up by an unlimited good.

Many years ago, I had a student who was doing her best in all ways, as far as I could see. One evening after a class, she asked to talk with me privately.

"I think I understand this, but I have not been able to demonstrate anything as yet that proves I do understand. How long does it take?" she asked.

Surprised by this admission, I asked, "What is it that you are desiring to see manifest?"

"Mostly, that my husband be better, and my children good," was the comment.

"Your husband is not well?"

"No, no, I didn't mean that. I mean better, you know, not always arguing and yelling around the place. My kids are into everything; oh, we have a terrible time." She snickered a little, "They do the darndest things; maybe it's just normal, for they're little, but he blames me, and I'm always after 'em."

By the time she had finished, she had given me a picture of a pretty hectic household. I made several suggestions about changing beliefs and a good training pattern for the little boy and girl.

Several weeks later, she invited me to come to dinner. I found her husband to be a pleasant host, the children well-behaved, the dinner good and the house neat. In fact, everything was quite nice.

When the children were in bed and the husband excused himself to go take care of a business matter, she turned to me and said, "See what I mean?"

"About what?"

"See how nasty he is? Always making sarcastic remarks. He just isn't happy unless he is running me down some way. I was embarrassed over the way my kids acted."

"Considering their ages, I thought they did remarkably well," I amazed her by saying (and I meant it), "I didn't hear anything sarcastic."

I'd been thinking how nicely she had done ridding herself of a belief, for certainly this was a pleasant little family group.

If she was allowed to continue imagining something which didn't as yet exist, it wouldn't be too long before it would become an actual fact. How could I help her?

We had many talks, many visits outside if actual class instruction, then one day when I was in her neighborhood, I dropped in without calling ahead of time. Such an action on my part was unprecedented, and I could only conclude that it was a guidance in order that I might see the real reason for her beliefs hanging on as they seemed to do.

Her own conduct, her nagging, and quick temper was what she was seeing reflected, but only in her imagination. Her failure to understand how to apply her thought correctly was due solely to this misconduct. I learned something vitally important about teaching this subject, namely, that a student's own conduct must be of a nature that he approves.

Until self-approval is established, no further understanding of the Law of Mind can be comprehended.

How to Establish Self-Approval

We have dealt with this before, but now we are going to add something further. You are not going to do YOUR best, if you are too busy trying to make others do their best.

Your attention is divided. There is nothing selfish about being the best you know how to be, but it is a mark of selfishness to think that you cannot do better. Room for improvement is a big room.

Successful people got that way by doing everything just a little bit better every day. The learned something more every day. They don't spend time, they use time, to their advantage.

It may not matter what others think about you, or how they regard you, but what you think of yourself is so important that I advise you to get a good book on social manners, and read it and apply it. Knowing what are the accepted customs of courtesy will stand you in good stead, for this knowledge stems from a love of graciousness. If you want gracious living, you will have to learn how to express it.

Good business practices are based upon fairness and justice. To lie or cheat is to sell yourself short, for in the long run, though you may be ahead financially, the loss of self-approval is the real loss. You *"sell your soul for a mess of pottage.*

If, through ignorance of the importance of this, you have already strayed far away, there are two, ways you can regain self-approval:

1. Consider each day a *new* day, in which you amend all seen-to-be-faulty ways. You make up your mind that for this one day, at least, you are strong enough to do just what you know is right.

2. You can remember who you really are, the Joyous You.

What Awareness of Joy Does for You

The Joyous YOU knows Itself to be eternal. It has no fear of death, for it understands. It knows no gluttony nor greed. It never frets, stews, nor grumbles, at any time. It is only the "mask," the personality, that does this sort of thing. It is strong or weak, and when it is weak it is inclined to conform to the ways of those who are just as weak. You can easily tell where your viewpoint is, by what you are doing, and how you feel.

The Joyous YOU knows that when an idea comes as desire, it means this thing or event is on its way to being "stepped down" into visibility. It says, "Thank you, Father." It is completely grateful and appreciative, and never asks "when?" or "how?" It knows it is worthy, and never has to ask how to be made so. Being heir to the Kingdom of Perfect Ideas, it accepts its inheritance.

The Joyous YOU knows there are no circumstances beyond your control, for being authority over your beliefs, this YOU knows how to remove what seems to show up as such.

Someone will always argue at this point, especially about having no fears, and also about others being "to blame." Fear and caution are so frequently used interchangeably, that I am often asked if fear isn't needful for protection. When you are using intelligence, you will be heedful, of course, will you not? It is the emotion of dread and anxiety that you should rid yourself of. There is nothing wrong with being circumspect. To blame or censure another is, at the very point you see wrong, to, deny the Allness of God.

You lose contact with the Joyous YOU when you fear or blame. As we noted before, when a person knows himself to be at fault, he becomes angry. Why? Because the real YOU knows. it needn't have been like that. It is not the real YOU that is angry, it is a belief born in sense consciousness which says, "I've done it wrong" that is angry. If another person is angry, what you are witnessing is his belief about himself, which can become your belief about him, if you aren't quick to see beyond it.

As you glimpse the reasons for anger and blame, and all the unpleasant emotions which stand between you and YOU, you see how your spiritual vision was made opaque, until the ability to comprehend appeared to be impossible.

Can you now listen to the deeper teachings of the Impersonal God? Can you take your mental attention off the world of effects long enough to perceive the Allness of God?

Have you ever gone to a masquerade and worn an all-over face mask? It was hot and uncomfortable and probably obstructed your vision somewhat. The personality mask is even worse, for it hobbles you in all ways.

You have *not* found your Joyous YOU just because you have had many hearings and blessings. You have found it only when you are no longer conscious of anything as a "problem." You may know there is a God, but you have not *found* HIM, nor do you *know* HIM, just because you have caught a glimpse of His goodness now and then. You have merely been playing peek-a-boo!

Strong words? Yes. As long as you still see others as wrong, mis-guided (because they do not see things your way), you have not *known* God.

Are we blaming anyone? Not at all! Are we accusing others of mis-teaching? Not a bit! We see all growing in understanding, even as you and I.

Are we blaming the little fellow in school when he writes on the blackboard, "6x6=35?" When we know the correct answer is 36 we are looking beyond his error, to the Truth. We are viewing the Principle and we know that his error didn't alter the multiplication table, nor effect us in the slightest way. We correct him without any emotion, show him the right answer and how we arrive at it.

To the question: "What is your authority?" God is my authority. God gave me the ability to read the Bible and understand it. I know it is true that the Real Self of everyone is the Divine Spirit. *"Prove me, and see . . ."* is the instruction. Can you prove it to yourself by letting it be revealed to you, from within?

Prove Me Now

God is unchangeable, all-good, and always present. Today, God is the Divine Love that *"never faileth."* YOU were created perfect. All your jewels are within.

Contemplate what is possible to Divine Intelligence. All thing, not just some things, are possible to God.

You, right here, right now, are one with this Joyous YOU. Can you feel it? You are more wonderful than you ever guessed, with abilities resting latent and dormant, which you can now call forth!

YOU and the Father (intelligent understanding) are One, not two. YOU and the Father (all joy and love and peace) are One, not two. Can you feel your union?

YOU know what action to take, what thought to think. This is "finding God." This is KNOWING God.

Don't Lose It

From the standpoint of spirit, all are "created equal." Watch that you don't deny that another has this same potential, or you will lose the feeling of Oneness.

A second reading of this book will reveal things to your awareness which you didn't grasp the first time. The more you use the lesson material, and the softener you contemplate the nature of God and your relationship to Divine Spirit, the smoother things will go for you in your world of effect.

There is always a tendency to return to the human reasoning of the senses. The desire to handle something with your hands is stronger than you may, at first, realize. This is why the contemplation of what God really *is*, is more necessary than *asking* for things, for deliverance from some so-called evil. He who wants much is always "wanting." Any shortage of good, or absence of good, on the relative level (to the senses), is showing because, it is held in mind. It is let go of only by contemplation of God.

What is Called "Healing"

Releasing these thought pictures, which have been brought into being by the senses, is what the world calls *healing*. How many ailments and diseases have you been freed from simply because you knew they *were* temporary? A good many, no doubt.

When someone comes along and tells you, "Here is an incurable disease," meaning that man's thought has not arrived at a point where a belief has created a serum, a medication, or a surgical skill which will eradicate it, and you accept his findings, you are doomed, or so you think. And, *"As a man thinketh, in his heart, so is he."*

A scientist, who realizes that it is the Father within him who doeth the works, can produce the right idea, and bring it forth into manifestation which will aid in giving relief. The one suffering can aid a great deal if he will contemplate the nature of Life to heal.

Science Advances Through a Law of Unfoldment

The spiritual system which we call the Universe is governed by the Laws of Mind. The Mind, which is God, is pushing out into what man calls his mind. Our power to *know* comes from this Universal mind. The urge to unfold is in everyone, showing to a greater or is lesser degree, and this is why each individual can advance by using his own thought correctly.

No Strain in Finding the Joyous You

Freeing the nature of the Divine Spirit into expression is, in itself, a joyful experience. You merely dwell serenely and quietly upon the idea that, in Truth, you are now wonderful.

It does not matter what you have done in the past. If you are good right now, aren't you just as good as is possible to be? Comprehension of the law of unfoldment helps you see that everyone else's past contains some stupid, faulty, and perhaps greatly regretted beliefs and actions. As you learn how to think about others, to see that they too, learned what not to continue doing, you are doing what is called "forgiving." You do not hold anything against them, for you are now able to understand that these were all simply wrong beliefs, which came to you through your senses. Your debts and transgressions are forgiven to the exact degree that you are able to let loose of those beliefs. When the "bad thing" you did has been seen to be a way in which you learned to do the right thing, the sense of guilt is gone.

This Joyous YOU sees beyond the three-dimensional, relative world, beyond the pairs of opposites, into the heart of Reality. You love every experience, moment after moment, knowing that every one of them discloses to you some new joy. This Self never bothers with trying to change appearances, or present conditions. It isn't trying to "get" anything, for it knows It is One with the Father, heir to the Kingdom. It knows everything is working out beautifully. It never bothers to look to see if things are getting better, but every person it meets represents a new experience of enlightenment, every telephone call a thrill, each piece of mail a delight. It sees nothing but progress. It delights in everything for it has no ability to know limitation. It sees the solutions, never the problems.

How Long Will It Take?

How much time will you spend contemplating what you really are? How much time do you spend thinking about what you seem to be? How much time are you giving now to thinking about others? How much time do you allot to thinking of the past?

When more time is used in knowing that you are heir to the Kingdom than is used up in these other categories, you will find the Joyous YOU.

It Is Already Present

Do you see how it is that you cannot possibly want anything which you know is already present? "*To him that hath, it shall be given,*" says a world of things to us; but when you read the rest of the quotation, "*and to him who hath not, that which he hath shall be taken away,*" and *still* declare that you have no joy, just sorrow, *then* even the *small* joys which were left begin to disappear! You cry out, "What have I done to deserve this?" You misused the Law of Mind! You grasp the point—to deny good anywhere is to push it away from you.

You would not knowingly condemn anything, or anyone, now . . . and hold off your *own* good!

Happy Laughter of Red Joy

You laugh with merry exhilaration; everything was here all the time! Never was the possibility of the presence of good missing, it was always possible. You just hadn't realized it. The still, small voice chuckles with glee, and your intellect (with its servants, the senses), and your real Self become ONE.

This is the "*marriage that is made in heaven,*" and you know it has nothing to do with man-made systems, laws for state, or clergy.

How wonderful to know that you are done with trying to get something, accumulate something—that all you need do is express what you are, and all that you need will find its way to you!

How wonderful to realize that the best of all scientific findings are ways in which the Intelligence of the Universe makes Its way into expression by means of Mankind!

How wonderful to comprehend the meaning of the "rich man who could not enter into heaven" and see that he was "rich" in having too many sense beliefs, thinking there were many minds, all working against one another!

How wonderful to understand that the outer things known by means of the senses were only reflections of ideas and beliefs, and that all your striving to hold on to them was like trying to hold a shadow in your hand!

How wonderful to turn within and be at peace!

How wonderful the JOYOUS ME!

CHAPTER 16

The Garments of Joy

"Do the beliefs and opinions we hold during our embodiment on earth, cease and become null and void at the point of death?" a student queried. He was a tranquil man, a retired minister, who had followed the traditional teachings of his denomination.

"Could they?" I countered, "when the soul is the mental body? Until they are corrected by knowledge of the Truth, they would endure, would they not?"

"Then," he said wearily, "death is no help, really?"

"There is no death," I reminded.

"I see . . . I see . . ." He rubbed a spot on his forhead with the back of his hand. "It must be God first, the Universal Law."

"Yes, all good follows the observance of the first Commandment." I knew he was wondering why when he has taught what he believed was true, preached Bible texts every Sunday morning for years, he had experienced so few moments of real unmitigated joy.

"As I see it now," he said more to himself than to me, "I allowed myself to feel sorrow for the mistakes I saw going on all around me. I so much wanted to show thern the way, but they seemed so blind . . . so blind."

The Old Way and the New

We have come to understand that the source of all there is is not a separate Being, outside and unattainable until we give up physical life, or some mysterious Force, present only to men or women of "the cloth." We know that it is the actual

239

spirit of life; that it is eternal in essence. We know that Everyman is using and mis-using the Law of Mind because he does not understand, but that as soon as he is apprised of the facts of the natural order of the cosmos, he will stop mis-using what was given him for his benefit.

Interpreting Scripture

Anyone who moves his attention above and beyond the many limitations of the physical-material plane, can and does correctly interpret the Scripture. Many already have.

First of all, do you know who Solomon is? Look at it: Solo Man. Solo means alone, does it not? Alone, with God. Ah! the Wisdom of Solo Man!

You already are aware that the image and likeness of God is spirit. You know spirit is not visible, nor limited. You know it is Life, and that you are alive. Your first awareness is of your body, which is called "Adam." Later on, the Scripture refers to the first Adam and the last Adam. When the intellect begins its functioning, this is called "Eve." You are Adam and Eve, the body and intellect, and it is the intellect which accepts the findings of the senses (the serpent in the garden).

When God comes to your attention, and you are asked, "Who told you that you are naked?" It is the same as "What is it that makes you think you do not have what you need?" You know now that it was by means of what your senses reported to the intellect, but you may not have known that the Bible said it. Your senses also read into this text that Adam and Eve were "*other people*." Now and then questions arose which bothered you.

Today, it is more clear to you that unless you begin from a correct premise, a right knowledge of God, you'll have questions again with no answers.

Symbols of Key Ideas

Just as the name "Solomon" gives you the Key Idea to

the subject of Wisdom, not all proper names are as easily discernable as this one, but all do represent types of thought and stages of consciousness.

"Egypt" means your brain, not a geographical location. The "Egyptians" are sense impressions and their burdens are fears, worries, and anxieties. "Priests and Pharisees" are the kinds of thoughts which help to support the claims of the senses.

When the conviction begins to grow that Life is not all that it appears to the senses to be, the key idea is called "Moses." It wants to take the "people" (your sense beliefs) to the Promised Land.

In this "Moses" state of consciousness, you become aware of "I Am," not "What I was," or even "What I hope to become." At this point, you say to yourself, "I am alive . . . I am that Life which is Intelligence."

The total aggregation of your beliefs are called "waters." Anything called "Sea" or "Seas" refer to the confused beliefs. In the Book of Revelation, you are told that there will be seas no longer.

The "Throne" means "origin of thought," and suggests government. A "river" means "a channel of thought," as does also a highway, a street, or a path. "Hands" means thoughts. The "right hand of God" is the right thought of God.

A "day" is a period of prayer when you get enlightenment, and "night" is when you have returned to sense beliefs. "Beast" means theory; the "mark of the beast" is suppositional knowledge, or that which is merely talked about and not practised. Can you imagine what chaos might result if some folks "preached" what they were practising? Only ignorance could perpetrate such teaching.

Every time you formulate an opinion due to what appears. you have discarded the Garment of Joy, to some degree, even if what appears is good, unless you remember

"Look what God has done!" To think, "Look what I have done," is to move away from the Universal. To think, "Look what my son, John, has done," or "Look what this fine woman has done," commendable as this thought is, (it certainly is an improvement over looking for flaws), it is still not quite the same as glorifying *God*. It means, simply, that your thought has moved back to the relative and is off the Universal.

This does not by any means imply that you are not to thank some individual, in whatever way you feel you would like to express such thanks, because you know God was the cause of some good action from which you benefited. The action you make of showing appreciation is YOUR recognition of God's Presence, everywhere, in you as well as in the other. Neglect in expressing gratitude is non-recognition of this quality of God in yourself.

The Ten Commandments

The word "commandment" means "to direct with authority." The first one reads, "And God spake all these words saying, *"I am the Lord thy God, which have brought thee out of the land of Egypt, out of the house of bondage. Thou shalt have no other gods before me.' "* (Exo. 20:1); the other nine statements tell you things which you are no longer inclined toward doing, once you have found your place of authority.

To *"have no other gods"* is to understand that to limit yourself to a mortal and physical sense of life, with attention forever fixed upon material forms, is to manifest limitations in various ways. You comprehend that *"graven images"* aren't just idols made of wood or stone, crucifixes or statues, but anything at all in the world of form. You understand that all things of form are symbols of ideas, and you can make way for the Ideas of Truth.

Haven't you often checked with "things that appear" to see how you are doing? Haven't you, at some time, attempted to "judge" your progress by looking to see if you are getting more money, or if your health is better, or your "demonstration" of some desire getting closer? Have you never looked at some teacher of such subjects as this and asked yourself, "Why doesn't he drive a better car, or have a nicer house?"

You find, as is shown in the story of Moses, that the people (your beliefs) are having a pretty wild time. It is up to you to bring every one of them into correction. Your wrong thoughts are "the heathen," and only *you* can convert them.

What happens to the Garment of Joy when you look around you at others, thinking, "his one or that one hasn't 'made it' yet?" Sometimes, it is rent, torn into shreds. When you allow your doubt to come up, due to what you observe, it has a way of taking over in all departments. Not only that, but the appearances upon which you formed such judgment may be far from presenting the true picture. That one you so criticize may have a bank account or properties which he may have good reasons for not revealing. To display it may have brought about an equally erroneous opposite reaction; namely, that his teaching was "a racket."

Do you see why the Ten Commandments were given to you?

Life Is Not Purposeless

You are told that you will not take on the nature of God *"in vain."* It is saying that you are to be delivered out of your difficulty, for the wrong belief will be corrected. Whatever good seemed to be missing from your experience was due only to this belief, even if that belief was *not* about yourself, but about another.

Holding to the first Commandment, you know that in Spirit, all are one, and the belief about another is in YOUR mind, and must be changed there.

Next, you are reminded to remember the Sabbath Day and keep it holy (wholly, entirely). The Sabbath has nothing whatsoever to do with a calendar day, no matter what you have formerly been taught. The six "days" before the Sabbath are periods of thought, steps of awareness, and they can take place in a flash, or move slowly month after month. They can also take place year after year, or life after fife, if we mean, by life, physical embodiment.

Some folks are reluctant to give up what has been washing into their intellect over a long period of what we call "time." The *"blind leaders of the blind,"* mentioned in Matthew 15:14, *"both fall into the ditch."* Do you see how the "priests and pharisees" (your physical senses) *"were offended, after they heard this saying?"* Yet, Jesus answered them and said, *"Every plant, which my heavenly Father hath not planted, shall be rooted up."*

Yes, you have been fooled about what the Sabbath is whether you think it to be Saturday or Sunday, for both are of the sense mind.

To *"keep the Sabbath"* then would be to hold all of your thoughts still. It is a listening attitude, a waiting for God, a freeing of the attention from any thought about the world of form.

There is a purpose is this, and you are so made that you can accomplish it. You already do it, more often than you may realize, but you can learn to do it consciously. The method has already been set down in the lessons.

The Fifth Commandment

Here you have, *"Honor thy father and thy mother,"* while in Matthew 23:9, we have, *"Call no man your father upon the earth; for one is your Father, which is in heaven."*

Confusing? Contradicting? Not at all, unless only your senses are giving you the meaning. There is no contradiction when you are reading with spiritual comprehension, for you do understand that God is the only Father, or Source, you ever had!

What a real blessing this realization is to your earthly parents, no matter how degrading they might have seemed to the senses! Do you know there are some who have turned away from God simply because He is called "Father?" When the sense impressions of the earthly male parent were unfavorable, cruel, thoughtless or unkind, God was believed to be a larger edition of the same thing, so He was shunned and actually feared.

God is the Father and Mother of all, an Androgynous Principle, and our earthly parents symbolize or reflect the understanding of this which we have.

Do remember that Jesus asked. *"Who is my mother? and who are my brethren?"* (Matt. 12:47), then told them that whoever does the will of God is his mother, sister, and brother.

You will wear and keep your Garment of Joy intact when you understand these passages. If you have read Luke 14:26, *"If any man come to me and hate not his father, mother, and wife and children, and brethren and sisters, yea, his own life also, he cannot be my disciple,"* you may have been greatly puzzled.

In a Gospel of Love, you are told to "hate?" Unthinkable! Yet, when you know that the word translated into our language as hate was taken from a word which meant "to turn away from," your puzzlement clears up. It is some help to know that it is not an injunction to entertain a disagreeable emotional attitude, which heretofore you have been cautioned about avoiding. To turn away from them, then, can only mean that you are not to lean upon them, nor permit them to lean upon you. You and all others are to lean only upon the Divine Spirit. Only now it is growing more clear to you that all you see and hear, touch and know, by means of your senses, are reflections of your own beliefs.

"Thou Shalt Not!"

Having now moved your attention from the senses and intellect, the following *commands* are not really orders, but explanations of how you could not act, when you are thinking from your Real Self, the God Mind.

You won't "kill."

Many persons who would not even think of using a gun or knife, or any means by which the soul would depart from its body, are busy denying the God-self of others! Unwittingly, they deny good is present there, because the senses do not see it. They discourage others from doing what the Divine Spirit in them would like to express. "They say such things as, *Don't be so generous, nobody will thank you for it. You aren't strong enough to do that. You aren't smart enough to accomplish Such a big thing."* In short, they are "killing" in a much worse way. They are often called "killjoys", aren't they? You must see that they exist only as a Sense-belief, representing your own doubt, and following your own convictions.

You do not "mix" or adulterate a true spiritual concept with a reflection which comes from the brain and senses. To do so would be to "commit adultery."

Therefore, knowing yourself to be Pure Spirit, you could not possibly do so, could you?

The sense interpretation of the man-made marriage law and meaning of adultery is only a reflection of the spiritual idea. Cohabiting with another outside the legal circle displays an unsolved problem, a feeling of unsureness and confusion. Those who thus engage themselves have problems which multiply like rabbits, as well as opeing a door, figuratively speaking, for the mate to do likewise. It brings us back again to the importance of self-approval. Do unto others, as though you *are* the others. When you hurt another, the hurt always comes home to roost.

The only "marriage" known to God is the true concept when it is known by the intellect. Such "marriages" are always made "in heaven," or, within yourself. "Marriage" and "adultery" as spoken of in the Bible has nothing to do with human-beings, state or federal laws, or the dictates of any church group. Sense interpretations of Bible texts are all that have brought about such legislation.

When men and women have learned who they are, and how to think, they will get married and stay married, rear their children properly, and live happy, productive lives.

The Allocation of True Values

You do not rid yourself of your false beliefs until you have taught yourself to trust God. Wisdom teaches you to look to the inner, not to the outer, for all that you need. Naturally, you would not steal, for within, All is already yours.

A sense-level belief could say, "Why, I can go take anything I want: it's all mine."

It is interesting to note that most who have normal reasoning powers see right away that being heir to the Kingdom does *not* mean you can run around helping yourself to whatever you want. We know that the reason for other sense-level beliefs about Bible texts is that people are still in the process of becoming aware of their *true* meanings.

"Thou shalt not steal" like the others, is not talking about the things of form but of how you are going to think when you follow the first order of Divine Spirit. The old beliefs about yourself were thieves and robbers, but you have gotten rid of them. You will no longer steal from yourself the good which is yours by believing that anything, or anyone, can keep it from you. All is Spirit, and Spirit is always expressing Itself for greater good.

You have laid the axe to the very root of the Tree of Knowledge of Good and Evil when you have ceased *"bearing false witness against your neighbor."* False testimony is always a *belief*, and is done away with by a correct Idea.

Let me show you. Little Mary is a child you know. Someone comes in and says to you, "*Mary is dreadfully ill, we have to call the doctor.*" Your ears have heard the belief, and your eyes see a worried and concerned countenance. You might even go have a look at Mary for yourself. What happens? You're convinced!

You now know that all means of persons in the Bible stand for qualities of thought, or the *way* thought is characterized. "Jacob" is the name of the kind of thought which is double-minded.

At this point, you are "Jacob." Your unbelief now must wrestle with your understanding of the Truth. What your senses have informed you about departs.

When any moment such as this comes to Your attention, when you see anyone sick or ailing, or in any difficulty, a belief is clashing with your awareness of the Presence of Perfect Life. It is trying to "steal." Your understanding of Truth will always be sufficient to erase the wrong picture.

The name "Israel" is conferred upon the victor, and the "*children of Israel*" are those purified thoughts which must be victorious.

So, you see, you cannot "*bear false witness,*" nor "*covet thy neighbor's house, wife, etc.*" You recognize that all forms are but reflections of beliefs, and that to lust, or covet, is to have your thought entangled with the reflections, not the real.

The Burning Bush

Everything in the natural world is a symbol of a spiritual truth, but you have never seen a bush that burned when the flames did not consume it. Moses did.

You are always on the "Mount," and you have decided to overcome the human, sense arguments (your people who are wild and raucous, and have made themselves an idol), and you want to lead them on to the Promised Land.

The Red Sea

Confusion looms up ahead; clear human thinking is difficult. Human thought is hungry for power, and wrong when it appears to be right. "Moses" represents a correct idea, a key thought that has helped you understand that all life is Spirit; but "Moses has to cross the Red Sea"—and the *Red Sea* is all the discord and confusion which has come from your sense beliefs and all the suggestions of fear and trouble you have been accepting.

The Real Self which has this key thought, *Moses,* will have the Red Sea part for you. That conviction you have so long entertained, that the world was material and your body was you, was the root of all your disturbance.

If you have been trying to believe that a body of water divided itself down the middle so that hordes of human-beings might cross to the other side of it, and thus continue their journey, no wonder you questioned the Bible!

Skilled movie makers have done all they could to kelp you to hold on to this illusion, and more's the pity.

Now and then, theologians who were unable to grasp the real meaning, have offered the flimsy excuse, "It could be done, in those days; but of course, not now."

Who Are the "Dead?"

Dormant ideas of whose existence you have no knowledge, will be "resurrected." Did you think the corpses in all the cemeteries were going to get up and walk around? Not a thrilling sight, any way you look at it.

You have not "come to life" until you have spiritual awareness. "Galilee" is your Soul where newborn ideas originate.

A Veritable Fountain of Perfect Thoughts

The whole Bible is talking about you and your states of consciousness. Most persons are interested when they are being discussed, and much so when that discussion is favorable. We interpret the word Love as meaning, "to give favorable attention." So, you see, this book called the Bible is favorable attention to you!

Wonderful Experiences

You experience the birth of the infant, Jesus, which is your own newly discovered awareness that God is really your Father, not a Big Man up in the sky, or one you meet only after passing through pearl-studded gates." But there *are* "pearls" and there are "gates;" they are pearls of wisdom and gates which open to ever greater understanding.

Because they are already within you, you can find them when you cease looking for them in someone else. They are there, too, but you'll never know it until you find your own, for you look too far away.

As this "babe" within you grows and becomes stronger, it (this knowledge) takes over the government of your life. It really *is* a Prince of Peace.

Many key thoughts promised you that this would take Place, and you would know mastery of problems; indeed, better than that, you would no longer "create them."

You "feed and nourish" this "babe" by right thoughts, which result in right actions. You gain an understanding of Life, for yourself, by doing your own thinking. You no longer accept everything you hear because you *do* stop to consider that every thought you think is a thread you are weaving into your own loom of life.

Your Birthright

The sense of dominion which comes as you decide to be an independent thinker gives living a fullness of joy never before known, which keeps expanding. You are intended to reach the place of comprehension where you find this glorious Self, which takes its wisdom from an unlimited source within.

Contrast this with the tendency to have to always ask someone else what to do. What if those to whom you go cannot think of the right advice to give you? What if that one's best knowledge turns out to be wrong? What if the one upon whom you depend, goes away, is unreachable?

If you believe something just because another has said it was right, where is your own individuality?

The same wisdom that is given to those you consider wise, is also given to you. Why don't you use it?

There could only be one reason, which is that you aren't sure of it. How will you make yourself sure, certain?

There Is an Overall Design

Consider the great Reality, the Universal Plan. Intelligence is manifested as many forms. This giving of Itself into form is called Divine Love. This Principle is power-*full*. It is an infinite thinker, thinking eternally. It does not and cannot destroy Itself. It is, was, and will ever be, an *Original Force,* an energy and essence which passes into form eternally. It is First Cause, the Universal *I Am.*

The Bible says, "In Him we live and move and have our being;" it also says, "No man hath seen God at any time." You cannot observe by means of any of your senses this Original Cause, but you do know that you live and think. The Bible adds, after that last quotation, only the Son, he hath revealed Him," which means that since you-observe an effect, you feel there is a Cause which produced it.

Now you can understand how it is that you "walk in God's presence." What a difference than the old belief that God was only present while you were in church, and that you might do as you pleased the rest of the time.

You ask, "But since God is in all, why not rely upon one who knows God better than I do?"

I didn't say you couldn't, or that there was anything wrong with it, but the day must come when you know for yourself, Why? Because you are "educating" your senses.

Conquering Unruly Thoughts

Being unsure of yourself is an adverse thought which tears away the Garment of Joy. While true convictions are lacking, you can be very miserable. You are like one who sits in a dark room, fearing the dark, with a light switch within reach.

If you will take great care not to drop into a forgetfulness of the unchanging goodness of this Life which you are, you can pass through the "seas" of erring thoughts and beliefs.

Here again, you must watch that you do not take on a self-righteous state of mental attention, which comes in this way, "I am so good and these others so mistaken . . . or bad." Look out for those comparisons, for that is an arrangement of thought forms, so prevalent in race-conscious thought, that is easy to adopt. When it happens, and it does with most of us who are still growing in our awareness (and all are), move your thought away from the *lack* of love, intelligence, or whatever it is that arrested your attention to cause you to so think.

I have done it here, whenever I have brought to your attention the points of apparent ignorance of those "who walk after the flesh." It is needful to do this for you, with you, as you read along, so that you get into the habit of seeing the fine line of demarkation between what are sense beliefs and what is true.

Improper Use of Imagination

As was pointed out earlier, to adulterate anything is to mix it up, so that it is no longer "pure." When you, understanding your relationship to the Divine, no longer mix sense impressions with Truth, you will find the right use of imagination.

While the senses remain in a negative state, or are only partially educated, the emotions are easily upset and correct use of the imagination is rare. Constructive use of the imagination has been said by many to be within the power of visualizing what you want. It does seem to "work" for some, but only when there are no negative thought forms still within the mental realm. Those for whom it does not seem to be an answer have not learned how to be happy, grateful, and sufficiently satisfied with present good. They have not moved away such conflicting blocks of belief as pride, pretense, and ego-satisfactions. The imagination works negatively when one interprets dominion to mean being tyrannical, possessive, or authoritative over others.

It is always your own beliefs that you take dominion over; other persons have a right to think as they choose; yes, even your nearest and dearest. See them as growing, with a Source the same as your own. If this is confusing to you yet, the time will come when you will understand with amazing clarity.

You can *imagine* what a wonderfully easy world this would be to live in when all understood what to do, and did it!

That time will come; and your thought, directed correctly, win help it along. But you don't have to wait until all know. Your world is already changing for the better.

Free From Error

Knowing the Truth, you are "set free" from error. The negative, unpleasant thing, that shouldn't be, *isn't*. But, to the senses, it *is*. See quickly that only because of a belief that such things *could* happen, *do* they happen. See that it is a belief, and that you can cast it out.

Don't throw it into someone else's lap, by saying that is the way he thinks. Don't blame your sinus infection upon the smong, the smoke from the smelter, or anything else the senses know. Recognize that it comes from a belief, and change the belief. It isn't "coming from" anywhere. It is a place in your mental realm where Truth has not been introduced!

Mortal Man

Mortal Man is mental concepts based upon what is known by mean of the senses, which, even at best, give you only a partial picture of Good.

God	True man
Is an infinitude of Per-fect Ideas, the unfolding of which is creation.	*Is God's Idea whole.* *Divine Love.* *Pure Spirit*

Personal Sense of Mortal Self

No one can do *your* thinking for you. Only your senses make it seem that they do. None takes your freedom; you have to give it up. The belief that another takes it is made by you.

You Increase in Wisdom and Stature

The "babe" is growing and "waxing strong." It is you who says, "Now I must be about my Father's business.

If your earthly male parent was to take you into his firm, providing he had one, you would have to learn something about what his business ways were. Common sense says that you would learn only by being on the premises. It also says that you aren't going to know all about it just because someone told you. If the company had a manual you could read, that might be quite an aid, but you would only learn the business by being there day after day, getting acquainted with all sides of this operation.

You are ready to ask of your Creative Intelligence what it wants done by means of you. It's will is always something you find enjoyment in; it will be constructive, for the Intelligence only operates constructively. It will progress you and prosper you, for that too, is It's nature. You will do it increasingly better.

As recorded in Luke you will notice that "Jesus" does not spring full-panoplied from the God-head. Neither do you; you grow one step at a time. Every step of the way he had obstacles to meet and met them. He trained his disciples, just as you are training the various faculties you have, disciplining them, until they know who you are.

Brotherly Love

You have wanted to rid yourself of those feelings of inadequacy, and to have a satisfying feeling of being able to know what you needed to do, and how to do it. You didn't know that every true thought bolsters up other true thoughts, and does away with the false ones, nor that this was the "brotherhood of man" rather than some lodge organization, where you pretended to be a friend of a lodge "brother."

When you truly love all your thoughts, and they love you, you will experience no inferiority feelings. How easily you could step across if the human ego self did not keep getting in the way!

The Loaves and Fishes

What does the story of the multiplying of the loaves and fishes really say? The senses have tried to make it into everything from an act of necromancy to the employment of a law as yet unknown to the rest of us.

You are told that if you already have, an idea and you bless it, that is, think correctly about it, the good from the idea, already inherent in it, multiplies itself many times.

I once heard of a woman who sat in front of a tableful of dollar bills, trying to "bless" them into multiplying themselves. No, nothing happened.

If you base everything upon the altar of Mammon (the reality of matter), you are not worshipping God, and you have forgotten that you cannot worship both God and Mammon.

Had she contemplated the abundance of substance, invisible and unlimited, and followed the next good idea she had, she might not have reaped a fortune the same day, but she could have been on her way to it.

I know a woman who asked for a fifty-thousand dollar bill and got it, but it was old Chinese currency, worthless at that time as to buying power.

There are those who go repeatedly to another to "pray for them," or, as they tell it, "know the truth for them," rather than learn how to correct their own faulty beliefs.

Using Prayer as a Last Resort

A garment is something you wear, and if all you want is to be comfortably fed, clothed, sheltered, and amused, your Garment is hanging in the closet.

It is not something to be put on only when the way grows rough. It might be a little hard to locate when you need it the most. If all you use prayer for is to get something to show off, you are likely to discover that a good many unfortunate things can take place while you are searching anew for the right state of mind.

When you are on the plane of enlightenment, you will not see one event as destructive and another as a savior. Everything is beneficial.

Anyone can be joyous when things go well, but it takes real understanding to *keep* wearing the Garment of Joy. knowing that God is not self-destructive. You can do it if you remember from which source comes your information. When it is of the senses, it can be either good or evil.

Take the letters of that last word, they will also spell "veil" and reversed they spell "live."

You don't use prayer as a last resort, once you have become acquainted with your inner Lord; you won't try everything and everyone else first, because you will have discovered that from within you can be told exactly what to do, whether it be a health condition, a business problem, or something having to do with human relationships.

History

Our Bible, read as history (and *that* is an interesting, word, *His Story*), tells us of the states of consciousness Everyman goes through. (Using the word generically, it means every woman, also). As long as the senses make the proper names into persons who lived long ago, you haven't begun to understand the meanings.

"But our minister said," "our doctrine teaches," "the Church says" —yes, I know. They are all of your senses, also. Are they not? Be honest with yourself.

When I tell you that we have more jails, penetentiaries, mental institutions, then we ever had, in which there are many who claim to have "accepted Jesus," how will you respond? How about the many hospitals in which there are many good, sincere church-members? If you say that the former group "didn't really believe," what will you say about these?

The Bible is Man's Story and depicts his discords and conflicts and does how him the way out of them.

Do you want to don a Garment of Enlightenment? Then you had better know that the "firmament" is your ability to identify God's ideas, and distinguish the difference between them and the beliefs you entertain which are untrue.

Not Curiosity, but Sincerity

A man once told me that as a young boy he had gone down "the sawdust trail," and thereafter believed that he was "saved." Then he added, with a whimsical smile, "I don't think it did me much good; I've had my share of tribulations."

"What prompted you get up and walk down there?" I asked him.

"Curiosity," he answered tersely.

Curiosity is not a key to the gates to the Kingdom; sincerity is. Until there is a sincere desire to find God, not more money, better health, a shining romance, and more pleasures, it remains pretty much of a foggy concept. Financial ease, freedom from pain, a sweetheart, or a bigger automobile are the "graven images." But finding God, locating the Kingdom, causes all these nice things to come. They come gradually for some, rapidly for others. Why? Some work harder at it.

Life Gives Us What It Is as We Know What It Is

The more frightening a wrong thing appears to be the closer it is to being eliminated, when you shift attention.

All which contradicts the supremacy of this Greater Good doesn't just vanish for the moment, it leaves forever, as far as you are concerned.

Is it worth it? A million times *yes!*

When the Last False Belief Goes

To know no fear, to feel entirely adequate because you have learned to listen to the still, small voice, and can reach the Kingdom at with any time, any place, is better than a Doctorate in any subject!

The feeling of peacefulness, followed by an indescribable joy, with a love for all, sets you free. You feel ageless, light, and joyous, for you have found out how to say to your thoughts, "Be still," and they have obeyed you!

You have "followed the Master," found the "Secret Place of the Most High," and entered the "Kingdom."

Stay Alert

You will never forget what you have found, but you must make an effort to remain in this awareness; it can expand so that you are always alert to hear the guidance. The veil is lifted for you; you have a job to do. The virtues, or qualities worth expressing, are yours to express.

It is clear to you that the Truth, the All Good must exist and be primal. Any error, or non-good, cannot be primal for there must first be that of which *it* is the negative. You know all error is untrue, therefore unreal, so you have turned all your attention to the real, the true.

Now, you wear the Garment of Light and gain further satisfaction.

CHAPTER 17

Gaining Satisfaction

The dormant Idea, Jesus, can be "killed," that is, discouraged, by sense impressions. This refusal to bring it into expression is symbolized by the "crucifixion." Your richly-loaded wealth within is often felt by you, whenever you have allowed expression of the Divine attributes. The things "of Spirit" must be discerned spiritually, not given temporal meanings.

Are the Senses Good?

Have you asked yourself many times who put the Tree of Knowledge of Good and Evil into the Garden, if not God? If this was done by your Creator, then the senses must be good, you reason. Exactly! In themselves, they are good, for how else would you be able to discern what you were believing? They show you with amazing accuracy your false beliefs and your true ideas.

They perform a valuable service by letting you know what you are accepting as true which is not true, and showing you, when you have accepted the truth, a better existence in every way. Your health, finances, love-life, and human relationships all improve. They disclose to you beauty, harmony, joy and ease of living in that same realm of effect, which formerly looked so disturbing.

The Resurrection

We are shown that the dormant Idea of your Perfect Self, is not "dead" in the sense that it will never again exist. It is merely sleeping, unrecognized by conscious awareness of its reality, so you recieve the instruction: "Awake, thou that sleepest!"

The next time *"Christ died for us"* comes to your mental attention, remember that it means *"Christ lies dormant because of sense impressions"*.

Your Saviour is present all the time, waiting only for your recognition. All the time you were struggling for a display of affection, or love from another individual, you had the ability to recognize that quality within yourself and express it. When you did, it was exhibited to your awareness by means of your sense. But the moment your turned away, judging again by appearances which you didn't understand, the imagination worked negatively and you conjured up beliefs which, being fed by the Life Force, made pictures in the outer to substantiate the composite of those beliefs.

It is possible to bring this Savior to your awareness and keep it there.

It is Characteristic of the Sense to Fight This

Because it is so much easier to believe "another man" did all that is given in the Gospels, and you know the Joyous YOU, the Enlightened YOU, also the Son of man, there will be meetings with those who cannot accept this, as yet.

Just as Jesus found the blind, the lame, the poor, and knew them to be experiencing the results of their sense beliefs, so will you find them. They do not represent your false beliefs, for you know *none* of these things, depicted as lack of good, are true of God. There will be those who are close enough to the borderline of understanding who will *"touch the hem of your Garment"* and be made whole All may not be healed, because of their, *not your,* lack of belief.

Those deeply immersed in sense awareness, you bless; that is, keep the correct thought, knowing the Law of Growth is operating right there, from the Divine Source. If you looked over a field of grain, part of which was ripe and part of which was not, you would not condemn that which had not arrived at its fullness.

God lovingly unfolds His creation and maintains it with Infinite Love; He reveals in unlimited ways all that is beautiful, desirable and harmonious to you. This does not meant that because you have discovered the Spirit of Life to be an all-inclusive good, that you will do nothing but sit and twiddle your thumbs! That would be to miss out on all the fun.

The philosophy that if you do nothing, you would not make mistakes, is an error you will not be guilty of making. You know that you continue to grow in grace, and if you make an error, you learn something new; you will not make the same mistake twice.

Your senses may try to convince you that an error is more real than the Truth. They may shake your poise, attempt to confuse you. If you listen too long to human opinions—the reasoning done from sense level that others are so willing to pour into your ears—your confidence and poise can become wobbly. It is then you must remember, *they* don't know, but YOU do.

How to Rise Above What Others Believe

Come back often to the words of Hosea 11:9 *"For I am God, and not man; the Holy One in the midst of thee."* Recognize immediately that God is the only Thinker, therefore the Only Mind.

It you catch yourself with a question about malpractice, remember this would be believing in two minds, at least, yours and anothers, which might work against you. This inconsistency is one which has harassed humanity for ages.

Go back to the beginning—God created all Ideas. God not the sense, created all your beliefs. Check back with yourself often to see if you are holding to the thought that all good attends you on your way, even when the senses have not as yet confirmed it. They will confirm it if you hold to it, this Right Idea.

Remember again, that God created Ideas, not the forms you look upon, the things you handle.

Someone may ask you, "Am I to say that God created the idea that this woman is sick?"

Your answer would be, "No, God created the Idea of Perfect Life. What have you and this woman done with it?"

Another says, "God must have created the idea of crime and poverty.

"Of course he didn't," you answer, "He created the ideas of intelligence and wealth. Mankind sees and hears such things because he is not sufficiently evolved to grasp the Truth.

It is now the beliefs and opinions of others which you "speak to," for these are not your own. They are mis-interpretations about Life. You are simply being careful that you do not allow them to again become real to you. Because YOU know that what the Bible calls "wicked" is to become bewitched by the relative findings of the senses, you keep your confidence and poise lasting by speaking the Truth.

Refuse to Respond Emotionally

Remain serene while others dramatize the results of their negative beliefs.

YOU are not tempted to side with the findings of their senses, for you know full well that the confidence which comes only from having a fat bank account and a good income can be shattered in an instant by an earthquake. You know, also, that the poise which comes only from knowledge of bring well-dressed leaves quickly during a shipwreck, and an automobile skidding out of control on an icy highway can uproot both confidence and poise if they aren't more deeply rooted. You listen with no emotion. You listen with no emotion because you know God was never the another of such confusion.

You may listen to those who have expressions of resentment, knowing that the belief they hold comes from a sense-recognized injustice, but you know there is no lack of justice, for justice is a quality of God. You know it is present, though not recognized here, by these, and you speak out, "There is Divine Justice." As an emotional habit, belief in injustice leads into self-pity, a greater wrong, which *you* refuse to accept as true.

While these others still believe themselves to be physical forms, only (still crusifying their Savior) by believing Him to be *someone else*, you hold to the constructive progress of Intelligence and Love, you are fanning the Divine Spark which blazes into their own enlightenment.

If it seems to take a while, you are not dismayed, for you know that Intelligence produces evolution, *not* that evolution produces intelligence, as many have thought.

You may tell them they although the Bible speaks of "body," it means to all manifestations of thought, including the physical form.

You are aware that all that God created is perfect, whole, complete; they are ideas of life, love, joy, success, strength and progress. You know they Intelligence, wherever there is life, reveals more and ever more of Itself, so you smile serenely, undisturbed by the sense findings of these others.

All Are Here by the Power of God

FOR WE WALK BY FAITH, NOT BY SIGHT. WE ARE CONFIDENT—I SAY, AND WILLING RATHER TO BE ABSENT FROM THE BODY, AND TO BE PRESENT WITH GOD THE LORD.

(II Cor. 5:7, 8)

You are, at times, conscious of a lively dispute going on in another, between what his senses have told him and what he is trying to comprehend as Truth. You know that the Father within you and within this other one is the same Spirit, and it is *"doing the work."* The right words are "given to you" to help speed his awareness when something needs to be said.

Oftentimes, just your knowledge that God is All, in All, is All, opens many channels for good to come forth into expression. You are not tempted, then, to glance over at his incorrect sense belief and think, "No wonder he has such a problem!" Rather, you regard such sense beliefs as you would a mirage, knowing God is there.

You will not think you see someone who wants to be a Somebody on his own, and who cannot give credit to God, because he, himself, wants all the credit for his skill and talent and abilities; nor will you think that such a separation is bound to produce an incapacitating illness, or loss of something they want. Your Real Self does not see such things, and if ever such seems to you to be the case, know that you have somehow accepted someone's *opinion* which took you back into the sense realm.

The God Concept of the Senses

The ancient Jews said Deity was "inhaling and exhaling," for this was Life, was it not? In their writing, they used a small mark, called a *Yodh,* or *Jodh.* This mark was used to form all the characters in their alphabet, and was a symbol of First Principle, from which all things were made. Originally, *J.H.V.H.* meant Life passing into manifestation through the breath, and there were no vowels but finally they were placed between the letters to make them pronounceable. Jehovah then become the concept of Deity when one was just beginning to discern what God is. It never was the name of anything, or anyone.

Jehovah is a concept derived from the senses, and is not mentioned further on in the Scriptures when *Elohim* is introduced as the True God.

Human consciousness, that is, the senses only, is called *"saul",* and if you know your Bible you know *"Soul"* never met Jesus.

You remember that *"Saul's"* name, or nature, was changed to *"Paul"* when he experienced a change of viewpoint.

Your Changed Viewpoint Affects Others for Good

When you listen and converse with these others, who are still in human sense consciousness, your office is *"Paul"*. They are confused and unsettled because their beliefs are aware at sense level and, to some degree yet, at war with Truth. It is not easy for them to see that Truth must be primal, and that all that they know of *lack of good* is due to their own inability to reach the Throne of David. The office of *"Paul"* points out that only the senses believe in both good and evil as realities.

Those who you do awaken, understand how it is that a change for the worse in material thinking brings about epidemics, calamities, and wars. They comprehend a value, perhaps dimly, at first, in contemplation of the nature of Mind, and see how a misuse of thought brings greater bondage.

They probably know someone who retorts sharply to anything which sounds to them like a slur or an insult, and are able to see how this one has conditioned his thought to negative emotions. The awakening enables one to understand how to handle his own belief, because he is able to observe how his acquaintance often puts the wrong interpretation upon what is said to him.

Now, he is aware that quite possibly he has sometimes done the same thing, not wanting to be hurt, but looking for hurts. He begins to put the best possible interpretation upon all that is said to him.

You Know What Conscience Is

To those who say, "I do only what my conscience tells me to do", you can explain. "What you call your conscience is only a bundle of beliefs which have been taught to you, such as moral ethics and appropriate behaviour. You may have been taught incorrectly, or something important may have been omitted.

Some persons have never been taught that it was not right to fright or kill, and to do so doesn't effect their conscience one iota. Others have been so taught and being drafted into war, have been taught to kill. Loyalty to country, and loyalty to what he has been taught is God's commandment, has reduced many a man's inner feelings to ashes. The conflict in his thought world can become great.

Popular literature has often brought up the question, "Why is it *wrong* to kill a man when you are a citizen if that man offends you, or endangers you, and *right* to kill a man when you are in the service of your country?" Such inconsistencies exist at sense level. But he have noticed that the man who has removed the belief in the need for killing another, is not placed in a position where he has to, or is called upon to do so.

What Have You Been Telling Yourself?

It is you who have been telling your legs they can walk, yours hands they can grasp, your eyes that they see.

What else have you been telling yourself? That there are those who *don't* understand, who *can't* understand? No, not the Real YOU: it would never do this. But your sense concept of yourself might, and this is what you are gradually moving more and more away from.

Today, you know that if you keep telling a child he is bad, he will become ever more difficult to deal with, so it is clear to you that you would not say of anyone's ears, that they could not hear. Neither would you deny anyone's comprehension.

Only to your senses does this absence first appear, but these are being trained by the Mind within.

FOR FLESH AND BLOOD HATH NOT REVEALED IT UNTO
THEE, BUT MY FATHER WHICH IS IN HEAVEN.

(Matt. 16:17)

The Greatest Glory

We know that the wise man builds his house upon a
rock, not upon sand, for if he builds, it upon the latter, when
the rain descends, and the flood comes, and the wind blows,
the house will fall.

You know that to the thinking which is at sense level
only, "being realistic" means the dealing with things which
can be seen and handled. All that is in form is subject to
age, decay, and destruction, so isn't so realistic, is it? In
Mind, in idea is called a "seed" and an idea grows in Mind
just like a seed grows in soil.

The training of the mind, just as in the buildings of a
house, must begin with the proper foundation. You have it
as long as you protect the idea that you are God's offspring
and never argue.

Only when the sense concept of Jesus Christ goes, do
you find that the name-nature of Jesus is *I Am,* and that the
only Son is awareness of Life as *Whole I-ness.* You know
that this I Am becomes the Christ, or savior, to you, for It
is your true selfhood.

To all who hold to mistaken sense beliefs about this
teaching, the Christ, their savior, is still "dead," dormant as
an idea. It has not been "resurrected", that is, brought to
conscious awareness. But YOU know it is there, within,
unrecognized. Can you bring it to recognition?

What Would It Be Worth to You?

It means doing what you love doing, and being amply
recompensed for it. It's value is unlimited in joy given and
received. It means constructive use of the imagination,
continuously. It is being able to hold in consciousness a right

idea until it becomes rational to you, and when rational, it has to appear in the world of form. It is understanding that what you have been looking *with* is what you have been looking *for*. It is correct knowledge at the instant you require it.

What price would you pay? Yes, it will cost you something, because this is a lasting benefit? When you buy anything in the world of form, you pay for its degree of excellence. When it is something you intend to use every day, and it is guaranteed to last, you are happy to own it. You will not hide it, nor discard it.

CHAPTER 18

Receiving Your Inheritance

Vision

Radiant light waves cover a scale of fifty-five octaves and even good mortal vision covers only one octave. Man has known, by the power of his mind, how to make microscopes and telescopes to extend his mortal vision.

The saying, *"without vision, the people perish,"* implies that we are to look ahead with the mind, to a brighter future.

The world as it exists for you appears to be a series of changing states of consciousness. Conditions and events are shifting. What you call good has a direct opposite and you are a mental see-saw most of the time, with both sides appearing equally real. When the strain of believing in both becomes too great, *"men die."*

While you believed that your mind was encased in a physical body, and your brain did your thinking, instead of being merely a computing organ which registered and took in sense impressions, you were "carnal-minded."

FOR TO BE CARNALLY MINDED IS DEATH; BUT TO BE SPIRITUALLY MINDED IS LIFE AND PEACE. BECAUSE THE CARNAL MIND IS ENMITY AGAINST GOD; FOR IT IS NOT SUBJECT TO THE LAW OF GOD, NEITHER INDEED CAN BE, SO THEY THAT ARE IN THE FLESH CANNOT PLEASE GOD.

(Romans 8:6-8)

"They that are in the flesh," are any beliefs that the flesh is *all* there is to you.

"The end of the world" is the end of these kind of thoughts, and it is the only end of the world which could possibly be!

270

Spirit Is Infinite and Eternal

Your Soul, your mental body, is bed by Spirit, and produced by It. Infinite Spirit is the nucleus of your Soul. The Intelligent, Infinite Spirit is always whole, complete, and eternal.

The Golden Rule

One who fails to grasp this line of thought, or who considers it impractical, *lives* from the sense interpretation of the Golden Rule. It he does a good deed, it is only because he has an axe to grind, an I'll-scratch-your-back-if-you'll-scratch-mine attitude. These clichés are familiar to us all as a favor-for-favor business, and are strictly of the human intellect, and by no means are the Golden Rule. Anyone who practices them knows one party benefits more than the other . . . for the time.

If you are one who has just had the union you belong to "go to bat" for you, and your salary is raised, perhaps you have realized that in due time the price of the product your company produces will go up in price, so that they may have the funds with which to pay the higher salaries. When you purchase these products, you have to pay more for them. How much more "good" did you really get?

Doing to others as you would like them to do to you doesn't mean to do to them what they *are* doing to you. A good many seem to think that is what it means.

How Will You Offset It?

"Flee from the man whose breath is in his nostrils." You do not have to do business with such persons. You do not have to buy the product of those whose advertisements are misleading. You *do* have to change your belief. When you do, you will be led to places and products which give value for value.

Unfair persons think God is unfair. Unreliable ones are sure God is unreliable, so they cannot know the value of

prayer. Why associate with them? What does the Christ
have to do with such? Nothing whatever.

When Faith Is Weak and Doubt Is Strong

Look for the jewel you have not brought out to the light
of day and expressed, if your understanding is moving
slowly. When things at sense level remain the same for too
long, there is something you are overlooking by not
expressing. What thought do you harbor which is inimical
to God, the all-good?

Are you thinking of all the ways in which you have been
duped, abused, or kept from having your chance? From
such a soured viewpoint comes much mischief, and to fix
your attention upon those who thusly deport themselves,
simply means that you have again made "real" the senses,
and moved out of the Kingdom.

The Creator of Perfect Ideas did not "create" these
imperfections. God created YOU, so that YOU might
express what He is. Want to shirk your right?

Two opposite things cannot both be true. One of them
must be primal. If evil were primal, there would be no way
of proving it false. Look at it this way: the truth that $5 \times 5 = 25$
is primal, but the error that $5 \times 5 = 26$ is not true. "Evil" is error,
and it is always a supposititious opposite. The error, or evil,
isn't true; therefore, what an errant one believes in and acts
upon is not true, and is therefore unreal.

The Battle of Armageddon

You are fighting a battle between your own thoughts, but
you win when your attention is upon what is true.

No matter what a mess you may seem to be in at any
particular time, you can turn frustration and disappointment
into greater satisfaction if you will make the effort to turn
within. Get just a little better acquainted with what God's
qualities are, and express them yourself.

"Gethsemane" is the word that explains how you feel when sense beliefs have manifested and are seemingly over-powering you. Those are the kind that tell you there is "no way out."

Turn Water Into Wine

You already know that "water" is thought and "wine" means spirit, don't you? You know it was not some magical trick, nor even a ritual done to amaze the senses. Of course, this esoteric use of words was telling us that thought was turned to Spirit. Contemplating It's nature is Holy Communion. It is possible to do it anywhere, but if you feel you require the aid of one who is more accustomed to thinking thusly, by all means become their guest.

Calvary

That personal sense of "I" which for so long you believed yourself to be, that one with so many years of Adam-thought, with academic degress, or the lack of them, who owns a house, or doesn't, is taken to "Calvary". You probably know that it means "death to the skull." The skull harbors the brain, the repository of all sense impressions. I'm sure you see the symbology.

Walking Unseen Through Crowds

Haven't you, the Real YOU, always been present, unseen in the crowds of sense beliefs? The false sense of what you thought yourself to be, is all that is "taken." Your limitations removed, YOU are "set free" to express, or show forth, your jewels.

You are receiving your inheritance, for you know that the Ideas that the eyes do not yet see, and that the hands do not touch, are the Real World of Mind. From It now, you are taking your good, which will appear to your enlightened senses.

No longer do you mentally view a man who could make himself invisible at will, or who made his ascent up an earthly hill, burdened with a heavy wooden cross. You no longer imagine the Roman soldiers "shooting craps" to see who will win possession of the "seamless Robe."

YOU know that by means of parable, allegory, and metaphor, Divine ideas have been presented.

Sinner Might Get to Heaven First

Incorrect sense beliefs are the first ones to be straightened out. What things which you *don't* do, which seem "wrong" to you, do you think are "wrong" for others?

This is pretty subtle. Let's take smoking as an example, and say you don't indulge. Do you want all these others to stop, because you think it's wrong? Well, suppose you're tolerant of this one, but you have strong feelings about the use of alcoholic beverages. You believe it promotes foolish, as well as dangerous, acts.

What so you suppose such thoughts will have to do with *your* inheriting of your good? Do you know there is nothing in tobacco or whisky that has more power than God? If you don't know that, what aren't you knowing it?

Yes, we are dealing with the *effects* known as tobacco and alcohol, which appear to be powerful enough to hold a man or woman in bondage to them. They are held because there are so many people believing this thought. Their problem is not with the effect, but with the *belief!*

Narcotic addiction is no different.

The search to relieve pain, worthy as it is, has been seen to need to begin where the patient thinks. Mental tensions can set the physical organism awry.

Again, those with strong beliefs in such addictions are the ones who see them; others are never where these things are.

The Know-How is Built-in

The world God created is still here, even if the world of man's thought seems to some to be a far cry from it. It is as ridiculous to say or believe that some do not wish to find God's world, as it would be to say that some do not wish to be happy, healthy, and well-supplied!

It, the know-how, is already present in everyone, and it is just as foolish to say that anyone has a "closed mind" as it would be to say that anyone didn't enjoy good food and a comfortable place to sleep.

The statement you might hear from some whom you might so label are only a plea for understanding. They want things explained to them. They want to be "awakened." YOU, who know of your inheritance, will not shut off your own supply of good by a craven attitude. You will give, freely and kindly, just enough, as you would water a precious plant.

A House Divided

When you meet those, who are trying to learn and they tell you that there are good and bad, as people, on both the seen and unseen planes, in other words "evil spirits," don't neglect to explain to them that God is Spirit, the *only* spirit. It is only an excuse to place the blame somewhere else, and it is a "house divided against itself."

Until God is known to be One Power, not two, there will be much turbulence on the sea.

Who Are the Criminals?

Imbedded within the very nature of Life is the desire for Fair Play. Anything achieved by man's will power alone, by plotting and scheming, putting others at a disadvantage in order to bring about some temporary gain, will disappear more quickly than it has accomplished and leave things worse than before.

Great fortunes and great power can be built up by such methods, but for every person who was taken advantage of, a penalty is given to the one who perpetrated it, often following quickly.

Anyone guilty of violation of God's Laws is a criminal. To think that anyone does not know what these are, when they are built-in, is to refuse to look at something quite fundamental. This belief, which is that anyone is ignorant of what is fair and right, must be changed. True, the sense hold tightly to it, for evidence of it at sense level is strong.

Those who have jettisoned this belief are never harassed by thieves or gangsters. Every car in a parking lot might be broken into and something taken from it, but theirs will go unmolested. Hordes may be taken in by some scheme, or fake stock, but such as these never even hear of it! Should anyone attempt as these never even hear of it! Should anyone attempt to lay a trap for these, the trap springs back upon the plotter.

What would happen if all ceased believing is "crocked politics" unfair practices, robberies and thefts! Do you care to try it?

Aren't crime and vice believed in by the very ones who try to stop it? Why are they believed in by legislators who pass the laws?

How Are You Using Your Inheritance?

This knowledge you now have, that there is nothing wrong anywhere in the Universe, is not something you can keep to yourself. Its nature demands expression. You have joined with those who are always safe, sane, serene, and secure.

You take time to count all that you like, and you have no unsolved problems. You know that you are always adequately supplied, and you are, for you can see the evidence.

You know that you will never hurt or harm anyone at all, in your profession, business or home.

You have rejected the thought of germs, of malfunctioning or organs of the body, and of such things as malignant growths. Have you also rejected the possibility of others having such experiences? Our own prayers are answered when we include all others. Have you ever said, "Well, he, or she, is still thinking from sense level, and believes in such things, so what can you expect?" No, YOU would not say that, but you might.

If you discuss the surgery, medication, and ailments of others as if they were *real*, what are you doing but solidifying a belief which may some day manifest in your own body?

Remember, I am not saying that your correct thought will affect a healing for that others person you discuss. It may, or it may not, because of that one's unbelief. He may need to suffer his penalty. But you had better think correctly about his life, unless you want to accept another false belief.

Pray Unceasingly

Prayer is *continual recognition* of the nature of what God created. While you hold to the idea of your Perfect Life, you remember that it is the same life every-where.

Persistence Is a Must

A constancy in turning the attention away from every example of non-good also means to pay no attention to the world of effect. This persistency will remove every adverse effect; it will also produce the good you wish to personally experience.

This is another subtle one, and a puzzle to many, but stay with it, and you will soon see for yourself.

Someone asks, "What about my work at the office? That is in the realm of effect. I have to think about it and know what I am doing."

The Universal Intelligence which is expressed by means of you, through your body, your hands, your eyes, and yes, even your brain, muscles, and nerves, knows exactly what to accomplish. You will find that this thought of the limitless life moving through you into expression, causes you to execute your tasks with joy-effortlessly, tirelessly, and better than you have done before.

A young mother says, "I have to bathe and care for the baby, Surely, I shouldn't keep my attention off him!

Isn't it God's love that is caring for the body? And won't she do her tasks exceptionally well, with happy ease, and enjoy even the washing of the diapers?

"Keep my attention off effect?" says a mechanic, "my job depends upon knowing what I'm doing. I repair things."

Isn't it God's energy and intelligence as this man's very life that makes him capable of what he does? He sees the mechanical parts as ideas, and knows instantly how to fit them together. Everything goes together so smoothly, he is hardly aware of the passage of time.

It is easy to carry out every task, when you place your thought upon the Intelligence which is doing it. This persistency that you exercise in remembering that the perfect Life is your life now, and the Perfect Mind is your mind, now, will put the effects where they belong, as perfect ideas.

How to Regard Another's Penalty

From this higher standared, this elevated awareness which is yours, you can easily see a compassionate, understanding thought would not be, "He deserved it." You have merely observed what happens when a law is broken. Neither glee nor regret is felt by YOU, merely enlightenment.

Personal faults, which one will not recognize and correct, are often regarded by them as "bad luck." Sometimes, these faults are hidden from themselves, but anyone who knows them could have (and probably *have*), told them more than once what they are. Supposing the fault is tardiness, they have a habit of being late. The penalty for this would be missing out on something which would given them joy.

The cure lies in the discovery of the fault, and that one's willingness to correct it. He must make the effort to be on time, just the same as a man who has a habit of cheating must learn not to by forcing himself into a new habit of honesty. Such as these cannot be "handled with kid gloves" and allowed to go on repeating their mistake. That is not kindness, that is foolishness. Dinners have been ruined, guests disturbed, and hostesses made frantic, because of a habit.

In all such cases, you do what benefits the largest number of persons. Strike such from your list that do not benefit all, and wait for Intelligence to take over.

There Is No "Bad Luck"

What appears to these folks as their bad luck, is nothing more than a faulty habit of thinking, which produces a habit action. What he once thought consciously becomes memory, so even though the thought is submerged, it is still active.

Any thought habit, which results in an action that disturbs, inconveniences, or robs another of his peace of mind, can be eliminated by causing the one so afflicted to become sharply aware of what he does, so that he is stimulated into making an effort to correct it.

It you were making a mistake which robbing you of your good, your joy, your best friends, or you job, wouldn't you want to be told about it? If subjective thought patterns kept denying every correct objective statement you made, you would like to know what habit pattern of thought kept you in such bondage. Yes, you'd want to know, and so does the person you see.

We are speaking as if there were two minds, but we are also remembering that there is only One Mind. When you speak out to the other, you are using that One Mind, in which he also has his being. You are speaking in calm trust to his conscious mind a new thought which will counteract his subjective memory pattern. If tardiness is the subject, you praise his efforts to be no time; you call forth his ability to make the effort. Tardiness is nothing but a false thought. As he gets the right idea, it will produce the effect like its cause. As he feels your interest in his welfare, he will be grateful. Know this, no matter what your senses report at the moment.

See the difference in praising the right idea as you call it to attention, and simply saying, "The trouble with you is you are always late."

Examples

A mother says to her little girl, "You are feeling better this morning, aren't you?"

The child smiles and nods.

Suppose she says, "You feel terrible this morning Honey? Are you still sick?"

The child nods.

An employer speaks to one of his men, "Joe, you're doing real good work; I wonder if you'd be able to speed it up just a little bit?"

But suppose he had said, "Joe, you're so slow we're going to lose money on this job!"

Practice Will Verify

Only as you utilize what you have been made aware of herein, will you attract to yourself what makes you happy. The correction of everything comes through a reversal of thought and action, because this intelligent Life Force in you responds to you on the terms of its own nature.

You are so much a part of the creative power, that you never wonder whether or not you are in touch with it, just *how* you are using it, negatively to positively.

Everything is mental before it can become material, so evil has to be *believed* in before it can become a fact. It you have a continuous string of problems in your private world of effect, health, finances, or human relationships, you need only to fulfill the requirements of the first Commandment and the negative events will cease.

Your Proficiency Increases With Practice

When your thoughts choose God as their only Creator and you no longer consider the importance of some material thing, or the behaviour of some human is allowed to sway your thought and emotion into negative patterns, all of your ideas will give you joy. The Divine lovingly unfolds Heaven *("as in heaven so in earth")* and in unlimited ways with infinite variation, the beautiful, the desirable, and harmonious is revealed.

You will bring in whatever is True by knowing what *is* True. When you know the Truth, that knowledge itself will manifest.

Isn't it a lovely inheritance?

CHAPTER 19

The Overall Design

This is a book about you, written for you, to you. YOU have all the qualities you yearn to see others express, and you know that you can, and now are, expressing them.

Right into the world of your sense beliefs came the awareness of your Self, as this Perfect Life, Love and Intelligence. At times it seemed difficult to see how this could be so, of you, but gradually it became easier to comprehend.

When God said (thought), *"Let us make man in our image and likeness,"* the pattern of mankind, male and female, was formed. YOU came into being as a Perfect Idea. Then, you became a "living soul," incorporating all the attributes of your Creator, an expression of His Idea. You were in Paradise, but you did not know it, so a physical form had to be manifested, with sense organs, so that you might become aware of what you knew.

Then, the senses "look over," and you began to believe what they "created" was the only true and real. You believed what you saw, and you saw what you believed. As time went on, you began to believe what others told you, what you heard, and if this could be confirmed by your sense of sight, then it was accepted as factual.

After a while you are aware of the sense of smell and taste and touch, as well as imagination and an intuitive sense.

What Intuition Is

Intuition has been said to be "being taught from within," and it really *is* immediate perception, an instinctive knowledge that comes without reasoning. But, what so frequently passes for intuitive knowledge is hypnotic suggestion, sometimes coming from an individual, sometimes from race consciousness.

What all believe, or most are believing, can become such a powerful thought pattern that it is often accepted as something coming from Divine Mind.

How You May Discern the Difference

The Original Source of Life, Pure Spirit, *never* gives off even the smallest degree of *non*-good. If what you call your "intuition" gives you even a slight degree of a negative happening, or condition, it is *not* intuition, but suggestion.

To "intuitively know" that someone is going to have an accident, or be sick, is pure suggestion. It is a thought-form, and intellectual belief, which it is your privilege to dissolve. It comes from sense level, even though unseen. YOU dissolve it by knowing that Spirit did not ordain it.

All the Senses Are Re-educated

Slowly, but surely, you move away from the belief in *Karma,* the law of cause and effect at sense level. You are now able to see how this belief kept you chained to the senses, and continually on a rescue mission, never able to look away from the undesirable.

It becomes increasingly more clear to you that the parables and allegories of Scripture are words put together to illustrate ideas, and aid interpretation by the use of already familiar subjects.

Comes the day when the *"stone-is rolled away,"* not a big hunk of rock shaped to fill a doorway, but a "hard place" in your own belief realm where nothing was "real" unless it had form or was happening.

The "wine" of Spirit helps you to understand this: the witness to the empty tomb were two women (intellectual beliefs now able to dimly accept). They saw a man (thought) walking in the garden, whom they believed to be the gardener.

A gardener is a servant and when you first get this idea, you, too, think it is a servant, someone who will do things for you. You do not know it is the Master, within yourself, and that YOU will do these things yourself, for yourself!

Who Is Judas Iscariot?

Sense interpretations have done ridiculous things with all of the disciples, but particularly with Judas. He has been called the betrayer because he revealed the where-abouts of the Christ.

Stop thinking of the Last Supper, the Roman soldiers, and the thirty pieces of silver as artists and motion pictures have depicted them, and your senses have accepted them, and see the meaning with your Mind.

When you have a desire for something, you have a thought which tells you that you do not have it, or that it is not attainable. "Judas" represents that thought which tells your negative beliefs how they may find. It is written that Judas committed suicide. Doesn't your desire "die" when the manifestation is forthcoming?

All Limitations Are the Result of Ignorance

While Intelligence is present, always available, need anyone remain in any sort of bondage? All you have been asked to give up is an incorrect viewpoint. You are completely equipped to make the discovery.

Just look at all the freedom you've had, to make this discovery for yourself! Hasn't the teaching, *"It is done unto you, as you believe,"* caused you to be more determined to believe after a Divine Pattern?

Giving up the false concept of yourself is as easy as walking away from your mirrored image. The Christ, the

Holy One, in the midst of you, is the Son, and only the Son "sees" the Father, or can understand the Father.

The *"last enemy, death"*—and an enemy is a lie—is given up, because the Truth is understood. Time after time you have made a new body form after the pattern of your Soul. Spencer was right when he said:

> *For of the soul the body form doth take;*
> *For soul is form and doth the body make.*

New Heaven and Earth

With the new concept if yourself, you know that you are already in possession of everything good, and that you are *entitled* to it. Illusions are dispelled, doubts vanish, and the unknown becomes known.

The key has turned, the gate have opened wide, and you are on the pinnacles of ecstasy, realizing that YOU are an embodiment of God, the Almighty Father. While there was "war in heaven" (conflicting beliefs in your soul), Michael (the right thoughts which rose above sense beliefs) fought the Dragon (those sense thoughts).

AND HE THAT SAT UPON THE THROWN SAID, BEHOLD. I MAKE ALL THINGS NEW. AND HE SAID UNTO ME, WRITE: FOR THESE WORDS ARE TRUE AND FAITHFUL.

AND HE SAID UNTO ME, IT IS DONE. I AM ALPHA AND OMEGA, THE BEGINNING AND THE END. I WILL GIVE UNTO HIM THAT IS A THIRST OF THE FOUNTAIN OF THE WATER OF LIFE FREELY. HE THAT OVERCOMETH SHALL INHERIT ALL THINGS; AND I WILL BE HIS GOD AND HE SHALL BE MY SON.

(Rev. 21:5, 6, 7)

You Are the Overall Design

Your body is a chemical laboratory; your eyes are a camera. All that appears to be outside of you is in your Mind. You are free to qualify all of it in any manner you choose. *"Adam names all things."*

Yes, even the vast and orderly intelligence of the Universe is in your Mind. Isn't it by means of your intelligent comprehension that you know the sun is still shining, even on cloudy or foggy days?

Everything has its beginning as an idea in Mind. YOU began that way, and YOU are tremendously important in this Universe! YOU are the creative Principle of Life. YOU are one in nature with God, to the degree that you are expressing those qualities inherent within you. When you turn your thought to the Allness of Love and Intelligence and Power, you are consciously unified with it.

LO! I AM WITH YOU ALWAYS.

Glossary of Bible Meanings

To Aid Your Comprehension

PROPER names used in the Scripute which seem to be the names of persons are actually names of *beliefs* and *ideas.* God is the maker of all Ideas: the senses are the makers of all Beliefs.

Other word meanings are given also to help you move away from the sense-made, storybook interpretations.

ABRAHAM. Consecrated Spiritual Faith, where you "touch" the source of true ideas.

ABRAM. Faith in what you cannot as yet perceive but feel is true.

ADAM. The "First Adam" is your first concept of your-self as body and personality. The "Last Adam" mentioned in I Corinthians, Chapter 15, and elsewhere is YOU, when you discover your Real Self.

BEAST. Theory based on Sense Findings. The *"Mark of the Beast"* is the wisdom of the Sense Findings when the True Idea is not discovered.

BETHLEHEM. The place where Ideas come forth. It means "house of bread."

BREAD. The "bread of heaven" is the Substance, itself, from which all thought is formed.

BROTHER, OR BRETHREN. Your own thoughts.

CHILD. A place in your thought realm where wise or foolish thoughts do not exist, nor any prior knowledge. It order to enter the Kingdom of Heaven, you are told to find such a place: *"Become as a child".*

CHILD OF ISRAEL.. A true idea, still hidden in your heart or in the "midst of you."

CHILDREN OF ISRAEL. Are not a race of people, such as your senses would see walking around, but True Ideas which have become obscured by your senses.

DAVID. The Throne of Pure Thought.

DEVIL. (Satan and the Great Red Dragon). Represent beliefs made at sense-level only; the judging by appearances.

EARTH. The reflection of a concept, or a belief, known to the physical senses.

EDEN. The brain knowledge, or intellect.

EGYPT. When you are aware of what the senses perceive. (*"Burdens of Egyptians"*: Fears and worries brought about by the sense testimony.)

FIRMAMENT. Not the earth your sense know, but the ability to identify God's Ideas. Distinguishing the difference between Universal Law and what the senses tell you.

FISH. New Ideas. A fish lives in water, and *water* is *thought*.

GALILEE. A place in your soul where right thoughts originate.

GENTILES. Your own false beliefs.

HEAVEN. The *within* where your thoughts go to become manifest and apprised by your senses.

ISAAC. A feeling of Joy.

JACOB. A concept of self while you learn.

JORDAN. A channel of thought to the God-Mind.

JOSHUA. A key Idea that is willing to make right thoughts.

KINGDOM. Place of authority. Control and discipline of emotions by right thoughts.

LAND. Has to do with mental or spiritual environment.

MAN. A thought, or idea. Man is what he thinks, and as he thinks.

MIND OF CHRIST. Enlightenment; understanding; comprehension.

MOSES. A state of consciousness; a point in your awareness where you perceive your True self and view the wild beliefs you had made and begin to want to change them.

MOUNT, OR MOUNTAIN. Greater knowledge of God's Laws.

NEW BIRTH. Having a new viewpoint—discovering that you are a new starting-point for creative action.

NEW HEAVEN AND EARTH. New ideas from your new viewpoint are reflected—that is, made manifest—in ever better ways.

NOAH AND THE FLOOD. The correct concept of yourself as Spirit is called "Noah" and the word of God washes away false sense beliefs. The spitirual concept of each Idea brings its own reflection, and the correct Idea and its reflection are yours.

RIVERS. Channels of thought.

SABBATH. Gratitude and appreciation for your Real Self.

SEAS. The mental confusion brought on by judging from appearances.

SHIPS. Key Thoughts.

SIN. A mistake, an error coming from sense perception only. An incorrect conviction which produces a faulty effect. *You* do not "sin", but you are mistaken about the "you" you believe yourself to be.

SOUL. The mental realm of each entity which has at its center

Pure Spirit. Since your life is comprised of what you allow in your mental realm, it is up to you to find the Christ, or Pure Spirit, from which good emanates.

TEMPTATION. Looking outside of yourself for a greater Good. God does not lead you to do this, for the Mind which is God, is the Pure Spirit, within.

THE NEW "TONGUES". Not a different language, nor some gibberish merely mouthed, meaningless to all, but a *code* mentioned in Mark 16:17.

TREE OF KNOWLEDGE OF GOOD AND EVIL. The physical senses, which deliver messages back to you, showing you what your beliefs are, are called a "tree," meaning a source of thought.

TREE OF LIFE. The True Source of True Ideas. God; Deity; the Creative Principle.